KETO DIET

1500 Days

Cookbook
for Beginners

Super Delicious, Simple, Low-carb Keto Recipes
Cookbook to Manage Your Body in a Healthier Way

Brian Vanfleet

Warning-Disclaimer

The purpose of this book is to educate and entertain. The author or publisher does not guarantee that anyone following the techniques, suggestions, tips, ideas, or strategies will become successful. The author and publisher shall have neither liability or responsibility to anyone with respect to any loss or damage caused, or alleged to be caused, directly or indirectly by the information contained in this book.

Table of Contents

Chapter 4 Poultry

Chapter 5 Fish and Seafood

Chapter 7 Salads
54

Chapter 8 Stews and Soups
61

INTRODUCTION

As a nutritionist and foodie, I have always been fascinated by the effects of different diets on the human body. After years of studying various dietary plans, I have come to the conclusion that the ketogenic diet is one of the most effective and healthy ways to nourish the body.

The ketogenic diet involves drastically reducing carbohydrate intake and increasing healthy fat consumption to force the body to enter a state of ketosis, where it burns fat for energy instead of glucose. This metabolic state has been shown to have numerous benefits, including weight loss, improved blood sugar control, and increased energy levels.

But while the benefits of the keto diet are clear, many people struggle with finding delicious and satisfying meals that fit within the guidelines of the diet. That's where this recipe book comes in.

In this book, I have compiled a wide variety of recipes that are both delicious and keto-friendly. From hearty breakfasts to filling dinners and everything in between, there is something here for every meal and every craving.

But this book is more than just a collection of recipes. I have also included a wealth of information on the principles of the ketogenic diet, including what foods to eat and what to avoid, as well as tips and tricks for staying on track.

Whether you are just starting out on the keto diet or are a seasoned pro looking for some new recipe ideas, this book is for you. With easy-to-follow recipes and helpful advice, you will be able to enjoy all the benefits of the keto diet while still enjoying delicious and satisfying meals.

So let's get started on this journey to better health and delicious food.

Chapter 1 A Complete Guide to the Keto Diet

The Keto diet is a low-carb, high-fat diet that has gained popularity in recent years due to its potential benefits for weight loss, improved blood sugar control, and increased energy levels. This diet works by forcing your body to enter a metabolic state called ketosis, where it burns fat for fuel instead of carbohydrates.

To follow the Keto diet, you must drastically reduce your carbohydrate intake and replace it with healthy fats and protein. This means eliminating or severely limiting bread, pasta, rice, and sugary foods, while eating plenty of meat, fish, eggs, nuts, seeds, and low-carb vegetables.

One of the biggest challenges of the Keto diet is sticking to the strict guidelines for carbohydrate intake. Most people on the Keto diet aim to consume no more than 50 grams of carbs per day, but some may need to reduce this even further to achieve ketosis. This can be difficult, especially for those who are used to eating a high-carb diet.

Another challenge of the Keto diet is ensuring that you are consuming enough healthy fats to maintain energy levels and support bodily functions. This means incorporating foods like avocado, coconut oil, olive oil, and fatty fish into your diet.

Despite these challenges, many people have found success with the Keto diet. In addition to weight loss and improved blood sugar control, it may also have benefits for those with neurological disorders, such as epilepsy and Alzheimer's disease.

However, it is important to consult with a healthcare professional before starting the Keto diet, as it can have potential risks for certain individuals, such as those with liver or pancreatic issues. Additionally, the long-term effects of the diet are still being studied.

Overall, the Keto diet can be a powerful tool for improving health and achieving weight loss goals, but it requires dedication and careful attention to nutrient intake. With proper guidance and support, it may be a viable option for those looking to improve their overall well-being.

Types of keto diets

There are four types of keto diets: the Standard Ketogenic Diet, the Cyclical Ketogenic Diet, the Targeted Ketogenic Diet, and the High-Protein Ketogenic Diet. The Standard Ketogenic Diet is the most common and involves consuming high amounts of fat, moderate amounts of protein, and very low amounts of carbs. The Cyclical Ketogenic Diet involves periods of high carb consumption followed by periods of strict keto eating. The Targeted Ketogenic Diet involves consuming carbs before or after workouts to enhance athletic performance. The High-Protein Ketogenic Diet involves consuming higher amounts of protein, while still maintaining low carb intake.

The Benefits of the Keto Diet

The Keto diet has numerous potential health benefits, including weight loss, improved blood sugar control, increased energy levels, reduced inflammation, and improved heart health. It may also be beneficial for people with certain medical conditions such as epilepsy, type 2 diabetes, and neurological disorders. Additionally, the Keto diet has been shown to improve brain function and cognitive performance. However, it is important to note that some of these benefits are based on limited research, and the long-term effects of the Keto diet are still being studied. Furthermore, the diet can be challenging to follow, and may not be appropriate for everyone, particularly those with certain medical conditions or a history of disordered eating.

Keto Food Pyramid

There is no official keto food pyramid, but many people on the keto diet use a pyramid or chart to help them understand which foods they should focus on and which ones they should limit or avoid. The general idea is to eat mostly healthy fats, moderate amounts of protein, and very few carbohydrates.

At the base of the pyramid are high-fat foods like avocados, olive oil, and nuts. These are the foods that should make up the bulk of your calories on the keto diet. Next up are moderate protein sources like meat, fish, and eggs. These should make up a smaller portion of your calories than fat.

In the middle of the pyramid are low-carb vegetables like leafy greens, cauliflower, and broccoli. These foods are important for getting vitamins and minerals, but you need to be careful not to eat too much of them because they do contain some carbs.

At the top of the pyramid are foods you should avoid or eat very sparingly. This includes high-carb fruits, grains, and sugars. These foods will kick you out of ketosis and make it much harder to stay in fat-burning mode.

Foods to Avoid

There are many foods that we are discouraged from eating while on keto. I found the challenge of ignoring the prohibited foods from my keto diet daunting. However, I realized we could introduce small servings of off-limit foods now and again. The foods we should avoid are the following.

Grains

We should avoid eating all grain-based foods when we are on keto. Included here are crackers, pasta, cereal, and rice. What's more, all bread, including gluten-free varieties, has a high carbohydrate content.

Starchy Vegetables

I discovered that starchy vegetables low in fiber and high in carbohydrates should be avoided when we are on keto. Included here are beets, corn, and all types of potatoes. In addition, chips, crisps, and French fries are prohibited on keto.

High-Sugar, Fruits

We should avoid fruits like bananas, dates, and mangoes as they spike our blood sugar due to their increased carbohydrate content.

Sweetened Yogurt

We should avoid artificially sweetened foods as the added sugars boost our carbs. Instead, we can choose plain Greek yogurt which is rich in proteins and low in carbs.

Juices

Most fruit juices have a high sugar content and are thus not recommended for keto.

Syrup, Honey, and Sugar

We should avoid all high-carb, sugar-based foods, syrup, and honey, no matter how delicious.

Five Best Keto Tips and Tricks for Beginners

Plan ahead: One of the biggest challenges of the keto diet is figuring out what to eat. Spend some time planning your meals and snacks for the week ahead. This will help you stay on track and avoid the temptation to reach for carb-heavy options.

Focus on healthy fats: Since the keto diet is high in fat, it's important to choose healthy sources of fat like avocados, nuts, seeds, and fatty fish. Avoid processed and fried foods as they often contain unhealthy trans fats.

Stay hydrated: The keto diet can be dehydrating, so it's important to drink plenty of water throughout the day. You may also want to consider supplementing with electrolytes to help maintain proper fluid balance.

Be mindful of carb counts: To stay in ketosis, you'll need to limit your carb intake to 20-50 grams per day. Be mindful of the carb content of foods, and use apps or nutritional guides to help you track your intake.

Find keto-friendly substitutes: There are many keto-friendly substitutes for your favorite carb-heavy foods. For example, cauliflower rice can replace regular rice, and zucchini noodles can replace pasta. Finding these substitutes can help you stay satisfied and motivated on the keto diet.

Here are some tips for eating out when following the keto diet:

Research before you go: Check out the restaurant's menu online before you go, and look for dishes that are keto-friendly. Most restaurants offer some kind of meat or fish dish that can be paired with low-carb vegetables or a salad.

Ask questions: Don't be afraid to ask your server questions about the menu items. Ask if they can modify a dish to make it low-carb or if they have any keto-friendly options that aren't listed on the menu.

Skip the bread and pasta: Most restaurants offer bread or pasta as a starter or side dish, but these are high in carbs and should be avoided on the keto diet. Ask for a salad or extra vegetables instead.

Choose healthy fats: On the keto diet, it's important to get enough healthy fats. Choose dishes that contain avocado, nuts, seeds, or olive oil. Avoid dishes that are cooked in vegetable oil or contain unhealthy trans fats.

Be careful with sauces and dressings: Many sauces and dressings contain hidden sugars and carbs. Ask for them on the side, so you can control how much you consume, or choose a simple dressing like olive oil and vinegar.

Remember, it's okay to indulge every once in a while, but be mindful of your choices and try to stick to the keto diet as much as possible when eating out.

【30 Days Keto Diet Meal Plan】

DAYS	BREAKFAST	LUNCH	DINNER	SNACK/DESSERT
1	Almond Flour Tortillas	Korean Ground Beef Bowl	BLT Chicken Salad	Parmesan Artichoke
2	Smoked Salmon and Cream Cheese Roll-Ups	Swedish Meatloaf	Sesame Chicken with Broccoli	Bone Broth Fat Bombs
3	Chocolate Raspberry Smoothie	Sausage and Cauliflower Arancini	Chicken and Mixed Greens Salad	Gourmet "Cheese" Balls
4	Savory Zucchini Cheddar Waffles	Rosemary Mint Marinated Lamb Chops	Chicken Piccata	Salami Chips with Pesto
5	Coconut Flour Macadamia Pancakes	Sausage and Peppers	Chicken Patties	Lemon-Butter Mushrooms
6	Sausage & Squash Omelet with Swiss Chard	Parmesan-Crusted Steak	Kung Pao Chicken	Tuna Cucumber Boats
7	Keto Chai	Herb-Crusted Lamb Chops	Coconut Curry Chicken	Cheese Stuffed Mushrooms
8	Three-Cheese Quiche	Loaded Burger Bowls	Turkey Enchilada Bowl	Curried Broccoli Skewers
9	Mini Shrimp Frittata	Cardamom Beef Stew Meat with Broccoli	Zucchini Spaghetti with Turkey Bolognese Sauce	Cheese and Charcuterie Board
10	Kimchi Eggs	Pork Loin Roast	Sage Chicken Thighs	Chicken Tinga Wings
11	Chocoholic Granola	Salisbury Steak with Mushroom Sauce	Chicken Thighs with Feta	Pickled Herring
12	Cheesy Keto Hash Browns with Avocado Mayo	Weeknight Chili	Chicken with Mushrooms and Shallots	Grandma's Meringues
13	Something Different Breakfast Sammy	Garlic Balsamic London Broil	Paprika Chicken	Greens Chips with Curried Yogurt Sauce
14	Cheesy Cauliflower Grits	Better Than Take-Out Beef with Broccoli	Crunchy Chicken Tacos	Cabbage and Broccoli Slaw
15	Baklava Hot Porridge	Hawaiian Pulled Pork Roast with Cabbage	Poulet en Papillote	Cauliflower Cheese Balls
16	Overnight "Noats"	Pan-Seared Steak with Mushroom Sauce	Classic Whole Chicken	Crispy Bacon Wrapped Onion Rings
17	Super Breakfast Combo	Garlic Lamb Vindaloo	Shredded Chicken	Salmon-Stuffed Cucumbers
18	Cheddar Soufflés	Beef and Sausage Medley	Turkey with Mushroom Gravy	Bacon-Wrapped Avocado Fries

DAYS	BREAKFAST	LUNCH	DINNER	SNACK/DESSERT
19	Rocket Fuel Hot Chocolate	Pancetta Sausage with Kale	Easy Turkey Tenderloin	Keto Taco Shells
20	Traditional Porridge	Ground Beef Stroganoff	Chicken Skewers with Peanut Sauce	Citrus-Marinated Olives
21	Blender Cinnamon Pancakes with Cacao Cream Topping	Filipino Pork Loin	Harissa-Rubbed Cornish Game Hens	Broccoli Cheese Dip
22	Brussels Sprouts, Bacon, and Eggs	Fried Rice with Ham	Crack Chicken Breasts	Brownie Cake
23	Cinnamon Muffins	Blue Cheese Stuffed Steak Roll-Ups	Chili Lime Turkey Burgers	Bacon-Wrapped Avocados
24	Yogurt Parfait with Creamy Blueberry Crumble	Breaded Pork Chops	Chicken Alfredo	Easy Peasy Peanut Butter Cookies
25	Low-Carb Egg Curry	French Dip Chuck Roast	Chicken Bacon Burgers	Low-Carb Granola Bars
26	Pumpkin Spice Smoothie	Deconstructed Egg Rolls	Chicken Meatballs with Green Cabbage	Granola Clusters
27	Allspice Muffins	Pork Mushroom Stroganoff	Chicken and Grape Tomatoes	Crunchy Jicama Fries
28	Egg and Cheese Biscuit Casserole	Feta-Stuffed Burgers	Tuscan Chicken Drumsticks	Keto Trail Mix
29	Gyro Breakfast Patties with Tzatziki	Chili-Stuffed Avocados	Fried Chicken Breasts	Baked Crab Dip
30	Pumpkin Spice Latte Overnight "Oats"	Beery Boston-Style Butt	Roasted Chicken Breasts with Capers	Mac Fatties

Chapter 2 Breakfasts

Smoked Salmon and Cream Cheese Roll-Ups

Prep time: 25 minutes | Cook time: 0 minutes | Serves 2

4 ounces cream cheese, at room temperature

1 teaspoon grated lemon zest

1 teaspoon Dijon mustard

2 tablespoons chopped scallions, white and green parts

Pink Himalayan salt

Freshly ground black pepper

1 (4-ounce) package cold-smoked salmon (about 12 slices)

1. Put the cream cheese, lemon zest, mustard, and scallions in a food processor (or blender), and season with pink Himalayan salt and pepper. Process until fully mixed and smooth. 2. Spread the cream-cheese mixture on each slice of smoked salmon, and roll it up. Place the rolls on a plate seam-side down. 3. Serve immediately or refrigerate, covered in plastic wrap or in a lidded container, for up to 3 days.

Per Serving:
calories: 268 | fat: 22g | protein: 14g | carbs: 4g | net carbs: 3g | fiber: 1g

Overnight "Noats"

Prep time: 5 minutes | Cook time: 0 minutes | Serves 1

2 tablespoons hulled hemp seeds

1 tablespoon chia seeds

½ scoop collagen powder

½ cup unsweetened nut or seed milk (hemp, almond, coconut, cashew)

1. In a small mason jar or glass container, combine the hemp seeds, chia seeds, collagen, and milk. 2. Secure tightly with a lid, shake well, and refrigerate overnight.

Per Serving:
calories: 263 | fat: 19g | protein: 16g | carbs: 7g | net carbs: 2g | fiber: 5g

Coconut Flour Macadamia Pancakes

Prep time: 5 minutes | Cook time: 10 minutes | Makes 8 pancakes

3 large eggs

¼ cup (½ stick) unsalted butter, melted

¼ cup heavy cream

¼ cup full-fat coconut milk

½ teaspoon vanilla extract

¼ cup coconut flour

¼ teaspoon kosher salt

½ teaspoon baking powder

½ teaspoon ground cinnamon

Keto-friendly sweetener of choice, to taste (optional)

¼ cup macadamias, chopped or

ground to desired coarseness

Coconut oil to grease griddle

1. In medium bowl, whisk together the eggs, butter, cream, coconut milk, and vanilla. 2. In a small bowl, stir together the flour, salt, baking powder, cinnamon, and sweetener with a fork, breaking up clumps of coconut flour. Stir the dry ingredients into the wet. 3. Add the macadamias to the batter and stir. Batter will be thick. Add water a little bit at a time until it is the consistency of thick pancake batter. 4. Heat a large, flat-bottomed skillet or griddle over medium-low heat. When warm, grease lightly with coconut oil. Drop big spoonfuls of the batter onto the griddle. It will not spread like traditional pancake batter, so use the back of a spoon or spatula to gently spread the batter into a thinner pancake. 5. Allow to cook slowly, several minutes per side until bubbles form, then flip. Serve hot.

Per Serving:
calories: 154 | fat: 14g | protein: 4g | carbs: 4g | net carbs: 3g | fiber: 1g

Savory Zucchini Cheddar Waffles

Prep time: 10 minutes | Cook time: 18 minutes | Makes 4 medium-sized waffles

WAFFLES:

2 large zucchini

2 large eggs

⅔ cup shredded cheddar cheese (about 2⅔ ounces)

2 tablespoons coconut flour

½ teaspoon garlic powder

½ teaspoon red pepper flakes

¼ teaspoon pink Himalayan salt

FOR GARNISH (OPTIONAL):

Sour cream

Shredded cheddar cheese

Minced fresh chives

1. Preheat a waffle iron on the medium setting. 2. Using a vegetable or cheese grater, grate the zucchini into a large colander set inside of a bowl. Squeeze the excess water out of the grated zucchini using your hands and drain. 3. Add the eggs and cheese to the drained zucchini and combine with a fork. Add the coconut flour, garlic powder, red pepper flakes, and salt and use the fork to combine once more. 4. Open the waffle iron and grease the top and bottom with coconut oil spray. 5. Using a ⅓-cup measuring cup, scoop out some of the batter, place it in the center of the waffle iron, and close the lid. Cook the waffle for 4 to 4½ minutes, until golden brown and fully cooked through. Use a fork to lift it off the iron and set on a plate. 6. Repeat with the remaining batter, making a total of 4 waffles. Garnish with sour cream, shredded cheddar cheese, and/or minced chives, if desired.

Per Serving:
calories: 292 | fat: 19g | protein: 20g | carbs: 14g | net carbs: 9g | fiber: 5g

Kimchi Eggs

Prep time: 4 minutes | Cook time: 5 minutes | Serves 2

1 tablespoon Paleo fat	1 cup kimchi
4 large eggs	For Garnish (optional):
Fine sea salt and freshly ground	Sliced green onions
black pepper, to taste	Red pepper flakes

1. Heat the fat in a cast-iron skillet over low heat. Crack the eggs into the skillet. Season with salt and pepper. Cover with a lid and cook until the whites are cooked through on top and the yolks are still runny, about 4 minutes. 2. Meanwhile, divide the kimchi between two serving bowls. When the eggs are done, remove them from the heat and place 2 eggs into each bowl. Garnish with green onions and red pepper flakes, if desired.

Per Serving:
calories: 240 | fat: 16g | protein: 16g | carbs: 8g | net carbs: 5g | fiber: 3g

Cheesy Keto Hash Browns with Avocado Mayo

Prep time: 15 minutes | Cook time: 20 minutes | Serves 4

2 cups riced cauliflower, fresh or frozen	2 tablespoons minced scallions, green and white parts
2 ounces (57 g) cream cheese, room temperature	6 tablespoons extra-virgin olive oil, divided
2 tablespoons ground flaxseed or flax meal	1 small very ripe avocado, peeled, pitted, and mashed
2 tablespoons almond flour	1 teaspoon white wine vinegar or lemon juice
½ teaspoon garlic powder	¼ teaspoon freshly ground black pepper
1 teaspoon baking powder	
1 teaspoon salt, divided	
1 large egg, lightly beaten	

1. Steam or microwave the riced cauliflower, covered, until tender. For frozen, cook 2 to 3 minutes in the microwave or 4 to 5 minutes on the stovetop. For fresh, cook 1 to 2 minutes in the microwave or 3 to 4 minutes on the stovetop. Set aside until completely cooled. 2. Meanwhile, in a medium bowl, mix the cream cheese until smooth. Add the flaxseed, almond flour, garlic powder, baking powder, ½ teaspoon of salt, and the beaten egg and whisk to combine well. 3. When the cauliflower reaches room temperature, cover with a paper towel. Use your hands to press down, allowing the liquid to rise above the towel, and pour off the excess. Continue pressing until the cauliflower is mostly dried and drained of excess liquid. 4. Stir the cauliflower and scallions into the cream cheese mixture. 5. Heat 2 tablespoons of olive oil in a large skillet over medium heat. Drop heaping tablespoonfuls of the cauliflower batter onto the skillet, and press down with a spatula to form 4 to 6 small patties, depending on the size of the skillet. Cook for 2 to 4 minutes, until the bottom is browned, then flip and cook another 2 to 4 minutes. Repeat with another 2 tablespoons of olive oil and the remaining batter. 6. To prepare the avocado mayo, in a small bowl, blend the remaining 2 tablespoons of olive oil, the mashed avocado, the remaining ½ teaspoon of salt, the vinegar or lemon juice, and pepper and whisk or beat with a fork until smooth and creamy. 7. Serve the hash browns warm with avocado mayo.

Per Serving:
calories: 379 | fat: 37g | protein: 6g | carbs: 10g | net carbs: 4g | fiber: 6g

Sausage & Squash Omelet with Swiss Chard

Prep time: 10 minutes | Cook time: 10 minutes | Serves 1

2 eggs	4 ounces roasted squash
1 cup Swiss chard, chopped	1 tablespoon olive oil
4 oz sausage, chopped	Salt and black pepper, to taste
2 tablespoons ricotta cheese	Fresh parsley to garnish

1. Beat the eggs in a bowl, season with salt and pepper; stir in the swiss chard and the ricotta cheese. 2. In another bowl, mash the squash and add to the egg mixture. Heat ¼ tbsp of olive oil in a pan over medium heat. Add sausage and cook until browned on all sides, turning occasionally. 3. Drizzle the remaining olive oil. Pour the egg mixture over. Cook for about 2 minutes per side until the eggs are thoroughly cooked and lightly browned. Remove the pan and run a spatula around the edges of the omelet; slide it onto a warm platter. Fold in half, and serve sprinkled with fresh parsley.

Per Serving:
calories: 744 | fat: 62g | protein: 32g | carbs: 15g | net carbs: 12g | fiber: 3g

Chocoholic Granola

Prep time: 5 minutes | Cook time: 10 minutes | Makes 3½ cups

⅓ cup (65 g) erythritol	¾ teaspoon finely ground sea salt
2 tablespoons water	3 cups (190 g) unsweetened coconut flakes
1 teaspoon vanilla extract	
⅓ cup (27 g) cocoa powder	
1 teaspoon ground cinnamon	

1. Cover a cutting board or baking sheet with a piece of parchment paper and set aside. 2. Place the erythritol, water, and vanilla in a large saucepan over medium-low heat. Bring to a light simmer, stirring every 30 seconds. Continue to Step 3 if using confectioners'-style erythritol; if using granulated erythritol, continue to simmer until the granules can no longer be felt on the back of the spoon. 3. Reduce the heat to low and add the cocoa powder, cinnamon, and salt; mix until fully incorporated. 4. Add the coconut flakes and continue to stir frequently, keeping the temperature low to prevent burning. Cook for 6 to 7 minutes, until the bottom of the pan gets sticky. 5. Remove from the heat and transfer the granola to the parchment paper. Allow to cool completely, about 20 minutes, before enjoying, or transfer to a 1-quart (950-ml) or larger airtight container for storage.

Per Serving:
calories: 106 | fat: 9g | protein: 1g | carbs: 5g | net carbs: 2g | fiber: 3g

Traditional Porridge

Prep time: 5 minutes | Cook time: 4 minutes | Serves 4

2 tablespoons coconut oil	½ cup chopped cashews
1 cup full-fat coconut milk	½ cup chopped pecans
2 tablespoons blanched almond flour	½ teaspoon ground cinnamon
2 tablespoons sugar-free chocolate chips	½ teaspoon erythritol, or more to taste
1 cup heavy whipping cream	¼ cup unsweetened coconut flakes

1. Set the Instant Pot to Sauté and melt the coconut oil. 2. Pour in the coconut milk, 1 cup of filtered water, then combine and mix the flour, chocolate chips, whipping cream, cashews, pecans, cinnamon, erythritol, and coconut flakes, inside the Instant Pot. 3. Close the lid, set the pressure release to Sealing, and hit Cancel to stop the current program. Select Manual, set the Instant Pot to 4 minutes on High Pressure, and let cook. 4. Once cooked, perform a quick release by carefully switching the pressure valve to Venting. 5. Open the Instant Pot, serve, and enjoy!

Per Serving:
calories: 533 | fat: 51g | protein: 7g | carbs: 16g | net carbs: 11g | fiber: 5g

Blender Cinnamon Pancakes with Cacao Cream Topping

Prep time: 10 minutes | Cook time: 10 minutes | Serves 4

Cinnamon Pancakes:	1 cup coconut cream
2 cups pecans	1½ tablespoons raw cacao powder
4 large eggs	Optional: low-carb sweetener, to taste
1 tablespoon cinnamon	
½ teaspoon baking soda	To Serve:
1 teaspoon fresh lemon juice or apple cider vinegar	9 medium strawberries, sliced
1 tablespoon virgin coconut oil or ghee	1 tablespoon unsweetened shredded coconut
Cacao Cream Topping:	

1. To make the pancakes: Place the pecans in a blender and process until powdered. Add all of the remaining ingredients apart from the ghee. Blend again until smooth. 2. Place a nonstick pan greased with 1 teaspoon of the coconut oil over low heat. Using a ¼-cup (60 ml) measure per pancake, cook in batches of 2 to 3 small pancakes over low heat until bubbles begin to form on the pancakes. Use a spatula to flip over, then cook for 30 to 40 seconds and place on a plate. Grease the pan with more coconut oil between batches. Transfer the pancakes to a plate. 3. To make the cacao cream topping: Place the coconut cream in a bowl. Add the cacao powder and sweetener, if using. Whisk until well combined and creamy. 4. Serve the pancakes with the cacao cream, sliced strawberries and a sprinkle of shredded coconut. You can enhance the flavor of the shredded coconut by toasting it in a dry pan for about 1 minute.

Per Serving:
calories: 665 | fat: 65g | protein: 14g | carbs: 17g | fiber: 9g | sodium: 232mg

Brussels Sprouts, Bacon, and Eggs

Prep time: 5 minutes | Cook time: 20 minutes | Serves 2

½ pound Brussels sprouts, cleaned, trimmed, and halved	6 bacon slices, diced
1 tablespoon olive oil	4 large eggs
Pink Himalayan salt	Pinch red pepper flakes
Freshly ground black pepper	2 tablespoons grated Parmesan cheese
Nonstick cooking spray	

1. Preheat the oven to 400°F. 2. In a medium bowl, toss the halved Brussels sprouts in the olive oil, and season with pink Himalayan salt and pepper. 3. Coat a 9-by-13-inch baking pan with cooking spray. 4. Put the Brussels sprouts and bacon in the pan, and roast for 12 minutes. 5. Take the pan out of the oven, and stir the Brussels sprouts and bacon. Using a spoon, create 4 wells in the mixture. 6. Carefully crack an egg into each well. 7. Season the eggs with pink Himalayan salt, black pepper, and red pepper flakes. 8. Sprinkle the Parmesan cheese over the Brussels sprouts and eggs. 9. Cook in the oven for 8 more minutes, or until the eggs are cooked to your preference, and serve.

Per Serving:
calories: 401 | fat: 29g | protein: 27g | carbs: 12g | net carbs: 7g | fiber: 5g

Cinnamon Muffins

Prep time: 10 minutes | Cook time: 14 minutes | Makes 12 muffins

1½ cups finely ground blanched almond flour	2 tablespoons salted butter, softened
1 tablespoon baking powder	1 tablespoon heavy whipping cream
1 tablespoon plus 1 teaspoon ground cinnamon, divided	½ teaspoon vanilla extract
2 large eggs	1/8 teaspoon liquid stevia
½ cup granular erythritol	

1. Preheat the oven to 350°F. Grease a standard-size 12-well muffin pan. 2. In a small bowl, whisk together the almond flour, baking powder, and 1 tablespoon of the cinnamon; set aside. 3. In a medium-sized bowl, whisk the eggs, then add the erythritol, butter, cream, vanilla extract, stevia, and remaining 1 teaspoon of cinnamon and stir until the ingredients are well combined. Slowly add the flour mixture, stirring with a spoon until the batter is smooth. 4. Pour the batter into the prepared muffin pan, filling each well about three-quarters full. Bake for 12 to 14 minutes, until a toothpick or tester inserted in the middle of a muffin comes out clean. 5. Allow the muffins to cool completely before removing from the pan. Leftovers can be stored in an airtight container at room temperature for up to 3 days or in the refrigerator for up to a week.

Per Serving:
calories: 218 | fat: 19g | protein: 7g | carbs: 6g | net carbs: 3g | fiber: 3g

Low-Carb Egg Curry

Prep time: 15 minutes | Cook time: 20 minutes | Serves 4

½ onion, finely diced

1 small (1-inch) knob fresh ginger

2 garlic cloves

1 small green chile pepper

1 large Roma tomato

1 tablespoon ghee

2 teaspoons ground turmeric

2 teaspoons chili powder

2 teaspoons ground coriander

2 teaspoons garam masala

½ cup water

Salt and freshly ground black pepper, to taste

4 hardboiled eggs, peeled

1. In a food processor or blender, combine the onion, ginger, garlic, and chile pepper. Process until a paste forms. Transfer to a small bowl and set aside. 2. Rinse out the blender then purée the tomato in it. Set aside. 3. In a small saucepan over medium heat, melt the ghee. Add the onion-ginger-garlic-chile paste to the pan. Stir and let it cook for 3 to 4 minutes or until fragrant. 4. Stir in the turmeric, chili powder, coriander, and garam masala. 5. Stir in the puréed tomato. Cook for 1 to 2 minutes then add the water, stirring to thoroughly combine. Season with salt and pepper, cover the pan, and cook for about 10 minutes over low heat. 6. Add the peeled eggs to the curry and gently stir to get all sides coated with the sauce. Cook for 3 to 5 minutes over low heat and serve.

Per Serving:
calories: 128 | fat: 8g | protein: 7g | carbs: 7g | net carbs: 5g | fiber: 2g

Egg and Cheese Biscuit Casserole

Prep time: 15 minutes | Cook time: 20 minutes | Serves 9

4 tablespoons (½ stick) butter, at room temperature, plus more for greasing the pan

½ cup coconut flour

2 teaspoons baking powder

¼ teaspoon salt

7 large eggs, divided

¼ cup sour cream

2 tablespoons heavy cream

1 teaspoon salt

1 teaspoon freshly ground black pepper

1 cup grated Cheddar cheese

1. Preheat the oven to 400°F (205°C). Grease a 9-by-9-inch casserole dish and set aside. 2. In a small bowl, whisk together the coconut flour, baking powder, and salt. 3. In a medium bowl, whisk together 3 eggs, the sour cream, and 4 tablespoons of butter. 4. Pour the dry mixture into the egg mixture, and mix well until just a few lumps remain. 5. Transfer the dough mixture to the casserole dish and mash to spread evenly across the bottom. 6. In a small bowl, whisk together the remaining 4 eggs and the heavy cream, salt, and pepper, and pour over the dough mixture. 7. Bake for 15 minutes. Pull the casserole out and sprinkle the Cheddar cheese across the top. Return to the oven for another 3 to 5 minutes or until the cheese is melted. 8. Allow to rest for 5 to 10 minutes before serving.

Per Serving:
calories: 280 | fat: 22g | protein: 14g | carbs: 9g | net carbs: 4g | fiber: 5g

Baklava Hot Porridge

Prep time: 5 minutes | Cook time: 5 minutes | Serves 2

2 cups riced cauliflower

¾ cup unsweetened almond, flax, or hemp milk

4 tablespoons extra-virgin olive oil, divided

2 teaspoons grated fresh orange peel (from ½ orange)

½ teaspoon ground cinnamon

½ teaspoon almond extract or vanilla extract

⅛ teaspoon salt

4 tablespoons chopped walnuts, divided

1 to 2 teaspoons liquid stevia, monk fruit, or other sweetener of choice (optional)

1. In medium saucepan, combine the riced cauliflower, almond milk, 2 tablespoons olive oil, grated orange peel, cinnamon, almond extract, and salt. Stir to combine and bring just to a boil over medium-high heat, stirring constantly. 2. Remove from heat and stir in 2 tablespoons chopped walnuts and sweetener (if using). Stir to combine. 3. Divide into bowls, topping each with 1 tablespoon of chopped walnuts and 1 tablespoon of the remaining olive oil.

Per Serving:
calories: 414 | fat: 38g | protein: 6g | carbs: 16g | fiber: 4g | sodium: 252mg

Keto Chai

Prep time: 3 minutes | Cook time: 10 to 15 minutes | Serves 7

8 whole cloves

7 cardamom pods

2 cinnamon sticks

1½ teaspoons black peppercorns

1 (2-inch) piece fresh ginger, sliced into thin rounds

5 cups cold water

5 bags black tea

2 cups unsweetened (unflavored

or vanilla-flavored) cashew milk, homemade or store-bought, or almond milk (or hemp milk for nut-free)

2 to 4 tablespoons Swerve confectioners'-style sweetener or equivalent amount of liquid or powdered sweetener

1 tablespoon coconut oil per cup of tea

1. Place the spices and ginger in a medium saucepan. Toast on low heat while lightly crushing the spices with the back of a spoon. 2. Add the water and bring to a boil. Once boiling, cover the pan, lower the heat, and simmer for 5 to 10 minutes (the longer time will create a stronger chai flavor). Remove from the heat. 3. Place the teabags in the saucepan and steep for 4 minutes. Remove the teabags and add the cashew milk and 2 tablespoons of the sweetener. Stir, taste, and add more sweetener if desired. 4. Bring the chai to a bare simmer over medium heat, then strain it into a teapot. Just before serving, place a tablespoon of coconut oil in each teacup, pour the hot tea over it, and whisk to blend the coconut oil into the tea. Store extra tea in an airtight container in the fridge for up to 1 week.

Per Serving:
calories: 35 | fat: 3g | protein: 1g | carbs: 1g | net carbs: 1g | fiber: 0g

Three-Cheese Quiche

Prep time: 10 minutes | Cook time: 6 minutes | Serves 6

6 eggs, beaten

2 tablespoon cream cheese

1 teaspoon Italian seasoning

¼ cup shredded Cheddar cheese

3 ounces (85 g) Monterey Jack

cheese, shredded

2 ounces (57 g) Mozzarella, shredded

1 cup water, for cooking

1. Pour water in the instant pot. 2. In the mixing bowl, mix up eggs cream cheese, Italian seasoning, and all types of cheese. 3. Pour the mixture in the baking cups (molds) and place them in the instant pot. 4. Close and seal the lid. 5. Cook the quiche cups for 6 minutes on Manual mode (High Pressure). 6. Make a quick pressure release.

Per Serving:

calories: 175 | fat: 13g | protein: 13g | carbs: 1g | net carbs: 0g | fiber: 1g

Pumpkin Spice Smoothie

Prep time: 5 minutes | Cook time: 0 minutes | Serves 2

1 cup full-fat coconut, nut, or dairy milk

¾ cup canned pumpkin

½ cup frozen riced cauliflower

1 cup water

1 teaspoon ground cinnamon, plus extra for garnish if desired

1 teaspoon pumpkin pie spice

1 teaspoon pure vanilla extract

Small handful of ice (optional)

2 scoops collagen peptides

⅛ teaspoon green stevia, or 2 or 3 drops stevia extract (optional)

1 tablespoon coconut chips, for garnish (optional)

1. Place all the ingredients except the coconut chips in a blender and blend until smooth. If you prefer a thinner smoothie, add more water or milk to your liking. 2. Garnish with ground cinnamon and coconut chips before serving, if desired.

Per Serving:

calories: 302 | fat: 24g | protein: 13g | carbs: 12g | net carbs: 9g | fiber: 3g

Allspice Muffins

Prep time: 15 minutes | Cook time: 25 minutes | Makes 12 muffins

DRY INGREDIENTS:

1½ cups (165 g) blanched almond flour

½ cup (64 g) roughly ground flax seeds

½ cup (80 g) confectioners'-style erythritol

2 teaspoons baking powder

1 tablespoon plus 1 teaspoon ground allspice

½ teaspoon finely ground gray

sea salt

WET INGREDIENTS:

6 large eggs

½ cup (120 ml) melted (but not hot) coconut oil

½ cup (120 ml) full-fat coconut milk

Grated zest of 1 lemon

1 teaspoon vanilla extract

TOPPING:

¼ cup (28 g) raw walnut pieces

1. Preheat the oven to 350°F (177°C) and line a muffin pan with 12 paper liners, or have on hand a 12-cavity silicone muffin pan. 2. Place the dry ingredients in a medium-sized bowl and mix until fully blended. 3. In a large bowl, whisk the eggs, coconut oil, coconut milk, lemon zest, and vanilla. Once combined, add the dry mixture to the wet. Stir with a spatula just until incorporated. 4. Pour the batter into the prepared muffin cups, filling each about three-quarters full. Sprinkle the tops with the walnuts. 5. Bake for 22 to 25 minutes, until the tops are golden and a toothpick inserted in the middle comes out clean. 6. Allow the muffins to cool in the pan for 30 minutes before removing and serving.

Per Serving:

calories: 273 | fat: 24g | protein: 8g | carbs: 6g | net carbs: 2g | fiber: 4g

Chocolate Raspberry Smoothie

Prep time: 5 minutes | Cook time: 0 minutes | Serves 1

¾ cup water

½ packed cup frozen raspberries

4 large ice cubes (approximately ½ cup)

¼ cup full-fat coconut, nut, or dairy milk

¼ medium avocado, peeled

2 tablespoons cacao powder

2 tablespoons ground chia or flax seeds

2 scoops grass-fed collagen peptides

¼ teaspoon pure vanilla extract

⅛ teaspoon green stevia, or 2 or 3 drops stevia extract (optional)

Pinch of sea salt

Cacao nibs, for garnish (optional)

Whole fresh raspberries, for garnish (optional)

1. Place all the ingredients in a blender and blend until smooth. If you prefer a thinner smoothie, add more water or milk to your liking. 2. Garnish with cacao nibs and fresh raspberries, if desired.

Per Serving:

calories: 444 | fat: 27g | protein: 28g | carbs: 27g | net carbs: 8g | fiber: 19g

Cheddar Soufflés

Prep time: 15 minutes | Cook time: 12 minutes | Serves 4

3 large eggs, whites and yolks separated

¼ teaspoon cream of tartar

½ cup shredded sharp Cheddar

cheese

3 ounces (85 g) cream cheese, softened

1. In a large bowl, beat egg whites together with cream of tartar until soft peaks form, about 2 minutes. 2. In a separate medium bowl, beat egg yolks, Cheddar, and cream cheese together until frothy, about 1 minute. Add egg yolk mixture to whites, gently folding until combined. 3. Pour mixture evenly into four ramekins greased with cooking spray. Place ramekins into air fryer basket. Adjust the temperature to 350°F (177°C) and bake for 12 minutes. Eggs will be browned on the top and firm in the center when done. Serve warm.

Per Serving:

calories: 184 | fat: 16g | protein: 9g | carbs: 1g | net carbs: 1g | fiber: 0g

Super Breakfast Combo

Prep time: 10 minutes | Cook time: 0 minutes | Serves 1

CHOCOLATE FAT BOMBS:

1 tablespoon coconut butter

2 teaspoons coconut oil

1 teaspoon cocoa powder

½ teaspoon confectioners'-style erythritol, or 1 drop liquid stevia

MATCHA LATTE:

1 cup (240 ml) boiling water

2 tablespoons collagen peptides or protein powder

1 tablespoon coconut butter, coconut oil, or nut butter

1 teaspoon erythritol, or 2 drops liquid stevia

1 teaspoon matcha powder

½ teaspoon maca powder (optional)

¼ teaspoon chaga powder or ashwagandha powder (optional)

1¼ cups (300 ml) full-fat coconut milk, hot

1. To prepare the fat bomb, place all the ingredients in a bowl and either set out in the sun to melt or microwave for 20 to 30 seconds. Once the coconut butter has melted, whisk thoroughly and transfer to a paper muffin liner, a silicone mold, a plastic container—anything will do. Place in the freezer for 5 minutes, or until hardened. 2. Meanwhile, place the boiling water, collagen, coconut butter, sweetener, matcha, and maca and chaga, if using, in a 20-ounce (600-ml) or larger mug. Whisk until the ingredients are incorporated and the lumps are gone, about 1 minute. Stir in the hot coconut milk. 3. Serve the latte with the chilled fat bomb.

Per Serving:

calories: 740 | fat: 65g | protein: 26g | carbs: 12g | net carbs: 2g | fiber: 9g

Gyro Breakfast Patties with Tzatziki

Prep time: 10 minutes | Cook time: 20 minutes per batch | Makes 16 patties

Patties:

2 pounds (907 g) ground lamb or beef

½ cup diced red onions

¼ cup sliced black olives

2 tablespoons tomato sauce

1 teaspoon dried oregano leaves

1 teaspoon Greek seasoning

2 cloves garlic, minced

1 teaspoon fine sea salt

Tzatziki:

1 cup full-fat sour cream

1 small cucumber, chopped

½ teaspoon fine sea salt

½ teaspoon garlic powder, or 1 clove garlic, minced

¼ teaspoon dried dill weed, or 1 teaspoon finely chopped fresh dill

For Garnish/Serving:

½ cup crumbled feta cheese (about 2 ounces / 57 g)

Diced red onions

Sliced black olives

Sliced cucumbers

1. Preheat the air fryer to 350°F (177°C). 2. Place the ground lamb, onions, olives, tomato sauce, oregano, Greek seasoning, garlic, and salt in a large bowl. Mix well to combine the ingredients. 3. Using your hands, form the mixture into sixteen 3-inch patties. Place about 5 of the patties in the air fryer and air fry for 20 minutes, flipping halfway through. Remove the patties and place them on a serving platter. Repeat with the remaining patties. 4. While the patties cook, make the tzatziki: Place all the ingredients in a small bowl and stir well. Cover and store in the fridge until ready to serve. Garnish with ground black pepper before serving. 5. Serve the patties with a dollop of tzatziki, a sprinkle of crumbled feta cheese, diced red onions, sliced black olives, and sliced cucumbers. 6. Store leftovers in an airtight container in the refrigerator for up to 5 days or in the freezer for up to a month. Reheat the patties in a preheated 390°F (199°C) air fryer for a few minutes, until warmed through.

Per Serving:

calories: 149 | fat: 10g | protein: 13g | carbs: 2g | net carbs: 2g | fiber: 0g

Rocket Fuel Hot Chocolate

Prep time: 5 minutes | Cook time: 0 minutes | Makes 2

2 cups (475 ml) milk (nondairy or regular), hot

2 tablespoons cocoa powder

2 tablespoons collagen peptides or protein powder

2 tablespoons coconut oil, MCT oil, unflavored MCT oil

powder, or ghee

1 tablespoon coconut butter

1 tablespoon erythritol, or 4 drops liquid stevia

Pinch of ground cinnamon (optional)

1. Place all the ingredients in a blender and blend for 10 seconds, or until the ingredients are fully incorporated. 2. Divide between 2 mugs, sprinkle with cinnamon if you'd like, and enjoy!

Per Serving:

calories: 357 | fat: 29g | protein: 13g | carbs: 11g | net carbs: 7g | fiber: 4g

Mini Shrimp Frittata

Prep time: 15 minutes | Cook time: 20 minutes | Serves 4

1 teaspoon olive oil, plus more for spraying

½ small red bell pepper, finely diced

1 teaspoon minced garlic

1 (4-ounce / 113-g) can of tiny

shrimp, drained

Salt and freshly ground black pepper, to taste

4 eggs, beaten

4 teaspoons ricotta cheese

1. Spray four ramekins with olive oil. 2. In a medium skillet over medium-low heat, heat 1 teaspoon of olive oil. Add the bell pepper and garlic and sauté until the pepper is soft, about 5 minutes 3. Add the shrimp, season with salt and pepper, and cook until warm, 1 to 2 minutes. Remove from the heat. 4. Add the eggs and stir to combine. 5. Pour one quarter of the mixture into each ramekin. 6. Place 2 ramekins in the air fryer basket and bake at 350°F (177°C) for 6 minutes. 7. Remove the air fryer basket from the air fryer and stir the mixture in each ramekin. Top each fritatta with 1 teaspoon of ricotta cheese. Return the air fryer basket to the air fryer and cook until eggs are set and the top is lightly browned, 4 to 5 minutes. 8. Repeat with the remaining two ramekins.

Per Serving:

calories: 114 | fat: 6g | protein: 12g | carbs: 1g | fiber: 0g | sodium: 314mg

Something Different Breakfast Sammy

Prep time: 5 minutes | Cook time: 10 minutes | Serves 1

1 medium Hass avocado, peeled and pitted (about 4 oz/110 g of flesh)	1 red onion ring
	1 tomato slice
	Pinch of finely ground sea salt
1 lettuce leaf, torn in half	Pinch of ground black pepper
1 tablespoon mayonnaise	Pinch of sesame seeds or poppy
2 strips bacon (about 2 oz/55 g), cooked until crispy	seeds (optional)

1. Cook the bacon in a medium-sized frying pan over medium heat until crispy, about 10 minutes. 2. Place the avocado halves cut side up on a plate. 3. Lay the lettuce pieces on top of one of the avocado halves, then slather the mayonnaise on the lettuce. Top the lettuce with the bacon, onion, and tomato, then sprinkle with the salt and pepper. 4. Cover the stack with the other avocado half and sprinkle with the seeds, if using. Enjoy immediately!

Per Serving:
calories: 545 | fat: 43g | protein: 19g | carbs: 20g | net carbs: 11g | fiber: 9g

Cheesy Cauliflower Grits

Prep time: 5 minutes | Cook time: 15 minutes | Serves 4

¼ cup heavy cream	black pepper
4 tablespoons unsalted butter, divided	2 cups riced cauliflower
	¾ cup shredded Cheddar cheese
1 teaspoon salt	¼ cup shredded Parmesan
½ teaspoon garlic powder	cheese
¼ teaspoon freshly ground	

1. In a medium saucepan over high heat, combine the heavy cream, 2 tablespoons of butter, salt, garlic powder, and pepper and bring to just below a boil. Add the riced cauliflower and reduce heat to low. 2. Simmer, stirring occasionally, for 8 to 10 minutes, until the cauliflower is tender, most of the water from the vegetable has evaporated, and the mixture is thick and creamy. 3. Remove from the heat and stir in the shredded cheeses and remaining 2 tablespoons of butter. Serve warm.

Per Serving:
calories: 280 | fat: 26g | protein: 8g | carbs: 5g | net carbs: 4g | fiber: 1g

Almond Flour Tortillas

Prep time: 10 minutes | Cook time: 25 minutes | Makes 5 tortillas

10 eggs	Salt and freshly ground black pepper, to taste
6 tablespoons almond flour	
3 tablespoons arrowroot powder	2 to 3 tablespoons butter,
1 teaspoon garlic powder	divided

1. Heat a large skillet over medium-high heat. 2. In a large bowl whisk the eggs. 3. Sift the almond flour and arrowroot powder into the bowl and add the garlic powder. Season with salt and pepper. 4. Add 1 tablespoon of butter to the skillet to melt. Pour in about ¼ cup of the batter. Tilt the skillet around so the batter evenly coats the bottom. Cook for 2 to 3 minutes or until the edges begin to pull away from the skillet. Use a spatula to flip the tortilla and let it cook on the other side for 1 to 2 minutes. Transfer to a plate and repeat, adding a bit more butter and another ¼ cup of batter until the ingredients have been used up. Serve immediately.

Per Serving:
1 tortilla: calories: 225 | fat: 17g | protein: 12g | carbs: 6g | net carbs: 6g | fiber: 0g

Ground Pork Breakfast Patties

Prep time: 5 minutes | Cook time: 15 minutes | Serves 4

1 pound (454 g) 84% lean ground pork	½ teaspoon garlic powder
	½ teaspoon salt
1 teaspoon dried thyme	¼ teaspoon pepper
½ teaspoon dried sage	¼ teaspoon red pepper flakes

1. Mix all ingredients in large bowl. Form into 4 patties based on preference. Press the Sauté button and press the Adjust button to lower heat to Less. 2. Place patties in Instant Pot and allow fat to render while patties begin browning. After 5 minutes, or when a few tablespoons of fat have rendered from meat, press the Cancel button. 3. Press the Sauté button and press the Adjust button to set heat to Normal. Sear each side of patties and allow them to cook fully until no pink remains in centers, approximately 10 additional minutes, depending on thickness.

Per Serving:
calories: 249 | fat: 16g | protein: 20g | carbs: 1g | net carbs: 1g | fiber: 0g

Hearty Spinach and Bacon Breakfast Bowl

Prep time: 10 minutes | Cook time: 10 minutes | Serves 2

1 tablespoon coconut oil	thoroughly washed
2 red bell peppers, chopped	8 cooked uncured bacon slices,
½ cup sliced white mushrooms	chopped
1 teaspoon minced garlic	½ cup grated Asiago cheese
½ teaspoon red pepper flakes	½ avocado, sliced
4 cups chopped spinach,	

1. Sauté the vegetables. In a large skillet over medium-high heat, melt the coconut oil. Add the red bell peppers, mushrooms, garlic, and red pepper flakes and sauté them until they've softened, about 3 minutes. Add the spinach and cook until it has wilted, about 4 minutes. 2. Finish cooking. Stir in the bacon and Asiago and cook for 2 minutes more. 3. Serve. Divide the mixture between four bowls and top with the avocado slices.

Per Serving:
calories: 445 | fat: 32g | protein: 26g | carbs: 14g | net carbs: 8g | fiber: 6g

Yogurt Parfait with Creamy Blueberry Crumble

Prep time: 10 minutes | Cook time: 25 minutes | Serves 4

6 tablespoons cold unsalted butter, divided

¼ cup almond flour

¼ cup ground flaxseed

¼ cup slivered almonds

¼ cup chopped roasted unsalted walnuts

1 cup fresh or frozen blueberries

2 to 4 tablespoons granulated

sugar-free sweetener

Zest of 1 lemon

1 teaspoon vanilla extract

½ teaspoon ground ginger or cinnamon

½ cup heavy cream

2 cups plain full-fat Greek yogurt

1. Preheat the oven to 350°F (180°C) and generously coat the bottom and sides of an 8-inch square glass baking dish or 8-inch pie pan with 2 tablespoons of butter. 2. In a medium bowl, cut the remaining 4 tablespoons of butter into very small pieces. Add the almond flour, flaxseed, almonds, and walnuts and mix until crumbly. Set aside. 3. In a separate bowl, combine the blueberries, sweetener, lemon zest, vanilla extract, and ginger or cinnamon. Toss to coat the blueberries well. 4. Add the blueberry mixture to the prepared baking dish (they won't quite cover the bottom), and pour the heavy cream over the blueberry mixture. 5. Top the blueberry mixture evenly with the flour-and-nut mixture, and bake for 20 to 25 minutes, until golden brown. Let rest for 10 minutes before serving to allow the mixture to thicken. 6. To serve, top one-quarter of the warm crumble mixture with ½ cup of Greek yogurt.
Per Serving:
calories: 500 | fat: 45g | protein: 10g | carbs: 18g | net carbs: 13g | fiber: 5g

Pumpkin Spice Latte Overnight "Oats"

Prep time: 5 minutes | Cook time: 0 minutes | Serves 2

½ cup (75 g) hulled hemp seeds

⅓ cup (80 ml) milk (nondairy or regular), plus more for serving

⅓ cup (80 ml) brewed coffee (decaf or regular)

2 tablespoons canned pumpkin puree

1 tablespoon chia seeds

2 teaspoons erythritol, or 3 drops liquid stevia

½ teaspoon vanilla extract

½ teaspoon ground cinnamon

¼ teaspoon ground nutmeg

⅛ teaspoon ground cloves

Pinch of finely ground sea salt

TOPPINGS (optional):

Chopped raw or roasted pecans

Ground cinnamon

Additional hulled hemp seeds

Toasted unsweetened shredded coconut

1. Place all the ingredients in a 12-ounce (350-ml) or larger container with a lid and stir until combined. Cover and set in the fridge to soak overnight, or for at least 8 hours. 2. The following day, add more milk until the desired consistency is reached. Divide between 2 small bowls, top as desired, and enjoy.
Per Serving:
calories: 337 | fat: 26g | protein: 15g | carbs: 9g | net carbs: 2g | fiber: 7g

Inside-Out Breakfast Burrito

Prep time: 10 minutes | Cook time: 5 minutes | Serves 2

Wrap:

¼ cup shredded low-moisture mozzarella cheese

2 large eggs

1 teaspoon coconut flour

Pink Himalayan sea salt

Freshly ground black pepper

2 teaspoons extra-virgin olive

oil, divided

Burrito:

½ cup cauliflower rice, cooked

4 ounces (113 g) breakfast sausage, cooked

½ cup shredded Cheddar cheese

1 medium avocado, sliced

1. To make the wrap: In a medium bowl, whisk together the mozzarella, eggs, and coconut flour. Season with salt and pepper. 2. In an 8-inch skillet, heat 1 teaspoon of olive oil over medium-low heat. 3. Pour half the egg mixture into the pan and rotate the pan to spread it evenly on the skillet bottom. 4. Cook for about 1 minute on each side, flipping once. 5. Remove the egg wrap from the heat and cool. 6. Repeat steps 2 to 5 for the second wrap. 7. To make the burrito: Onto each wrap, evenly spread half the cauliflower rice, sausage, Cheddar cheese, and avocado. 8. Fold the sides in, roll up like a burrito, and enjoy!
Per Serving:
calories: 654 | fat: 55g | protein: 29g | carbs: 15g | net carbs: 6g | fiber: 9g

Biscuits with Gravy

Prep time: 15 minutes | Cook time: 15 minutes |
Makes 12 biscuits with gravy

Biscuits:

½ cup coconut flour

2 teaspoons baking powder

¼ teaspoon salt

3 large eggs

¼ cup sour cream

4 tablespoons (½ stick) butter, at room temperature

Gravy:

1 pound (454 g) breakfast sausage

4 ounces (113 g) cream cheese

1 cup heavy (whipping) cream

1 teaspoon freshly ground black pepper

Make the Biscuits 1. Preheat the oven to 350°F (180°C). Line a baking sheet with parchment paper and set aside. 2. In a small bowl, whisk together the coconut flour, baking powder, and salt. 3. In a medium bowl, whisk together the eggs, sour cream, and butter. 4. Pour the dry mixture into the egg mixture and stir until well combined but still lumpy. 5. Scoop the biscuit mixture into 12 even mounds on the prepared baking sheet. Bake for 10 to 14 minutes or until golden brown. Make the Gravy 6. Meanwhile, in a skillet over medium heat, brown the breakfast sausage, then drain. 7. Add the cream cheese to the skillet and mix well. 8. Reduce the heat to low, add the heavy cream and pepper, and stir frequently for 10 to 15 minutes, until the gravy reaches the thickness you desire. If it gets too thick, add a little water. To Serve 9. Cut a biscuit in half and spoon a tablespoon of gravy on each half.
Per Serving:
calories: 301 | fat: 27g | protein: 9g | carbs: 5g | net carbs: 3g | fiber: 2g

Egg Roll in a Bowl

Prep time: 10 minutes | Cook time: 10 minutes | Serves 2

2 large eggs	(or bagged coleslaw mix; no
2 tablespoons sesame oil, divided	dressing)
	2 ribs celery, diced
2 tablespoons soy sauce, divided	½ small red bell pepper, diced
	2 tablespoons lime juice,
2 tablespoons extra-virgin olive oil	divided
	2 scallions, minced (green and
6 ounces (170 g) ground pork	white parts)
1 tablespoon chopped fresh ginger (or 1 teaspoon ground ginger)	2 tablespoons mayonnaise
	1 teaspoon sriracha or other hot sauce
2 cloves garlic, minced	½ teaspoon garlic powder
2 cups finely chopped cabbage	

1. In a small bowl, beat together the eggs, 1 tablespoon of sesame oil, and 1 tablespoon of soy sauce and set aside. 2. Heat the olive oil in a large skillet over medium heat. Sauté the ground pork, breaking it apart, until browned and no longer pink, 4 to 5 minutes. Add the ginger and garlic and sauté for an additional 30 seconds. 3. Add the cabbage, celery, and bell pepper and sauté, stirring constantly, until the vegetables are wilted and fragrant, another 2 to 3 minutes. 4. Push the vegetables and pork to one side of the skillet and add the egg mixture to the other side. Reduce heat to low and scramble the egg until cooked through, 1 to 2 minutes. Remove the skillet from the heat and mix the egg into the pork and cabbage. 5. In a small bowl, whisk together the remaining 1 tablespoon of sesame oil, the remaining 1 tablespoon of soy sauce, 1 tablespoon of lime juice, and the scallions. Pour over the cooked pork mixture and stir to combine well, reserving the bowl. 6. In the same small bowl, combine the remaining 1 tablespoon of lime juice, the mayonnaise, sriracha, and garlic powder. 7. Divide the pork mixture evenly between two bowls and drizzle each with half of the spicy mayo. Serve warm.

Per Serving:
calories: 695 | fat: 61g | protein: 25g | carbs: 16g | net carbs: 10g | fiber: 4g

No-Beans Hummus

Prep time: 5 minutes | Cook time: 0 minutes | Makes 2 cups

1 medium head cauliflower, cored and separated into florets (about 15½ ounces/445 g florets)	2 small cloves garlic, minced
	¾ teaspoon finely ground gray sea salt
¼ cup (65 g) tahini	½ teaspoon ground cumin
6 tablespoons (90 ml) extra-virgin olive oil, divided	Pinch of paprika, for garnish
	Pinch of dried parsley, for garnish
¼ cup (60 ml) fresh lemon juice	

1. Place the cauliflower florets, tahini, 4 tablespoons (60 ml) of the olive oil, lemon juice, garlic, salt, and cumin in a food processor or blender. Pulse until somewhat smooth, or until it reaches the desired hummus-like consistency. 2. Transfer the mixture to a serving bowl. Drizzle with the remaining olive oil and sprinkle with the paprika and parsley.

Per Serving:
calories: 162 | fat: 14g | protein: 2g | carbs: 5g | net carbs: 3g | fiber: 2g

Vegetable-Beef Hash with Nested Eggs

Prep time: 5 minutes | Cook time: 35 minutes | Serves 4

2 tablespoons good-quality olive oil	1½ cups low-carb tomato sauce
	1 tablespoon dried basil
½ pound grass-fed ground beef	1 teaspoon dried oregano
½ red bell pepper, diced	⅛ teaspoon sea salt
½ zucchini, diced	⅛ teaspoon freshly ground black pepper
¼ onion, diced	
2 teaspoons minced garlic	4 eggs

1. Cook the beef. In a large deep skillet over medium-high heat, warm the olive oil. Add the beef and, stirring it occasionally, cook until it is completely browned, about 10 minutes. 2. Make the sauce. Add the bell pepper, zucchini, onion, and garlic to the skillet and sauté for 3 minutes. Stir in the tomato sauce, basil, oregano, salt, and pepper, bring it to a boil, and cook for about 10 minutes. 3. Cook the eggs. Make four wells in the beef mixture using the back of a spoon. Crack an egg into each well, then cover the skillet, reduce the heat to medium-low, and simmer until the eggs are cooked through, about 10 minutes. 4. Serve. Divide the mixture between four bowls, making sure to include an egg in each serving.

Per Serving:
calories: 275 | fat: 19g | protein: 18g | carbs: 8g | net carbs: 6g | fiber: 2g

Blackberry Vanilla Cake

Prep time: 10 minutes | Cook time: 25 minutes | Serves 8

1 cup almond flour	4 tablespoons melted butter
2 eggs	¼ cup heavy cream
½ cup erythritol	½ teaspoon baking powder
2 teaspoons vanilla extract	1 cup water
1 cup blackberries	

1. In large bowl, mix all ingredients except water. Pour into 7-inch round cake pan or divide into two 4-inch pans, if needed. Cover with foil. 2. Pour water into Instant Pot and place steam rack in bottom. Place pan on steam rack and click lid closed. Press the Cake button and press the Adjust button to set heat to Less. Set time for 25 minutes. 3. When timer beeps, allow a 15-minute natural release then quick-release the remaining pressure. Let cool completely.

Per Serving:
calories: 174 | fat: 15g | protein: 10g | carbs: 17g | net carbs: 15g | fiber: 2g

Greek Breakfast Power Bowl

Prep time: 15 minutes | Cook time: 20 minutes | Serves 2

3 tablespoons extra-virgin avocado oil or ghee, divided
1 clove garlic, minced
2 teaspoons chopped fresh rosemary
1 small eggplant, roughly chopped
1 medium zucchini, roughly chopped
1 tablespoon fresh lemon juice
2 tablespoons chopped mint

1 tablespoon chopped fresh oregano
Salt and black pepper, to taste
6 ounces (170 g) Halloumi cheese, cubed or sliced
¼ cup pitted Kalamata olives
4 large eggs, soft-boiled (or hard-boiled or poached)
1 tablespoon extra-virgin olive oil, to drizzle

1. Heat a skillet (with a lid) greased with 2 tablespoons (30 ml) of the avocado oil over medium heat. Add the garlic and rosemary and cook for 1 minute. Add the eggplant, zucchini, and lemon juice. Stir and cover with a lid, then reduce the heat to medium-low. Cook for 10 to 15 minutes, stirring once or twice, until tender. 2. Stir in the mint and oregano. Optionally, reserve some herbs for topping. Season with salt and pepper to taste. Remove from the heat and transfer to a plate. Cover with the skillet lid to keep the veggies warm. 3. Grease the same pan with the remaining 1 tablespoon (15 ml) avocado oil and cook the Halloumi over medium-high heat for 2 to 3 minutes per side until lightly browned. Place the slices of cooked Halloumi on top of the cooked veggies. Top with the olives and cooked eggs and drizzle with the olive oil. 4. Always serve warm, as Halloumi hardens once it cools. Reheat before serving if necessary.

Per Serving:
calories: 748 | fat: 56g | protein: 40g | carbs: 25g | fiber: 10g | sodium: 275mg

Avocado Boats with Flax Crackers

Prep time: 10 minutes | Cook time: 0 minutes | serves 2

1 Roma tomato, chopped
2 tablespoons cold-pressed olive oil, plus more for drizzling
1 tablespoon fresh basil, plus more, cut into chiffonade, for serving
1 garlic clove, crushed

Sea salt
⅛ teaspoon freshly ground black pepper
1 avocado, halved and pit removed
Juice of ½ lemon
Flaxseed crackers

1. In a small mixing bowl, gently toss the tomato, olive oil, basil, garlic, salt, and pepper, and set aside. 2. Sprinkle the cut surface of the avocado halves with the lemon juice to prevent browning. 3. Generously stuff the avocado halves with the tomato mixture. 4. Plate the stuffed avocado, drizzle with olive oil, and top with a few ribbons of fresh basil. 5. Serve with flax crackers.

Per Serving:
calories: 286 | fat: 28g | protein: 2g | carbs: 12g | net carbs: 5g | fiber: 7g

Egg Tofu Scramble with Kale & Mushrooms

Prep time: 10 minutes | Cook time: 25 minutes | Serves 4

2 tbsp ghee
1 cup sliced white mushrooms
2 cloves garlic, minced
16 oz firm tofu, pressed and

crumbled
Salt and black pepper to taste
½ cup thinly sliced kale
6 fresh eggs

1. Melt the ghee in a non-stick skillet over medium heat, and sauté the mushrooms for 5 minutes until they lose their liquid. Add the garlic and cook for 1 minute. 2. Crumble the tofu into the skillet, season with salt and black pepper. Cook with continuous stirring for 6 minutes. Introduce the kale in batches and cook to soften for about 7 minutes. Crack the eggs into a bowl, whisk until well combined and creamy in color, and pour all over the kale. Use a spatula to immediately stir the eggs while cooking until scrambled and no more runny, about 5 minutes. Plate, and serve with low carb crusted bread.

Per Serving:
Per serving: Kcal 469, Fat 39g, Net Carbs 5g, Protein 25g

No-Bake Keto Power Bars

Prep time: 10 minutes | Cook time: 0 minutes | Makes 12 bars

½ cup pili nuts
½ cup whole hazelnuts
½ cup walnut halves
¼ cup hulled sunflower seeds
¼ cup unsweetened coconut flakes or chips
¼ cup hulled hemp seeds
2 tablespoons unsweetened cacao nibs
2 scoops collagen powder (I use 1 scoop Perfect Keto vanilla

collagen and 1 scoop Perfect Keto unflavored collagen powder)
½ teaspoon ground cinnamon
½ teaspoon sea salt
¼ cup coconut oil, melted
1 teaspoon vanilla extract
Stevia or monk fruit to sweeten (optional if you are using unflavored collagen powder)

1. Line a 9-inch square baking pan with parchment paper. 2. In a food processor or blender, combine the pili nuts, hazelnuts, walnuts, sunflower seeds, coconut, hemp seeds, cacao nibs, collagen powder, cinnamon, and salt and pulse a few times. 3. Add the coconut oil, vanilla extract, and sweetener (if using). Pulse again until the ingredients are combined. Do not over pulse or it will turn to mush. You want the nuts and seeds to still have some texture. 4. Pour the mixture into the prepared pan and press it into an even layer. Cover with another piece of parchment (or fold over extra from the first piece) and place a heavy pan or dish on top to help press the bars together. 5. Refrigerate overnight and then cut into 12 bars. Store the bars in individual storage bags in the refrigerator for a quick grab-and-go breakfast.

Per Serving:
calories: 242 | fat: 22g | protein: 6g | carbs: 4g | net carbs: 2g | fiber: 2g

Spicy Breakfast Scramble

2 tablespoons ghee

6 ounces Mexican chorizo or other spicy sausage

6 large eggs

2 tablespoons heavy (whipping) cream

Pink Himalayan salt

Freshly ground black pepper

½ cup shredded cheese, like pepper Jack, divided

½ cup chopped scallions, white and green parts

1. In a large skillet over medium-high heat, melt the ghee. Add the sausage and sauté, browning for about 6 minutes, until cooked through. 2. In a medium bowl, whisk the eggs until frothy. 3. Add the cream, and season with pink Himalayan salt and pepper. Whisk to blend thoroughly. 4. Leaving the fat in the skillet, push the sausage to one side. Add the egg mixture to the other side of the skillet and heat until almost cooked through, about 3 minutes. 5. When the eggs are almost done, mix in half of the shredded cheese. 6. Mix the eggs and sausage together in the skillet. Top with the remaining shredded cheese and the scallions. 7. Spoon onto two plates and serve hot.

Per Serving:
calories: 850 | fat: 70g | protein: 46g | carbs: 7g | net carbs: 6g | fiber: 1g

Mushroom Frittata

2 tablespoons olive oil

1 cup sliced fresh mushrooms

1 cup shredded spinach

6 bacon slices, cooked and chopped

10 large eggs, beaten

½ cup crumbled goat cheese

Sea salt

Freshly ground black pepper

1. Preheat the oven to 350°F. 2. Place a large ovenproof skillet over medium-high heat and add the olive oil. 3. Sauté the mushrooms until lightly browned, about 3 minutes. 4. Add the spinach and bacon and sauté until the greens are wilted, about 1 minute. 5. Add the eggs and cook, lifting the edges of the frittata with a spatula so uncooked egg flows underneath, for 3 to 4 minutes. 6. Sprinkle the top with the crumbled goat cheese and season lightly with salt and pepper. 7. Bake until set and lightly browned, about 15 minutes. 8. Remove the frittata from the oven, and let it stand for 5 minutes. 9. Cut into 6 wedges and serve immediately.

Per Serving:
calories: 379 | fat: 27g | protein: 16g | carbs: 1g | net carbs: 1g | fiber: 0g

Cream Cheese Muffins

4 tablespoons melted butter, plus more for the muffin tin

1 cup almond flour

¾ tablespoon baking powder

2 large eggs, lightly beaten

2 ounces cream cheese mixed with 2 tablespoons heavy (whipping) cream

Handful shredded Mexican blend cheese

1. Preheat the oven to 400°F. Coat six cups of a muffin tin with butter. 2. In a small bowl, mix together the almond flour and baking powder. 3. In a medium bowl, mix together the eggs, cream cheese–heavy cream mixture, shredded cheese, and 4 tablespoons of the melted butter. 4. Pour the flour mixture into the egg mixture, and beat with a hand mixer until thoroughly mixed. 5. Pour the batter into the prepared muffin cups. 6. Bake for 12 minutes, or until golden brown on top, and serve.

Per Serving:
calories: 247 | fat: 23g | protein: 8g | carbs: 4g | net carbs: 4g | fiber: 2g

Kale Pâté

2 tablespoons refined avocado oil, for the pan

4 cups (190 g) chopped kale

½ cup (75 g) sesame seeds

½ cup (120 ml) refined avocado oil or extra-virgin olive oil

8 green onions, green parts only, roughly chopped

3 tablespoons apple cider vinegar

1¼ teaspoons finely ground gray sea salt

1. Place 2 tablespoons of avocado oil and the chopped kale in a large frying pan over medium heat. Cover and cook until the kale is slightly crispy, stirring occasionally, 3 to 6 minutes. 2. Meanwhile, place the remaining ingredients in a blender or food processor.

Per Serving:
calories: 228 | fat: 22g | protein: 3g | carbs: 6g | net carbs: 4g | fiber: 2g

Chapter 3 Beef, Pork, and Lamb

Korean Ground Beef Bowl

Prep time: 5 minutes | Cook time: 10 minutes | Serves 4

1 tablespoon sesame oil	1 teaspoon minced garlic
1½ pounds (680 g) ground sirloin	¼ teaspoon ground ginger
1 teaspoon dried basil	1 teaspoon red pepper flakes
½ teaspoon oregano	¼ teaspoon allspice
Sea salt and ground black pepper, to taste	1 tablespoon coconut aminos
½ cup diced onion	½ cup roughly chopped fresh cilantro leaves

1. Press the Sauté button to heat up the Instant Pot. Then, heat the sesame oil until sizzling. 2. Add ground sirloin and cook for a few minutes or until browned. Add the remaining ingredients, except for cilantro. 3. Secure the lid. Choose Manual mode and High Pressure; cook for 5 minutes. Once cooking is complete, use a natural pressure release; carefully remove the lid. 4. Divide among individual bowls and serve garnished with fresh cilantro. Bon appétit!

Per Serving:
calories: 307 | fat: 17g | protein: 34g | carbs: 4g | net carbs: 3g | fiber: 1g

Swedish Meatloaf

Prep time: 10 minutes | Cook time: 35 minutes | Serves 8

1½ pounds (680 g) ground beef (85% lean)	Sauce:
¼ pound (113 g) ground pork	½ cup (1 stick) unsalted butter
1 large egg (omit for egg-free)	½ cup shredded Swiss or mild Cheddar cheese (about 2 ounces / 57 g)
½ cup minced onions	
¼ cup tomato sauce	2 ounces (57 g) cream cheese (¼ cup), softened
2 tablespoons dry mustard	
2 cloves garlic, minced	⅓ cup beef broth
2 teaspoons fine sea salt	⅛ teaspoon ground nutmeg
1 teaspoon ground black pepper, plus more for garnish	Halved cherry tomatoes, for serving (optional)

1. Preheat the air fryer to 390°F (199°C). 2. In a large bowl, combine the ground beef, ground pork, egg, onions, tomato sauce, dry mustard, garlic, salt, and pepper. Using your hands, mix until well combined. 3. Place the meatloaf mixture in a loaf pan and place it in the air fryer. Bake for 35 minutes, or until cooked through and the internal temperature reaches 145°F (63°C). Check the meatloaf after 25 minutes; if it's getting too brown on the top, cover it loosely with foil to prevent burning. 4. While the meatloaf cooks, make the sauce: Heat the butter in a saucepan over medium-high heat until it sizzles and brown flecks appear, stirring constantly to keep the butter from burning. Turn the heat down to low and whisk in the Swiss cheese, cream cheese, broth, and nutmeg. Simmer for at least 10 minutes. The longer it simmers, the more the flavors open up. 5. When the meatloaf is done, transfer it to a serving tray and pour the sauce over it. Garnish with ground black pepper and serve with cherry tomatoes, if desired. Allow the meatloaf to rest for 10 minutes before slicing so it doesn't crumble apart. 6. Store leftovers in an airtight container in the fridge for 3 days or in the freezer for up to a month. Reheat in a preheated 350°F (177°C) air fryer for 4 minutes, or until heated through.

Per Serving:
calories: 362 | fat: 29g | protein: 22g | carbs: 2g | net carbs: 1g | fiber: 1g

Cardamom Beef Stew Meat with Broccoli

Prep time: 10 minutes | Cook time: 50 minutes | Serves 2

9 ounces (255 g) beef stew meat, chopped	½ teaspoon salt
1 teaspoon ground cardamom	1 cup chopped broccoli
	1 cup water

1. Preheat the instant pot on the Sauté mode. 2. When the title "Hot" is displayed, add chopped beef stew meat and cook it for 4 minutes (for 2 minutes from each side). 3. Then add the ground cardamom, salt, and broccoli. 4. Add water and close the instant pot lid. 5. Sauté the stew for 45 minutes to get the tender taste. 6. Enjoy!

Per Serving:
calories: 256 | fat: 8g | protein: 40g | carbs: 4g | net carbs: 2g | fiber: 2g

Beef Provençal

Prep time: 10 minutes | Cook time: 35 minutes | Serves 4

12 ounces beef steak racks	½ cup apple cider vinegar
2 fennel bulbs, sliced	1 teaspoon herbs de Provence
Salt and black pepper, to taste	1 tablespoon swerve
3 tablespoons olive oil	

1. In a bowl, mix the fennel with 2 tablespoons of oil, swerve, and vinegar, toss to coat well, and set to a baking dish. Season with herbs de Provence, pepper and salt, and cook in the oven at 400°F for 15 minutes. 2. Sprinkle black pepper and salt to the beef, place into an oiled pan over medium heat, and cook for a couple of minutes. Place the beef to the baking dish with the fennel, and bake for 20 minutes. Split everything among plates and enjoy.

Per Serving:
calories: 251 | fat: 15g | protein: 19g | carbs: 8g | net carbs: 4g | fiber: 4g

Salisbury Steak with Mushroom Sauce

Prep time: 10 minutes | Cook time: 15 minutes | Serves 4

1 pound (454 g) 85% lean ground beef	½ cup sliced button mushrooms
1 teaspoon steak seasoning	1 cup beef broth
1 egg	2 ounces (57 g) cream cheese
2 tablespoons butter	¼ cup heavy cream
½ medium onion, thinly sliced	¼ teaspoon xanthan gum

1. In large bowl mix ground beef, steak seasoning, and egg. Form 4 patties and set aside. 2. Press the Sauté button and add butter, onion, and mushrooms to Instant Pot. Sauté 3 to 5 minutes or until onions are translucent and fragrant. Press the Cancel button. 3. Add broth, beef patties, and cream cheese to Instant Pot. Click lid closed. Press the Manual button and adjust time for 15 minutes. 4. When timer beeps, allow a 10-minute natural release. Quick-release the remaining pressure. Carefully remove patties and set aside. Add heavy cream and xanthan gum. Whisk until fully mixed. Press the Sauté button and reduce gravy until desired thickness, about 5 to 10 minutes. Press the Cancel button and add patties back to Instant Pot until ready to serve.

Per Serving:
calories: 420 | fat: 30g | protein: 25g | carbs: 3g | net carbs: 2g | fiber: 1g

Sausage and Cauliflower Arancini

Prep time: 30 minutes | Cook time: 28 to 32 minutes | Serves 6

Avocado oil spray	4 ounces (113 g) Cheddar cheese, shredded
6 ounces (170 g) Italian sausage, casings removed	1 large egg
¼ cup diced onion	½ cup finely ground blanched almond flour
1 teaspoon minced garlic	¼ cup finely grated Parmesan cheese
1 teaspoon dried thyme	
Sea salt and freshly ground black pepper, to taste	Keto-friendly marinara sauce, for serving
2½ cups cauliflower rice	
3 ounces (85 g) cream cheese	

1. Spray a large skillet with oil and place it over medium-high heat. Once the skillet is hot, put the sausage in the skillet and cook for 7 minutes, breaking up the meat with the back of a spoon. 2. Reduce the heat to medium and add the onion. Cook for 5 minutes, then add the garlic, thyme, and salt and pepper to taste. Cook for 1 minute more. 3. Add the cauliflower rice and cream cheese to the skillet. Cook for 7 minutes, stirring frequently, until the cream cheese melts and the cauliflower is tender. 4. Remove the skillet from the heat and stir in the Cheddar cheese. Using a cookie scoop, form the mixture into 1½-inch balls. Place the balls on a parchment paper-lined baking sheet. Freeze for 30 minutes. 5. Place the egg in a shallow bowl and beat it with a fork. In a separate bowl, stir together the almond flour and Parmesan cheese. 6. Dip the cauliflower balls into the egg, then coat them with the almond flour mixture, gently pressing the mixture to the balls to adhere. 7. Set the air fryer to 400ºF (204ºC). Spray the cauliflower rice balls with oil, and arrange them in a single layer in the air fryer basket, working in batches if necessary. Air fry for 5 minutes. Flip the rice balls and spray them with more oil. Air fry for 3 to 7 minutes longer, until the balls are golden brown. 8. Serve warm with marinara sauce.

Per Serving:
calories: 312 | fat: 26g | protein: 14g | carbs: 6g | net carbs: 4g | fiber: 2g

Rosemary Mint Marinated Lamb Chops

Prep time: 5 minutes | Cook time: 10 minutes | Serves 4

3 tablespoons extra-virgin olive oil, plus more for greasing	leaves
½ teaspoon sea salt	½ teaspoon garlic salt
1 tablespoon fresh rosemary leaves (from about 4 sprigs), plus more sprigs for garnish	4 (4-ounce / 113-g) lamb chops (about ½-inch thick)
1 tablespoon chopped mint	Freshly ground black pepper, to taste

1. In a blender, combine the olive oil, salt, rosemary, mint, and garlic salt and blend until smooth. Rub the mixture all over the lamb chops and let them marinate in an airtight container in the refrigerator for 30 minutes or up to 4 hours. 2. Oil a large skillet over medium-high heat. Add the lamb chops and cook for about 3 minutes on each side (for medium-rare), or to desired doneness. 3. Plate the chops and let them rest for 3 minutes. Pour the leftover extra juices over the lamb chops and garnish with rosemary sprigs and pepper.

Per Serving:
1 chop: calories: 254 | fat: 18g | protein: 23g | carbs: 0g | net carbs: 0g | fiber: 0g

Sausage and Peppers

Prep time: 7 minutes | Cook time: 35 minutes | Serves 4

Oil, for spraying	1 tablespoon olive oil
2 pounds (907 g) hot or sweet Italian sausage links, cut into thick slices	1 tablespoon chopped fresh parsley
4 large bell peppers of any color, seeded and cut into slices	1 teaspoon dried oregano
	1 teaspoon dried basil
1 onion, thinly sliced	1 teaspoon balsamic vinegar

1. Line the air fryer basket with parchment and spray lightly with oil. 2. In a large bowl, combine the sausage, bell peppers, and onion. 3. In a small bowl, whisk together the olive oil, parsley, oregano, basil, and balsamic vinegar. Pour the mixture over the sausage and peppers and toss until evenly coated. 4. Using a slotted spoon, transfer the mixture to the prepared basket, taking care to drain out as much excess liquid as possible. 5. Air fry at 350ºF (177ºC) for 20 minutes, stir, and cook for another 15 minutes, or until the sausage is browned and the juices run clear.

Per Serving:
calories: 378 | fat: 23g | protein: 39g | carbs: 6g | net carbs: 4g | fiber: 2g

Parmesan-Crusted Steak

Prep time: 30 minutes | Cook time: 12 minutes | Serves 6

½ cup (1 stick) unsalted butter, at room temperature	almond flour
1 cup finely grated Parmesan cheese	1½ pounds (680 g) New York strip steak
¼ cup finely ground blanched	Sea salt and freshly ground black pepper, to taste

1. Place the butter, Parmesan cheese, and almond flour in a food processor. Process until smooth. Transfer to a sheet of parchment paper and form into a log. Wrap tightly in plastic wrap. Freeze for 45 minutes or refrigerate for at least 4 hours. 2. While the butter is chilling, season the steak liberally with salt and pepper. Let the steak rest at room temperature for about 45 minutes. 3. Place the grill pan or basket in your air fryer, set it to 400ºF (204ºC), and let it preheat for 5 minutes. 4. Working in batches, if necessary, place the steak on the grill pan and air fry for 4 minutes. Flip and cook for 3 minutes more, until the steak is brown on both sides. 5. Remove the steak from the air fryer and arrange an equal amount of the Parmesan butter on top of each steak. Return the steak to the air fryer and continue cooking for another 5 minutes, until an instant-read thermometer reads 120ºF (49ºC) for medium-rare and the crust is golden brown (or to your desired doneness). 6. Transfer the cooked steak to a plate; let rest for 10 minutes before serving.

Per Serving:
calories: 319 | fat: 20g | protein: 32g | carbs: 3g | net carbs: 2g | fiber: 1g

Herb-Crusted Lamb Chops

Prep time: 10 minutes | Cook time: 5 minutes | Serves 2

1 large egg	leaves
2 cloves garlic, minced	½ teaspoon ground black pepper
¼ cup pork dust	4 (1-inch-thick) lamb chops
¼ cup powdered Parmesan cheese	For Garnish/Serving (Optional):
1 tablespoon chopped fresh oregano leaves	Sprigs of fresh oregano
1 tablespoon chopped fresh rosemary leaves	Sprigs of fresh rosemary
1 teaspoon chopped fresh thyme	Sprigs of fresh thyme
	Lavender flowers
	Lemon slices

1. Spray the air fryer basket with avocado oil. Preheat the air fryer to 400ºF (204ºC). 2. Beat the egg in a shallow bowl, add the garlic, and stir well to combine. In another shallow bowl, mix together the pork dust, Parmesan, herbs, and pepper. 3. One at a time, dip the lamb chops into the egg mixture, shake off the excess egg, and then dredge them in the Parmesan mixture. Use your hands to coat the chops well in the Parmesan mixture and form a nice crust on all sides; if necessary, dip the chops again in both the egg and the Parmesan mixture. 4. Place the lamb chops in the air fryer basket, leaving space between them, and air fry for 5 minutes, or until the internal temperature reaches 145ºF (63ºC) for medium doneness. Allow to rest for 10 minutes before serving. 5. Garnish with sprigs of oregano, rosemary, and thyme, and lavender flowers, if desired. Serve with lemon slices, if desired. 6. Best served fresh. Store leftovers in an airtight container in the fridge for up to 4 days. Serve chilled over a salad, or reheat in a 350ºF (177ºC) air fryer for 3 minutes, or until heated through.

Per Serving:
calories: 510 | fat: 42g | protein: 30g | carbs: 3g | fiber: 1g | sodium: 380mg

Loaded Burger Bowls

Prep time: 15 minutes | Cook time: 10 minutes | Serves 4

1 pound (454 g) 85% lean ground beef	2 cups shredded lettuce
½ teaspoon salt	1 cup shredded Cheddar cheese
¼ teaspoon pepper	4 pickle spears
½ medium onion, sliced	1 avocado, sliced

1. Press the Sauté button and add ground beef to Instant Pot. When meat is browned completely, drain if needed. 2. Add salt, pepper, and onion. Continue cooking until onion is soft and translucent. Press the Cancel button. 3. Divide lettuce into four sections. Top each section with a quarter of the ground beef. Add a quarter of the Cheddar, one pickle spear, and sliced avocado. Top with favorite sauce or dressing.

Per Serving:
calories: 429 | fat: 27g | protein: 29g | carbs: 3g | net carbs: 0g | fiber: 3g

Weeknight Chili

Prep time: 10 minutes | Cook time: 35 minutes | Serves 6

¼ cup extra-virgin olive oil	6 cloves garlic, minced
1 small yellow onion, diced	1 (14½-ounce / 411-g) can diced tomatoes, with juices
1 green bell pepper, diced	1 (6-ounce / 170-g) can tomato paste
1 pound (454 g) ground beef, preferably grass-fed	2 cups water
½ pound (227 g) ground Italian sausage (hot or sweet)	2 ripe avocados, pitted, peeled, and chopped
1 tablespoon chili powder	1 cup sour cream
2 teaspoons ground cumin	
1½ teaspoons salt	

1. Heat the olive oil in a large pot over medium heat. Add the onion and bell pepper and sauté for 5 minutes, or until just tender. 2. Add the ground beef and sausage and cook until meat is browned, 5 to 6 minutes, stirring to break into small pieces. Add the chili powder, cumin, salt, and garlic and sauté, stirring frequently, for 1 minute, until fragrant. 3. Add the tomatoes and their juices, tomato paste, and water, stirring to combine well. Bring the mixture to a boil, reduce heat to low, cover, and simmer for 15 to 20 minutes, stirring occasionally. Add additional water for a thinner chili if desired. 4. Serve hot, garnished with chopped avocado and sour cream.

Per Serving:
calories: 591 | fat: 49g | protein: 25g | carbs: 18g | net carbs: 10g | fiber: 8g

Ground Beef Stroganoff

Prep time: 10 minutes | Cook time: 20 minutes | serves 6

1½ pounds ground beef	1 cup beef broth
½ cup finely chopped onions	¼ cup heavy whipping cream
2 cloves garlic, minced	¼ cup water
4 ounces white mushrooms, sliced	1 tablespoon Worcestershire sauce
4 ounces cream cheese (½ cup), softened	Salt and ground black pepper
	½ cup sour cream

1. In a large skillet over medium heat, cook the ground beef with the onions, garlic, and mushrooms, crumbling the meat with a large spoon it as cooks, until the meat is browned and the onions are softened and translucent, about 10 minutes. Drain the fat, if necessary. 2. Stir in the cream cheese and cook until melted. Add the broth, cream, water, and Worcestershire sauce and stir to combine. Continue to simmer for 5 minutes. 3. Season to taste with salt and pepper. Stir in the sour cream and serve. Leftovers can be stored in an airtight container in the refrigerator for up to 5 days.

Per Serving:
calories: 396 | fat: 32g | protein: 22g | carbs: 23g | net carbs: 2g | fiber: 0g

Fried Rice with Ham

Prep time: 5 minutes | Cook time: 20 minutes | Serves 2

2 tablespoons butter	2 tablespoons coconut aminos or soy sauce
12 ounces (340 g) boneless cooked ham steak, cubed	½ teaspoon rice wine vinegar
¼ medium onion, chopped	¼ teaspoon pink Himalayan sea salt
1 teaspoon minced garlic	
1 (12-ounce / 340-g) package cauliflower rice, fresh or thawed frozen	¼ teaspoon freshly ground black pepper
¼ cup peas, fresh or thawed frozen	1 tablespoon extra-virgin olive oil
	2 large eggs

1. In a large sauté pan or skillet, melt the butter over medium heat. Add the ham cubes and cook for about 5 minutes, stirring, until slightly crisp on all sides. 2. Add the onion and cook for 3 to 5 minutes, until translucent. Then add the garlic and cook for an additional minute, until fragrant. 3. Mix the cauliflower rice and peas into the skillet and cook for 3 to 5 minutes, stirring from time to time. 4. In a small bowl, combine the coconut aminos, vinegar, salt, and pepper. 5. Add the sauce mixture to the pan and stir to coat well. Continue to stir and cook until the cauliflower rice and peas are warmed through. 6. Push the mixture to one side of the skillet, then add the olive oil to the other side. Heat the oil for 30 seconds to 1 minute, then add the eggs. Using a spatula or wooden spoon, scramble the eggs for 2 to 3 minutes, until cooked. 7. Stir the cauliflower mixture into the eggs, combining all ingredients in the skillet, until slightly browned and heated through. Serve.

Per Serving:
calories: 536 | fat: 32g | protein: 46g | carbs: 17g | net carbs: 10g | fiber: 7g

Indian Mint and Chile Kebabs

Prep time: 30 minutes | Cook time: 15 minutes | Serves 4

1 pound (454 g) ground lamb	½ teaspoon ground turmeric
½ cup finely minced onion	½ teaspoon cayenne pepper
¼ cup chopped fresh mint	¼ teaspoon ground cardamom
¼ cup chopped fresh cilantro	¼ teaspoon ground cinnamon
1 tablespoon minced garlic	1 teaspoon kosher salt

1. In the bowl of a stand mixer fitted with the paddle attachment, combine the lamb, onion, mint, cilantro, garlic, turmeric, cayenne, cardamom, cinnamon, and salt. Mix on low speed until you have a sticky mess of spiced meat. If you have time, let the mixture stand at room temperature for 30 minutes (or cover and refrigerate for up to a day or two, until you're ready to make the kebabs). 2. Divide the meat into eight equal portions. Form each into a long sausage shape. Place the kebabs in a single layer in the air fryer basket. Set the air fryer to 350ºF (177ºC) for 10 minutes. Increase the air fryer temperature to 400ºF (204ºC) and cook for 3 to 4 minutes more to brown the kebabs. Use a meat thermometer to ensure the kebabs have reached an internal temperature of 160ºF / 71ºC (medium).

Per Serving:
calories: 231 | fat: 14g | protein: 23g | carbs: 3g | fiber: 1g | sodium: 648mg

Hawaiian Pulled Pork Roast with Cabbage

Prep time: 10 minutes | Cook time: 1 hour 2 minutes minutes | Serves 6

1½ tablespoons olive oil	1 tablespoon liquid smoke
3 pounds (1.4 kg) pork shoulder roast, cut into 4 equal-sized pieces	2 cups water, divided
	1 tablespoon sea salt
3 cloves garlic, minced	2 cups shredded cabbage

1. Select Sauté mode and add the olive oil to the Instant Pot. Once the oil is hot, add the pork cuts and sear for 5 minutes per side or until browned. Once browned, transfer the pork to a platter and set aside. 2. Add the garlic, liquid smoke, and 1½ cups water to the Instant Pot. Stir to combine. 3. Return the pork to the pot and sprinkle the salt over top. 4. Lock the lid. Select Manual mode and set cooking time for 1 hour on High Pressure. 5. When cooking is complete, allow the pressure to release naturally for 20 minutes, then release any remaining pressure. 6. Open the lid and transfer the pork to a large platter. Using two forks, shred the pork. Set aside. 7. Add the shredded cabbage and remaining water to the liquid in the pot. Stir. 8. Lock the lid. Select Manual mode and set cooking time for 2 minutes on High Pressure. When cooking is complete, quick release the pressure. 9. Transfer the cabbage to the serving platter with the pork. Serve warm.

Per Serving:
calories: 314 | fat: 12.0g | protein: 46.5g | carbs: 2.7g | net carbs: 2.0g | fiber: 0.7g

Better Than Take-Out Beef with Broccoli

Prep time: 10 minutes | Cook time: 20 minutes | Serves 4

Marinade:

3 tablespoons coconut aminos (or 2 tablespoons liquid aminos)

2 tablespoons coconut oil, melted

2 tablespoons toasted sesame oil

2 tablespoons fish sauce

1 tablespoon coconut vinegar or apple cider vinegar

1 teaspoon onion powder

1 teaspoon garlic powder

½ teaspoon ground ginger

¼ teaspoon red pepper flakes

Beef and Broccoli:

1 pound (454 g) beef sirloin or flank, sliced thinly across the grain

2 cups broccoli florets

1 tablespoon coconut oil

2 garlic cloves, minced

½ teaspoon sea salt

¼ teaspoon freshly ground black pepper

1 tablespoon toasted sesame seeds (optional)

Make the Marinade 1. In a medium bowl, whisk together the coconut aminos, coconut oil, sesame oil, fish sauce, vinegar, onion powder, garlic powder, ginger, and red pepper flakes. Make the Beef and Broccoli 2. In a large plastic bag or medium bowl, pour one-third of the marinade over the beef and let marinate in the refrigerator for a few hours or overnight. Save the rest of the marinade in a small container to use for the sauce. 3. In a large pot, steam the broccoli until just tender. Transfer to a bowl with ice and cold water to stop the cooking. Drain and set aside. 4. In a large skillet or wok, heat the coconut oil over high heat. Remove the beef from the marinade (discard the marinade) and add the beef to the skillet. Let brown for 2 to 3 minutes. Flip the meat and cook for another 2 to 3 minutes. 5. Add the garlic, salt, and pepper and stir to combine. 6. Add the cooked broccoli florets and the reserved marinade. Stir well and let simmer on medium-low heat for 5 to 10 minutes or until the sauce thickens and the meat is cooked through. Top with sesame seeds (if using).

Per Serving:

calories: 356 | fat: 24g | protein: 29g | carbs: 6g | net carbs: 4g | fiber: 2g

Filipino Pork Loin

Prep time: 10 minutes | Cook time: 40 minutes | Serves 4

1 pound (454 g) pork loin, chopped

½ cup apple cider vinegar

1 cup chicken broth

1 chili pepper, chopped

1 tablespoon coconut oil

1 teaspoon salt

1. Melt the coconut oil on Sauté mode. 2. When it is hot, and chili pepper and cook it for 2 minutes. Stir it. 3. Add chopped pork loin and salt. Cook the ingredients for 5 minutes. 4. After this, add apple cider vinegar and chicken broth. 5. Close and seal the lid and cook the Filipino pork for 30 minutes on High Pressure (Manual mode). Then make a quick pressure release.

Per Serving:

calories: 320 | fat:19 g | protein: 32g | carbs: 0g | net carbs: 0g | fiber: 0g

Pork Loin Roast

Prep time: 30 minutes | Cook time: 55 minutes | Serves 6

1½ pounds (680 g) boneless pork loin roast, washed

1 teaspoon mustard seeds

1 teaspoon garlic powder

1 teaspoon porcini powder

1 teaspoon shallot powder

¾ teaspoon sea salt flakes

1 teaspoon red pepper flakes, crushed

2 dried sprigs thyme, crushed

2 tablespoons lime juice

1. Firstly, score the meat using a small knife; make sure to not cut too deep. 2. In a small-sized mixing dish, combine all seasonings in the order listed above; mix to combine well. 3. Massage the spice mix into the pork meat to evenly distribute. Drizzle with lemon juice. 4. Set the air fryer to 360ºF (182ºC). Place the pork in the air fryer basket; roast for 25 to 30 minutes. Pause the machine, check for doneness and cook for 25 minutes more.

Per Serving:

calories: 157 | fat: 5g | protein: 26g | carbs: 1g | fiber: 0g | sodium: 347mg

Garlic Balsamic London Broil

Prep time: 30 minutes | Cook time: 8 to 10 minutes | Serves 8

2 pounds (907 g) London broil

3 large garlic cloves, minced

3 tablespoons balsamic vinegar

3 tablespoons whole-grain mustard

2 tablespoons olive oil

Sea salt and ground black pepper, to taste

½ teaspoon dried hot red pepper flakes

1. Score both sides of the cleaned London broil. 2. Thoroughly combine the remaining ingredients; massage this mixture into the meat to coat it on all sides. Let it marinate for at least 3 hours. 3. Set the air fryer to 400ºF (204ºC); Then cook the London broil for 15 minutes. Flip it over and cook another 10 to 12 minutes. Bon appétit!

Per Serving:

calories: 240 | fat: 15g | protein: 23g | carbs: 2g | fiber: 0g | sodium: 141mg

Pan-Seared Steak with Mushroom Sauce

Prep time: 10 minutes | Cook time: 20 minutes | Serves 4

4 top sirloin steaks (6 ounces / 170 g each), at room temperature

½ teaspoon sea salt, or more to taste

¼ teaspoon black pepper, or more to taste

4 tablespoons (½ stick) butter, divided into 2 tablespoons and

2 tablespoons

2 cloves garlic, minced

8 ounces (227 g) baby portobello mushrooms, thinly sliced

¼ cup beef broth

1 teaspoon fresh thyme, chopped

¼ cup heavy cream

1. Season the steaks on both sides with the sea salt and black pepper. Let rest at room temperature for 30 minutes. 2. Heat a large sauté pan over medium-high heat. Add 2 tablespoons of the butter and melt. 3. Place the steaks in the pan in a single layer. Cook for the following number of minutes on each side, based on desired level of doneness (cook time will vary depending on the steak's thickness and the temperature of the pan). For best results, use a meat thermometer and remove the steak from the heat when it's 5°F lower than the desired final temperature. Steaks will rise another 5°F while resting. Rare: 2 to 4 minutes per side, or until 115°F (46°C) inside. Steak will reach 120°F (49°C) while resting afterward. Medium-rare: 3 to 5 minutes per side, or until 125°F (52°C) inside. Steak will reach 130°F (54°C) while resting afterward. Medium: 4 to 6 minutes per side, or until 135°F (57°C) inside. Steak will reach 140°F (60°C) while resting afterward. Medium-well: 5 to 7 minutes per side, or until 145°F (63°C) inside. Steak will reach 150°F (66°C) while resting afterward. Well-done: 7 to 9 minutes per side, or until 155°F (68°C) inside. Steak will reach 160°F (71°C) while resting afterward. 4. When the steaks in the pan reach the desired internal temperature, remove them from the pan, transfer to a plate, and cover with foil. Let the steaks rest without cutting: the steak's internal temperature will rise another 5°F to the desired final temperature. 5. Return the sauté pan to medium heat. Melt the remaining 2 tablespoons butter. Add the garlic and sauté for about 1 minute, until fragrant. 6. Add the mushrooms, beef broth, and thyme. Scrape any browned bits from the bottom of the pan. Adjust the heat to bring to a simmer (typically at medium-high), cover, and simmer, stirring occasionally, for 5 to 8 minutes, until the mushrooms are soft. 7. Reduce the heat to medium, add the cream, and simmer for 1 to 3 minutes, until the sauce thickens. Adjust salt and pepper to taste, if needed. 8. Spoon the mushroom sauce over the steaks to serve.

Per Serving:
calories: 420 | fat: 27g | protein: 39g | carbs: 3g | net carbs: 3g | fiber: 0g

Garlic Lamb Vindaloo

Prep time: 10 minutes | Cook time: 34 minutes | Serves 4

1 tablespoon unsalted butter (or coconut oil for dairy-free)	2 pounds (907 g) boneless lamb shoulder, cut into 1½-inch cubes
¼ cup diced onions	
6 cloves garlic, minced	1 (14-ounce / 397-g) can full-fat coconut milk
3 tablespoons grainy mustard	
2 teaspoons ground cumin	1 tablespoon lime juice
2 teaspoons turmeric powder	Fresh cilantro leaves, for garnish
½ teaspoon cayenne pepper	

1. Place the butter in the Instant Pot and press Sauté. Once melted, add the onions and garlic and cook, stirring often, for 4 minutes, or until the onions are soft. Press Cancel to stop the Sauté. 2. Place the mustard, cumin, turmeric, and cayenne in a small bowl and stir well. Place the lamb in the Instant Pot and cover with the mustard mixture. Pour in the coconut milk. 3. Seal the lid, press Manual, and set the timer for 30 minutes. Once finished, let the pressure release naturally. 4. Remove the lid and stir in the lime juice. Garnish with cilantro and serve.

Per Serving:
calories: 535 | fat: 35g | protein: 46g | carbs: 5g | net carbs: 4g | fiber: 1g

Beef and Sausage Medley

Prep time: 10 minutes | Cook time: 27 minutes | Serves 8

1 teaspoon butter	1½ cups roasted vegetable broth
2 beef sausages, casing removed and sliced	2 cloves garlic, minced
	1 teaspoon Old Bay seasoning
2 pounds (907 g) beef steak, cubed	2 bay leaves
1 yellow onion, sliced	1 sprig thyme
2 fresh ripe tomatoes, puréed	1 sprig rosemary
1 jalapeño pepper, chopped	½ teaspoon paprika
1 red bell pepper, chopped	Sea salt and ground black pepper, to taste

1. Press the Sauté button to heat up the Instant Pot. Melt the butter and cook the sausage and steak for 4 minutes, stirring periodically. Set aside. 2. Add the onion and sauté for 3 minutes or until softened and translucent. Add the remaining ingredients, including reserved beef and sausage. 3. Secure the lid. Choose Manual mode and set time for 20 minutes on High Pressure. 4. Once cooking is complete, use a quick pressure release. Carefully remove the lid. 5. Serve immediately.

Per Serving:
calories: 319 | fat: 14.0g | protein: 42.8g | carbs: 6.3g | net carbs: 1.8g | fiber: 4.5g
K

Pancetta Sausage with Kale

Prep time: 15 minutes | Cook time: 20 minutes | Serves 8

2 cups kale	2 garlic cloves, minced
8 cups chicken broth	Salt and black pepper, to taste
A drizzle of olive oil	A pinch of red pepper flakes
1 cup heavy cream	1 onion, chopped
6 pancetta slices, chopped	1½ pounds hot pork sausage, chopped
1 pound (454 g) radishes, chopped	

1. Set a pot over medium heat. Add in a drizzle of olive oil and warm. Stir in garlic, onion, pancetta, and sausage; cook for 5 minutes. Pour in broth, radishes, and kale, and simmer for 10 minutes. 2. Stir in salt, red pepper flakes, black pepper, and heavy cream, and cook for about 5 minutes. Serve.

Per Serving:
calories: 432 | fat: 36g | protein: 21g | carbs: 8g | net carbs: 6g | fiber: 2g

Pork Fried Cauliflower Rice

Prep time: 10 minutes | Cook time: 20 minutes | Serves 4

1 pound (454 g) ground pork	3 cups thinly sliced cabbage
Sea salt and freshly ground black pepper, to taste	1 cup chopped broccoli
	1 red bell pepper, cored and chopped
3 tablespoons toasted sesame oil	1 garlic clove, minced

1½ cups riced cauliflower

1 tablespoon sriracha

2 tablespoons liquid aminos or tamari

1 teaspoon rice wine vinegar

1 teaspoon sesame seeds, for garnish

1. Heat a medium skillet over medium-high heat. Add the pork and sprinkle generously with salt and pepper. Cook, stirring frequently, until browned, about 10 minutes. Remove the meat from the skillet. 2. Reduce the heat to medium and add the sesame oil to the skillet along with the cabbage, broccoli, bell pepper, riced cauliflower, and garlic. Cook for about 5 minutes until slightly softened, then add the sriracha, liquid aminos, and vinegar and mix well. 3. Return the browned pork to the skillet. Simmer together for about 5 minutes more until the cabbage is crisp-tender. Season with salt and pepper, then garnish with the sesame seeds and serve right away.

Per Serving:
calories: 460 | fat: 36g | protein: 23g | carbs: 11g | net carbs: 5g | fiber: 6g

Blue Cheese Stuffed Steak Roll-Ups

Prep time: 5 minutes | Cook time: 15 minutes | Serves 6

1 (1½-pound / 680-g) beef round tip roast, sliced into 6 steaks of equal thickness

6 ounces (170 g) blue cheese, crumbled

½ cup beef broth

¼ cup coconut aminos, or 1

tablespoon wheat-free tamari

4 cloves garlic, minced

Chopped fresh Italian parsley, for garnish

Cracked black pepper, for garnish

1. Place each steak in a resealable plastic bag and pound with a rolling pin or meat mallet until it is ½ inch thick. Lay the pounded steaks flat on a cutting board or other work surface. 2. Divide the blue cheese evenly among the steaks, placing the cheese on one side. Roll up each steak, starting at a shorter end, and secure with toothpicks. 3. Combine the broth, coconut aminos, and garlic in the Instant Pot. Add the steak roll-ups to the broth mixture. 4. Seal the lid, press Manual, and set the timer for 15 minutes. Once finished, turn the valve to venting for a quick release. 5. Remove the toothpicks from the steak roll-ups before serving. Garnish the roll-ups with chopped parsley and cracked black pepper.

Per Serving:
calories: 417 | fat: 28g | protein: 37g | carbs: 3g | net carbs: 1g | fiber: 2g

Breaded Pork Chops

Prep time: 5 minutes | Cook time: 20 minutes | Serves 2

2 (8-ounce / 227-g) boneless pork loin chops

¼ cup pork panko crumbs

1 teaspoon extra-virgin olive oil

1 teaspoon grated Parmesan cheese

¼ teaspoon pink Himalayan sea salt

¼ teaspoon onion powder

¼ teaspoon paprika

¼ teaspoon garlic powder

⅛ teaspoon freshly ground black pepper

⅛ teaspoon dried parsley

⅛ teaspoon dried basil

⅛ teaspoon dried oregano

Pinch of cayenne pepper

1. Preheat the oven to 425ºF (220ºC). Place a baking rack on a small baking sheet. 2. Pat the chops dry with a paper towel. 3. In a food processor, combine the pork crumbs, olive oil, Parmesan, salt, onion powder, paprika, garlic powder, pepper, parsley, basil, oregano, and cayenne and run on high until the mixture forms a uniform, fine powder. Transfer the mixture to a resealable 1-gallon plastic bag. 4. Add the chops to the bag, one at a time, shaking to coat them in the breading. 5. Transfer the chops to the rack and bake for 20 minutes, until an instant-read thermometer registers 160ºF (71ºC) or the juices run clear when the meat is pierced.

Per Serving:
calories: 435 | fat: 23g | protein: 57g | carbs: 0g | net carbs: 0g | fiber: 0g

French Dip Chuck Roast

Prep time: 5 minutes | Cook time: 70 minutes | Serves 6

2 tablespoons avocado oil

2 to 2½ pounds (907 g to 1.1 kg) chuck roast

2 cups beef broth

2 tablespoons dried rosemary

3 cloves garlic, minced

1 teaspoon salt

½ teaspoon black pepper

¼ teaspoon dried thyme

½ onion, quartered

2 bay leaves

1. Turn the pot to Sauté mode. Once hot, add the avocado oil. Add the roast and sear it on each side. This should take about 5 minutes. Press Cancel. 2. Add the broth to the pot. 3. Add the rosemary, garlic, salt, pepper, and thyme to the top of the roast. Add the onion and bay leaves. 4. Close the lid and seal the vent. Cook on High Pressure for 50 minutes. Let the steam naturally release for 15 minutes before Manually releasing. 5. Remove the roast to a plate and shred with two forks. Strain the jus though a fine-mesh sieve. Serve the roast au jus for dipping.

Per Serving:
calories: 548 | fat: 34g | protein: 55g | carbs: 2g | net carbs: 1g | fiber: 1g

Slow-Cooker Barbecue Ribs

Prep time: 10 minutes | Cook time: 4 hours | Serves 2

1 pound pork ribs

Pink Himalayan salt

Freshly ground black pepper

1 (1.25-ounce) package dry rib-

seasoning rub

½ cup sugar-free barbecue sauce

1. With the crock insert in place, preheat the slow cooker to high. 2. Generously season the pork ribs with pink Himalayan salt, pepper, and dry rib-seasoning rub. 3. Stand the ribs up along the walls of the slow-cooker insert, with the bonier side facing inward. 4. Pour the barbecue sauce on both sides of the ribs, using just enough to coat. 5. Cover, cook for 4 hours, and serve.

Per Serving:
calories: 956 | fat: 72g | protein: 68g | carbs: 5g | net carbs: 5g | fiber: 0g

Deconstructed Egg Rolls

Prep time: 10 minutes | Cook time: 15 minutes | Serves 6

1 pound (454 g) ground pork	ginger
1 tablespoon untoasted, cold-pressed sesame oil	1 tablespoon coconut aminos or wheat-free tamari
6 cups finely shredded cabbage	1 teaspoon fish sauce (optional)
2 teaspoons minced garlic	¼ cup chopped green onions,
1 tablespoon minced fresh	for garnish

1. Place the pork and oil in a large cast-iron skillet over medium-high heat and cook, crumbling the meat with a wooden spoon, until cooked through, about 10 minutes. (Do not drain the drippings from the pan.) 2. Add the cabbage, garlic, ginger, coconut aminos, and fish sauce, if using, to the skillet. Sauté until the cabbage is soft, 3 to 5 minutes. 3. Divide among six plates or bowls and serve garnished with the green onions.

Per Serving:
calories: 250 | fat: 19g | protein: 14g | carbs: 6g | net carbs: 3g | fiber: 3g

Pork Mushroom Stroganoff

Prep time: 10 minutes | Cook time: 25 minutes | Serves 4

½ cup chopped cremini mushrooms	½ cup coconut milk
1 teaspoon dried oregano	1 cup ground pork
½ teaspoon ground nutmeg	½ teaspoon salt
	2 tablespoons butter

1. Heat up butter on Sauté mode for 3 minutes. 2. Add mushrooms. Sauté the vegetables for 5 minutes. 3. Then stir them and add salt, ground pork, ground nutmeg, and dried oregano. 4. Stir the ingredients and cook for 5 minutes more. 5. Add coconut milk and close the lid. 6. Sauté the stroganoff for 15 minutes. Stir it from time to time to avoid burning.
Per Serving:
calories: 357 | fat: 29g | protein: 21g | carbs: 3g | net carbs: 2g | fiber: 1g

Feta-Stuffed Burgers

Prep time: 10 minutes | Cook time: 10 minutes | Serves 2

2 tablespoons fresh mint leaves, finely chopped	Freshly ground black pepper
1 scallion, white and green parts, thinly sliced	12 ounces (6 ounces each) ground beef and ground lamb mixture
1 tablespoon Dijon mustard	2 ounces crumbled feta cheese
Pink Himalayan salt	1 tablespoon ghee

1. In a large bowl, mix to combine the mint leaves with the scallion and mustard. Season with pink Himalayan salt and pepper. 2. Add the ground beef and lamb to the bowl. Mix together thoroughly, and form into 4 patties. 3. Press the feta crumbles into 2 of the patties, and put the other 2 patties on top so the cheese is in the middle. Pinch all the way around the edges of the burgers to seal in the feta cheese. 4. In a medium skillet over medium heat, heat the ghee. Add the burger patties to the hot oil. Cook each side for 4 to 5 minutes, until done to your preference, and serve.

Per Serving:
calories: 607 | fat: 48g | protein: 41g | carbs: 2g | net carbs: 2g | fiber: 1g

Chili-Stuffed Avocados

Prep time: 10 minutes | Cook time: 30 minutes | Serves 8

2 tablespoons tallow or bacon grease	¾ teaspoon finely ground gray sea salt
1 pound (455 g) ground beef (20% to 30% fat)	¼ teaspoon ground cinnamon
1 (14½-ounce/408-g/428-ml) can whole tomatoes with juices	2 tablespoons finely chopped fresh parsley
1½ tablespoons chili powder	4 large Hass avocados, sliced in half, pits removed (leave skin on), for serving
2 small cloves garlic, minced	
2 teaspoons paprika	

1. Place the tallow into a large saucepan. Melt on medium heat before adding the ground beef. Cook until beef is no longer pink, 7 to 8 minutes, stirring often to break the meat up into small clumps. 2. Add the tomatoes, chili powder, garlic, paprika, salt, and cinnamon. Cover and bring to a boil on high heat. Once boiling, reduce the heat to medium-low and simmer for 20 to 25 minutes, with the cover slightly askew to let steam out. 3. Once thickened, remove from the heat and stir in the chopped parsley. 4. Place an avocado half on a small serving plate or on a platter if you plan to serve them family style. Scoop ⅓ scant cup (180g) of chili into the hollow of

Per Serving:
calories: 385 | fat: 31g | protein: 17g | carbs: 10g | net carbs: 3g | fiber: 7g

Beery Boston-Style Butt

Prep time: 10 minutes | Cook time: 1 hour 1 minutes | Serves 4

1 tablespoon butter	Pinch of grated nutmeg
1 pound (454 g) Boston-style butt	Sea salt, to taste
½ cup leeks, chopped	¼ teaspoon ground black pepper
¼ cup beer	¼ cup water
½ cup chicken stock	

1. Press the Sauté button to heat up the Instant Pot. Once hot, melt the butter. 2. Cook the Boston-style butt for 3 minutes on each side. Remove from the pot and reserve. 3. Sauté the leeks for 5 minutes or until fragrant. Add the remaining ingredients and stir to combine. 4. Secure the lid. Choose the Manual mode and set cooking time for 50 minutes on High pressure. 5. Once cooking is complete, use a natural pressure release for 20 minutes, then release any remaining pressure. Carefully remove the lid. 6. Serve immediately.

Per Serving:
calories: 330 | fat: 13.1g | protein: 48.4g | carbs: 2.1g | net carbs: 0.4g | fiber: 1.7g

Keto Chili

Prep time: 20 minutes | Cook time: 5 TO 8 hours |
Serves 6

1 pound ground beef	1 (6-ounce) can tomato paste
1 pound bulk sausage, mild or hot	1 tablespoon chili powder
1 green bell pepper, diced	1½ teaspoons ground cumin
½ medium yellow onion, chopped	⅓ cup water
3 to 4 cloves garlic, minced, or 1 tablespoon garlic powder	Topping Suggestions
	Shredded cheddar cheese
	Sliced green onions
1 (14½-ounce) can diced tomatoes (with juices)	Sour cream
	Sliced jalapeños

1 In a large pot, brown the ground beef and sausage, using a wooden spoon to break up the clumps. Drain the meat, reserving half of the drippings. 2 Transfer the drained meat to a slow cooker. Add the reserved drippings, bell pepper, onion, garlic, tomatoes with juices, tomato paste, chili powder, cumin, and water and mix well. 3 Place the lid on the slow cooker and cook on low for 6 to 8 hours or on high for 5 hours, until the veggies are soft. 4 Serve topped with shredded cheese, green onions, sour cream, and/or sliced jalapeños, if desired.

Per Serving:
calories: 387 | fat: 25g | protein: 34g | carbs: 11g | net carbs: 8g | fiber: 3g

Crispy Baked Pork Chops with Mushroom Gravy

Prep time: 10 minutes | Cook time: 25 minutes | Serves 4

4 tablespoons extra-virgin olive oil, divided	4 (4-ounce / 113-g) boneless pork chops
½ cup almond flour	1 tablespoon unsalted butter
2 teaspoons dried sage, divided	4 ounces (113 g) chopped mushrooms
1½ teaspoons salt, divided	2 cloves garlic, minced
½ teaspoon freshly ground black pepper, divided	1 teaspoon dried thyme
1 large egg	8 ounces (227 g) cream cheese, room temperature
¼ cup flax meal	
¼ cup walnuts, very finely chopped	½ cup heavy cream
	¼ cup chicken stock

1. Preheat the oven to 400ºF (205ºC). Line a baking sheet with aluminum foil and coat with 1 tablespoon of olive oil. 2. In a small, shallow bowl, combine the almond flour, 1 teaspoon of sage, ½ teaspoon of salt, and ¼ teaspoon of pepper. In a second small bowl, whisk the egg. In a third small bowl, stir together the flax meal and walnuts. 3. One at a time, dredge each pork chop first in the flour mixture, then in the egg, then in the flax-and-walnut mixture to fully coat all sides. Place on the prepared baking sheet and drizzle the pork chops evenly with 1 tablespoon of olive oil. 4. Bake until cooked through and golden brown, 18 to 25 minutes, depending on the thickness of the pork. 5. While the pork is baking, prepare the gravy. Heat the remaining 2 tablespoons of olive oil and the butter in a medium saucepan over medium heat. Add the mushrooms and sauté until very tender, 4 to 6 minutes. Add the garlic, remaining 1 teaspoon of sage and 1 teaspoon of salt, thyme, and remaining ¼ teaspoon of pepper, and sauté for an additional 30 seconds. 6. Add the cream cheese to the mushrooms, reduce heat to low, and stir until melted and creamy, 2 to 3 minutes. Whisk in the cream and stock until smooth. Cook over low heat, whisking frequently, until the mixture is thick and creamy, another 3 to 4 minutes. 7. Serve each pork chop covered with a quarter of the mushroom gravy.

Per Serving:
calories: 799 | fat: 69g | protein: 36g | carbs: 11g | net carbs: 7g | fiber: 4g

Sweet Chipotle Grilled Ribs

Prep time: 5 minutes | Cook time: 50 minutes | Serves 4

2 tablespoons erythritol	1 teaspoon garlic powder
Pink salt and black pepper to taste	1 pound (454 g) beef spare ribs
1 tablespoon olive oil	4 tablespoons sugar-free BBQ sauce + extra for serving
3 teaspoons chipotle powder	

1. Mix the erythritol, salt, pepper, oil, chipotle, and garlic powder. Brush on the meaty sides of the ribs and wrap in foil. Sit for 30 minutes to marinate. 2. Preheat oven to 400ºF, place wrapped ribs on a baking sheet, and cook for 40 minutes to be cooked through. Remove ribs and aluminium foil, brush with BBQ sauce, and brown under the broiler for 10 minutes on both sides. Slice and serve with extra BBQ sauce and lettuce tomato salad.

Per Serving:
calories: 449 | fat: 37g | protein: 18g | carbs: 10g | net carbs: 9g | fiber: 1g

Mustard Lamb Chops

Prep time: 5 minutes | Cook time: 14 minutes | Serves 4

Oil, for spraying	¼ teaspoon freshly ground black pepper
1 tablespoon Dijon mustard	
2 teaspoons lemon juice	4 (1¼-inch-thick) loin lamb chops
½ teaspoon dried tarragon	
¼ teaspoon salt	

1. Preheat the air fryer to 390ºF (199ºC). Line the air fryer basket with parchment and spray lightly with oil. 2. In a small bowl, mix together the mustard, lemon juice, tarragon, salt, and black pepper. 3. Pat dry the lamb chops with a paper towel. Brush the chops on both sides with the mustard mixture. 4. Place the chops in the prepared basket. You may need to work in batches, depending on the size of your air fryer. 5. Cook for 8 minutes, flip, and cook for another 6 minutes, or until the internal temperature reaches 125ºF (52ºC) for rare, 145ºF (63ºC) for medium-rare, or 155ºF (68ºC) for medium.

Per Serving:
calories: 96 | fat: 4g | protein: 14g | carbs: 0g | fiber: 0g | sodium: 233mg

BBQ Beef & Slaw

Prep time: 10 minutes | Cook time: 45 minutes | Serves 4

BBQ BEEF:

1 pound (455 g) boneless beef chuck roast

1 cup (240 ml) beef bone broth

½ teaspoon finely ground sea salt

½ cup (80 g) sugar-free barbecue sauce

SLAW:

9 ounces (255 g) coleslaw mix

½ cup (120 ml) sugar-free poppy seed dressing

1. Place the chuck roast, broth, and salt in a pressure cooker or slow cooker. If using a pressure cooker, seal the lid and cook on high pressure for 45 minutes. When complete, allow the pressure to release naturally before removing the lid. If using a slow cooker, cook on high for 4 hours or on low for 6 hours. 2. When the meat is done, drain it almost completely, leaving ¼ cup (60 ml) of the cooking liquid in the cooker. Shred the meat with two forks, then add the barbecue sauce and toss to coat. 3. Place the coleslaw mix and dressing in a salad bowl and toss to coat. 4. Divide the BBQ beef and coleslaw among 4 dinner plates, placing the beef first and then the slaw on top, and enjoy.

Per Serving:

calories: 354 | fat: 27g | protein: 24g | carbs: 5g | net carbs: 3g | fiber: 2g

Cinnamon Beef with Blackberries

Prep time: 15 minutes | Cook time: 30 minutes | Serves 2

15 ounces (425 g) beef loin, chopped

1 tablespoon blackberries

1 cup water

½ teaspoon ground cinnamon

⅓ teaspoon ground black pepper

½ teaspoon salt

1 tablespoon butter

1. Pour water in the instant pot bowl. 2. Add chopped beef loin, blackberries, ground cinnamon, salt, and ground black pepper. Add butter. 3. Close the instant pot lid and set the Meat/Stew mode. 4. Cook the meat for 30 minutes. Then remove the meat from the instant pot. Blend the remaining blackberry mixture. 5. Pour it over the meat.

Per Serving:

calories: 372 | fat: 21g | protein: 39g | carbs: 4g | net carbs: 3g | fiber: 1g

Chile Verde Pulled Pork with Tomatillos

Prep time: 15 minutes | Cook time: 1 hour 3 minutes | Serves 6

2 pounds (907 g) pork shoulder, cut into 6 equal-sized pieces

1 teaspoon sea salt

½ teaspoon ground black pepper

2 jalapeño peppers, deseeded and stemmed

1 pound (454 g) tomatillos, husks removed and quartered

3 garlic cloves

1 tablespoon lime juice

3 tablespoons fresh cilantro, chopped

1 medium white onion, chopped

1 teaspoon ground cumin

½ teaspoon dried oregano

1⅔ cups chicken broth

1½ tablespoons olive oil

1. Season the pork pieces with the salt and pepper. Gently rub the seasonings into the pork cuts. Set aside. 2. Combine the jalapeños, tomatillos, garlic cloves, lime juice, cilantro, onions, cumin, oregano, and chicken broth in the blender. Pulse until well combined. Set aside. 3. Select Sauté mode and add the olive oil to the pot. Once the oil is hot, add the pork cuts and sear for 4 minutes per side or until browned. 4. Pour the jalapeño sauce over the pork and lightly stir to coat well. 5. Lock the lid. Select Manual mode and set cooking time for 55 minutes on High Pressure. 6. When cooking is complete, allow the pressure to release naturally for 10 minutes and then release the remaining pressure. 7. Open the lid. Transfer the pork pieces to a cutting board and use two forks to shred the pork. 8. Transfer the shredded pork back to the pot and stir to combine the pork with the sauce. Transfer to a serving platter. Serve warm.

Per Serving:

calories: 381 | fat: 24.8g | protein: 29.3g | carbs: 11.1g | net carbs: 8.3g | fiber: 2.8g

Chapter 4 Poultry

BLT Chicken Salad

Prep time: 15 minutes | Cook time: 17 minutes | Serves 4

4 slices bacon
2 (6-ounce / 170-g) chicken breasts
1 teaspoon salt
½ teaspoon garlic powder
¼ teaspoon dried parsley
¼ teaspoon pepper
¼ teaspoon dried thyme
1 cup water
2 cups chopped romaine lettuce
Sauce:
⅓ cup mayonnaise
1 ounce (28 g) chopped pecans
½ cup diced Roma tomatoes
½ avocado, diced
1 tablespoon lemon juice

1. Press the Sauté button to heat your Instant Pot. 2. Add the bacon and cook for about 7 minutes, flipping occasionally, until crisp. Remove and place on a paper towel to drain. When cool enough to handle, crumble the bacon and set aside. 3. Sprinkle the chicken with salt, garlic powder, parsley, pepper, and thyme. 4. Pour the water into the Instant Pot. Use a wooden spoon to ensure nothing is stuck to the bottom of the pot. Add the trivet to the pot and place the chicken on top of the trivet. 5. Secure the lid. Select the Manual mode and set the cooking time for 10 minutes at High Pressure. 6. Meanwhile, whisk together all the ingredients for the sauce in a large salad bowl. 7. Once cooking is complete, do a quick pressure release. Carefully open the lid. 8. Remove the chicken and let sit for 10 minutes. Cut the chicken into cubes and transfer to the salad bowl, along with the cooked bacon. Gently stir until the chicken is thoroughly coated. Mix in the lettuce right before serving.

Per Serving:
calories: 431 | fat: 32.6g | protein: 24.3g | carbs: 5.1g | net carbs: 2.4g | fiber: 2.7g

Sesame Chicken with Broccoli

Prep time: 15 minutes | Cook time: 12 minutes | Serves 2

½ teaspoon five spices
½ teaspoon sesame seeds
½ cup chopped broccoli
6 ounces (170 g) chicken fillet,
sliced
½ cup chicken broth
1 teaspoon coconut aminos
1 tablespoon avocado oil

1. In the mixing bowl, mix up avocado oil, coconut aminos, and sesame seeds. 2. Add five spices. 3. After this, mix up sliced chicken fillet and coconut aminos mixture. 4. Put the chicken in the instant pot. Add chicken broth and broccoli. 5. Close and seal the lid. 6. Cook the meal on Manual mode (High Pressure) for 12 minutes. Make a quick pressure release.

Per Serving:
calories: 195 | fat: 8g | protein: 27g | carbs: 3g | net carbs: 2g | fiber: 1g

Chicken Piccata

Prep time: 5 minutes | Cook time: 25 minutes | Serves 4

4 (6-ounce / 170-g) boneless, skinless chicken breasts
½ teaspoon salt
½ teaspoon garlic powder
¼ teaspoon pepper
2 tablespoons coconut oil
1 cup water
2 cloves garlic, minced
4 tablespoons butter
Juice of 1 lemon
¼ teaspoon xanthan gum

1. Sprinkle the chicken with salt, garlic powder, and pepper. 2. Set your Instant Pot to Sauté and melt the coconut oil. 3. Add the chicken and sear each side for about 5 to 7 minutes until golden brown. 4. Remove the chicken and set aside on a plate. 5. Pour the water into the Instant Pot. Using a wooden spoon, scrape the bottom if necessary to remove any stuck-on seasoning or meat. Insert the trivet and place the chicken on the trivet. 6. Secure the lid. Select the Manual mode and set the cooking time for 10 minutes at High Pressure. 7. Once cooking is complete, do a natural pressure release for 10 minutes, then release any remaining pressure. Carefully open the lid. 8. Remove the chicken and set aside. Strain the broth from the Instant Pot into a large bowl and return to the pot. 9. Set your Instant Pot to Sauté again and add the remaining ingredients. Cook for at least 5 minutes, stirring frequently, or until the sauce is cooked to your desired thickness. 10. Pour the sauce over the chicken and serve warm.

Per Serving:
calories: 338 | fat: 19.6g | protein: 32.2g | carbs: 1.8g | net carbs: 1.3g | fiber: 0.5g

Chicken Thighs with Feta

Prep time: 7 minutes | Cook time: 15 minutes | Serves 2

4 lemon slices
2 chicken thighs
1 tablespoon Greek seasoning
4 ounces (113 g) feta, crumbled
1 teaspoon butter
½ cup water

1. Rub the chicken thighs with Greek seasoning. 2. Then spread the chicken with butter. 3. Pour water in the instant pot and place the trivet. 4. Place the chicken on the foil and top with the lemon slices. Top it with feta. 5. Wrap the chicken in the foil and transfer on the trivet. 6. Cook on the Sauté mode for 10 minutes. Then make a quick pressure release for 5 minutes. 7. Discard the foil from the chicken thighs and serve!

Per Serving:
calories: 341 | fat: 24g | protein: 27g | carbs: 6g | net carbs: 6g | fiber: 0g

Chicken Patties

Prep time: 15 minutes | Cook time: 12 minutes | Serves 4

1 pound (454 g) ground chicken thigh meat	½ teaspoon garlic powder
	¼ teaspoon onion powder
½ cup shredded Mozzarella cheese	1 large egg
	2 ounces (57 g) pork rinds, finely ground
1 teaspoon dried parsley	

1. In a large bowl, mix ground chicken, Mozzarella, parsley, garlic powder, and onion powder. Form into four patties. 2. Place patties in the freezer for 15 to 20 minutes until they begin to firm up. 3. Whisk egg in a medium bowl. Place the ground pork rinds into a large bowl. 4. Dip each chicken patty into the egg and then press into pork rinds to fully coat. Place patties into the air fryer basket. 5. Adjust the temperature to 360ºF (182ºC) and air fry for 12 minutes. 6. Patties will be firm and cooked to an internal temperature of 165ºF (74ºC) when done. Serve immediately.

Per Serving:
calories: 265 | fat: 15g | protein: 29g | carbs: 1g | fiber: 0g | sodium: 285mg

Kung Pao Chicken

Prep time: 5 minutes | Cook time: 17 minutes | Serves 5

2 tablespoons coconut oil	½ teaspoon chili powder
1 pound (454 g) boneless, skinless chicken breasts, cubed	½ teaspoon finely grated ginger
	½ teaspoon kosher salt
1 cup cashews, chopped	½ teaspoon freshly ground black pepper
6 tablespoons hot sauce	

1. Set the Instant Pot to Sauté and melt the coconut oil. 2. Add the remaining ingredients to the Instant Pot and mix well. 3. Secure the lid. Select the Manual mode and set the cooking time for 17 minutes at High Pressure. 4. Once cooking is complete, do a quick pressure release. Carefully open the lid. 5. Serve warm.

Per Serving:
calories: 381 | fat: 25.0g | protein: 30.5g | carbs: 9.6g | net carbs: 8.6g | fiber: 1.0g

Coconut Curry Chicken

Prep time: 15 minutes | Cook time: 3 to 4 hours | Serves 6

1 tablespoon coconut oil	2 to 3 fresh green chiles, chopped
1 teaspoon cumin seeds	
2 medium onions, grated	1 cup coconut cream
7 to 8 ounces (198 to 227 g) canned plum tomatoes	12 chicken thighs, skinned, trimmed, and cut into bite-size chunks
1 teaspoon salt	
1 teaspoon turmeric	1 teaspoon garam masala
½ to 1 teaspoon Kashmiri chili powder (optional)	Handful fresh coriander leaves, chopped

1. Heat the oil in a frying pan (or in the slow cooker if you have a sear setting). Add the cumin seeds. When sizzling and aromatic, add the onions and cook until they are browning, about 5 to 7 minutes. 2. In a blender, purée the tomatoes and add them to the pan with the salt, turmeric, chili powder (if using), and fresh green chiles. 3. Stir together and put everything in the slow cooker. Pour in the coconut cream. Add the meat and stir to coat with the sauce. 4. Cover and cook on low for 4 hours, or on high for 3 hours. 5. Taste the sauce and adjust the seasoning. If the sauce is very liquidy, turn the cooker to high and cook for 30 minutes more with the lid off. 6. Add the garam masala and throw in the fresh coriander leaves to serve.

Per Serving:
calories: 648 | fat: 32g | protein: 78g | carbs: 9g | net carbs: 7g | sugars: 3g | fiber: 2g | sodium: 761mg | cholesterol: 363mg

Turkey Enchilada Bowl

Prep time: 10 minutes | Cook time: 25 minutes | Serves 4

2tbsp coconut oil	1 avocado, diced
1 lb boneless, skinless turkey thighs, cut into pieces	1 cup shredded mozzarella cheese
¾ cup red enchilada sauce (sugar-free)	¼ cup chopped pickled jalapeños
¼ cup water	½ cup sour cream
¼ cup chopped onion	1 tomato, diced
3 oz canned diced green chilis	

1. Set a large pan over medium heat. Add coconut oil and warm. Place in the turkey and cook until browned on the outside. Stir in onion, chillis, water, and enchilada sauce, then close with a lid. 2Allow simmering for 20 minutes until the turkey is cooked through. Spoon the turkey on a serving bowl and top with the sauce, cheese, sour cream, tomato, and avocado.

Per Serving:
Per serving: Kcal: 568, Fat: 40.2g, Net Carbs: 5.9g, Protein: 38g

Zucchini Spaghetti with Turkey Bolognese Sauce

Prep time: 10 minutes | Cook time: 35 minutes | Serves 6

3cups sliced mushrooms	1 cup diced onion
2 teaspoonsolive oil	2 cups broccoli florets
1 pound ground turkey	6 cups zucchini, spiralized
3 tablespoons pesto sauce	

1. Heat the oil in a skillet. Add zucchini and cook for 2-3 minutes, stirring continuously; set aside. 2. Add turkey to the skillet and cook until browned, about 7-8 minutes. Transfer to a plate. Add onion and cook until translucent, about 3 minutes. Add broccoli and mushrooms, and cook for 7 more minutes. Return the turkey to the skillet. Stir in the pesto sauce. Cover the pan, lower the heat, and simmer for 15 minutes. Stir in zucchini pasta and serve immediately.

Per Serving:
calories: 279 | fat: 19g | protein: 22g | carbs: 5g | net carbs: 3g | fiber: 2g

Sage Chicken Thighs

Prep time: 10 minutes | Cook time: 16 minutes | Serves 4

1 teaspoon dried sage	4 skinless chicken thighs
1 teaspoon ground turmeric	1 cup water
2 teaspoons avocado oil	1 teaspoon sesame oil

1. Rub the chicken thighs with dried sage, ground turmeric, sesame oil, and avocado oil. 2. Then pour water in the instant pot and insert the steamer rack. 3. Place the chicken thighs on the rack and close the lid. 4. Cook the meal on Manual (High Pressure) for 16 minutes. 5. Then make a quick pressure release and open the lid. 6. Let the cooked chicken thighs cool for 10 minutes before serving.

Per Serving:
calories: 293 | fat: 12g | protein: 42g | carbs: 1g | net carbs: 1g | fiber: 0g

Chicken with Mushrooms and Shallots

Prep time: 15 minutes | Cook time: 6 to 8 hours | Serves 2

1 teaspoon unsalted butter, at room temperature, or extra-virgin olive oil	1 shallot, minced
	3 tablespoons dry sherry
2 cups thinly sliced cremini mushrooms	2 bone-in, skinless chicken thighs, about 6 ounces (170 g) each
1 teaspoon fresh thyme	⅛ teaspoon sea salt
2 garlic cloves, minced	Freshly ground black pepper

1. Grease the inside of the slow cooker with the butter. 2. Put the mushrooms, thyme, garlic, and shallot into the slow cooker, tossing them gently to combine. Pour in the sherry. 3. Season the chicken with the salt and pepper and place the thighs on top of the mushroom mixture. 4. Cover and cook on low for 6 to 8 hours.

Per Serving:
calories: 243 | fat: 9g | protein: 35g | carbs: 4g | net carbs: 3g | sugars: 1g | fiber: 1g | sodium: 322mg | cholesterol: 165mg

Thanksgiving Turkey Breast

Prep time: 5 minutes | Cook time: 30 minutes | Serves 4

1½ teaspoons fine sea salt	1 teaspoon chopped fresh thyme leaves
1 teaspoon ground black pepper	
1 teaspoon chopped fresh rosemary leaves	1 (2-pound / 907-g) turkey breast
1 teaspoon chopped fresh sage	3 tablespoons ghee or unsalted butter, melted
1 teaspoon chopped fresh tarragon	3 tablespoons Dijon mustard

1. Spray the air fryer with avocado oil. Preheat the air fryer to 390ºF (199ºC). 2. In a small bowl, stir together the salt, pepper, and herbs until well combined. Season the turkey breast generously on all sides with the seasoning. 3. In another small bowl, stir together the ghee and Dijon. Brush the ghee mixture on all sides of the turkey breast. 4. Place the turkey breast in the air fryer basket and air fry for 30 minutes, or until the internal temperature reaches 165ºF (74ºC). Transfer the breast to a cutting board and allow it to rest for 10 minutes before cutting it into ½-inch-thick slices. 5. Store leftovers in an airtight container in the refrigerator for up to 4 days or in the freezer for up to a month. Reheat in a preheated 350ºF (177ºC) air fryer for 4 minutes, or until warmed through.

Per Serving:
calorie: 418 | fat: 22g | protein: 51g | carbs: 1g | sugars: 0g | fiber: 1g | sodium: 603mg

Paprika Chicken

Prep time: 10 minutes | Cook time: 25 minutes | Serves 4

4 (4-ounce) chicken breasts, skin-on	½ cup heavy (whipping) cream
	2 teaspoons smoked paprika
Sea salt	½ cup sour cream
Freshly ground black pepper	2 tablespoons chopped fresh parsley
1 tablespoon olive oil	
½ cup chopped sweet onion	

1. Lightly season the chicken with salt and pepper. 2. Place a large skillet over medium-high heat and add the olive oil. 3. Sear the chicken on both sides until almost cooked through, about 15 minutes in total. Remove the chicken to a plate. 4. Add the onion to the skillet and sauté until tender, about 4 minutes. 5. Stir in the cream and paprika and bring the liquid to a simmer. 6. Return the chicken and any accumulated juices to the skillet and simmer the chicken for 5 minutes until completely cooked. 7. Stir in the sour cream and remove the skillet from the heat. 8. Serve topped with the parsley.

Per Serving:
calories: 389 | fat: 30g | protein: 25g | carbs: 4g | net carbs: 4g | fiber: 0g

Chicken and Mixed Greens Salad

Prep time: 5 minutes | Cook time: 20 minutes | Serves 4

Chicken:	½ teaspoon freshly ground black pepper
2 tablespoons avocado oil	
1 pound (454 g) chicken breast, cubed	Salad:
	1 avocado, mashed
½ cup filtered water	1 cup chopped arugula
½ teaspoon ground turmeric	1 cup chopped Swiss chard
½ teaspoon dried parsley	1 cup chopped kale
½ teaspoon dried basil	½ cup chopped spinach
½ teaspoon kosher salt	2 tablespoons pine nuts, toasted

1. Combine all the chicken ingredients in the Instant Pot. 2. Secure the lid. Select the Manual mode and set the cooking time for 20 minutes at High Pressure. 3. Meanwhile, toss all the salad ingredients in a large salad bowl. 4. Once cooking is complete, do a quick pressure release. Carefully open the lid. 5. Remove the chicken to the salad bowl and serve.

Per Serving:
calories: 378 | fat: 23.3g | protein: 35.3g | carbs: 7.6g | net carbs: 3.5g | fiber: 4.1g

Classic Whole Chicken

Prep time: 5 minutes | Cook time: 50 minutes | Serves 4

Oil, for spraying	½ teaspoon salt
1 (4-pound / 1.8-kg) whole	½ teaspoon freshly ground
chicken, giblets removed	black pepper
1 tablespoon olive oil	¼ teaspoon finely chopped
1 teaspoon paprika	fresh parsley, for garnish
½ teaspoon granulated garlic	

1. Line the air fryer basket with parchment and spray lightly with oil. 2. Pat the chicken dry with paper towels. Rub it with the olive oil until evenly coated. 3. In a small bowl, mix together the paprika, garlic, salt, and black pepper and sprinkle it evenly over the chicken. 4. Place the chicken in the prepared basket, breast-side down. 5. Air fry at 360°F (182°C) for 30 minutes, flip, and cook for another 20 minutes, or until the internal temperature reaches 165°F (74°C) and the juices run clear. 6. Sprinkle with the parsley before serving.

Per Serving:
calories: 549 | fat: 11g | protein: 105g | carbs: 0g | fiber: 0g | sodium: 523mg

Crunchy Chicken Tacos

Prep time: 5 minutes | Cook time: 30 minutes to 8 hours | Serves 4

1 pound (454 g) frozen	2 teaspoons minced garlic
boneless, skinless chicken	8 slices provolone cheese
thighs	1 cup shredded lettuce
1 cup chicken broth	¼ cup chopped ripe tomato
1 cup low-carb green salsa	½ cup sour cream
½ medium onion, chopped	

1. In a slow cooker or electric pressure cooker, combine the chicken thighs, broth, salsa, onion, and garlic. 2. Place the lid on the pot. If using a slow cooker, cook on the low setting for 7 to 8 hours or on high for 3 to 4 hours. If using a pressure cooker, cook for 20 minutes on high pressure, then quick-release the pressure. 3. Place a slice of the provolone on a piece of parchment paper (not wax paper). Microwave on high power for 45 seconds; the cheese should just begin to turn a brownish orange in a few spots. 4. Quickly and carefully remove the parchment paper from the microwave. Holding opposite edges of the paper, form the melted cheese into a U shape. Hold it in this position for about 10 seconds, until it cools enough to hold its shape. (You can also hang the microwaved cheese slice over a wooden spoon handle to form the shape.) Remove the taco from the parchment paper. Repeat with the remaining 7 cheese slices. 5. Using a slotted spoon, remove the chicken from the cooker. Using 2 forks, shred the chicken, then return it to the cooker. 6. Use tongs or a slotted spoon to fill the tacos with equal portions of the chicken, being careful to drain off some of the liquid so the tacos don't get soggy. 7. Top the chicken filling with shredded lettuce, tomato, and sour cream, then serve.

Per Serving:
calories: 528 | fat: 40g | protein: 35g | carbs: 8g | net carbs: 6g | fiber: 2g

Roasted Chicken Breasts with Capers

Prep time: 10 minutes | Cook time: 55 minutes | Serves 6

3 medium lemons, sliced	2 tablespoons capers, rinsed
½ teaspoon salt	1¼ cup chicken broth
1 teaspoon olive oil	2 teaspoons butter
3 chicken breasts, halved	1½ tablespoons chopped fresh
Salt and black pepper to season	parsley
¼ cup almond flour	Parsley for garnish
2 teaspoons olive oil	

1. Preheat the oven to 350°F and lay a piece of parchment paper on a baking sheet. 2. Lay the lemon slices on the baking sheet, drizzle with olive oil and sprinkle with salt. Roast in the oven for 25 minutes to brown the lemon rinds. 3. Cover the chicken with plastic wrap, place them on a flat surface, and gently pound with the rolling pin to flatten to about ½ -inch thickness. Remove the plastic wraps and season with salt and pepper. 4. Next, dredge the chicken in the almond flour on each side, and shake off any excess flour. Set aside. 5. Heat the olive oil in a skillet over medium heat and fry the chicken on both sides to a golden brown, for about 8 minutes in total. Pour the chicken broth in, shake the skillet, and let the broth boil and reduce to a thick consistency, about 12 minutes. 6. Lightly stir in the capers, roasted lemon, pepper, butter, and parsley, and simmer on low heat for 10 minutes. Turn the heat off and serve the chicken with the sauce hot, an extra garnish of parsley with a creamy squash mash.

Per Serving:
calories: 366 | fat: 26g | protein: 27g | carbs: 6g | net carbs: 4g | fiber: 2g

Poulet en Papillote

Prep time: 10 minutes | Cook time: 45 minutes | Serves 4

4 chicken breasts, skinless,	1 medium celeriac, peeled,
scored	chopped
4 tablespoons white wine	2 cups water
2 tablespoons olive oil + extra	3 cloves garlic, minced
for drizzling	4 sprigs thyme, chopped
4 tablespoons butter	3 lemons, juiced
3 cups mixed mushrooms,	Salt and black pepper to taste
teared up	2 tablespoons Dijon mustard

1. Preheat the oven to 450°F. 2. Arrange the celeriac on a baking sheet, drizzle it with a little oil, and bake for 20 minutes; set aside. 3. In a bowl, evenly mix the chicken, roasted celeriac, mushrooms, garlic, thyme, lemon juice, salt, black pepper, and mustard. Make 4 large cuts of foil, fold them in half, and then fold them in half again. Tightly fold the two open edges together to create a bag. 4. Now, share the chicken mixture into each bag, top with the white wine, olive oil, and a tablespoon of butter. Seal the last open end securely making sure not to pierce the bag. Put the bag on a baking tray and bake the chicken in the middle of the oven for 25 minutes.

Per Serving:
calories: 333 | fat: 21g | protein: 29g | carbs: 7g | net carbs: 3g | fiber: 4g

Chicken Enchilada Bowl

Prep time: 10 minutes | Cook time: 35 minutes | Serves 4

2 (6-ounce / 170-g) boneless, skinless chicken breasts	¼ cup chicken broth
2 teaspoons chili powder	1 (4-ounce / 113-g) can green chilies
½ teaspoon garlic powder	¼ cup diced onion
½ teaspoon salt	2 cups cooked cauliflower rice
¼ teaspoon pepper	1 avocado, diced
2 tablespoons coconut oil	½ cup sour cream
¾ cup red enchilada sauce	1 cup shredded Cheddar cheese

1. Sprinkle the chili powder, garlic powder, salt, and pepper on chicken breasts. 2. Set your Instant Pot to Sauté and melt the coconut oil. Add the chicken breasts and sear each side for about 5 minutes until golden brown. 3. Pour the enchilada sauce and broth over the chicken. Using a wooden spoon or rubber spatula, scrape the bottom of pot to make sure nothing is sticking. Stir in the chilies and onion. 4. Secure the lid. Select the Manual mode and set the cooking time for 25 minutes at High Pressure. 5. Once cooking is complete, do a quick pressure release. Carefully open the lid. 6. Remove the chicken and shred with two forks. Serve the chicken over the cauliflower rice and place the avocado, sour cream, and Cheddar cheese on top.

Per Serving:
calories: 434 | fat: 26.1g | protein: 29.3g | carbs: 11.8g | net carbs: 7.0g | fiber: 4.8g

Fried Chicken Breasts

Prep time: 30 minutes | Cook time: 12 to 14 minutes | Serves 4

1 pound (454 g) boneless, skinless chicken breasts	cheese
¾ cup dill pickle juice	½ teaspoon sea salt
¾ cup finely ground blanched almond flour	½ teaspoon freshly ground black pepper
¾ cup finely grated Parmesan	2 large eggs
	Avocado oil spray

1. Place the chicken breasts in a zip-top bag or between two pieces of plastic wrap. Using a meat mallet or heavy skillet, pound the chicken to a uniform ½-inch thickness. 2. Place the chicken in a large bowl with the pickle juice. Cover and allow to brine in the refrigerator for up to 2 hours. 3. In a shallow dish, combine the almond flour, Parmesan cheese, salt, and pepper. In a separate, shallow bowl, beat the eggs. 4. Drain the chicken and pat it dry with paper towels. Dip in the eggs and then in the flour mixture, making sure to press the coating into the chicken. Spray both sides of the coated breasts with oil. 5. Spray the air fryer basket with oil and put the chicken inside. Set the temperature to 400ºF (204ºC) and air fry for 6 to 7 minutes. 6. Carefully flip the breasts with a spatula. Spray the breasts again with oil and continue cooking for 6 to 7 minutes more, until golden and crispy.

Per Serving:
calories: 319 | fat: 17g | protein: 37g | carbs: 5g | fiber: 3g | sodium: 399mg

Chicken Skewers with Peanut Sauce

Prep time: 10 minutes | Cook time: 15 minutes | Serves 2

1 pound boneless skinless chicken breast, cut into chunks	3 teaspoons toasted sesame oil, divided
3 tablespoons soy sauce (or coconut aminos), divided	Ghee, for oiling
½ teaspoon Sriracha sauce, plus	2 tablespoons peanut butter
¼ teaspoon	Pink Himalayan salt
	Freshly ground black pepper

1. In a large zip-top bag, combine the chicken chunks with 2 tablespoons of soy sauce, ½ teaspoon of Sriracha sauce, and 2 teaspoons of sesame oil. Seal the bag, and let the chicken marinate for an hour or so in the refrigerator or up to overnight. 2. If you are using wood 8-inch skewers, soak them in water for 30 minutes before using. 3. I like to use my grill pan for the skewers, because I don't have an outdoor grill. If you don't have a grill pan, you can use a large skillet. Preheat your grill pan or grill to low. Oil the grill pan with ghee. 4. Thread the chicken chunks onto the skewers. 5. Cook the skewers over low heat for 10 to 15 minutes, flipping halfway through. 6. Meanwhile, mix the peanut dipping sauce. Stir together the remaining 1 tablespoon of soy sauce, ¼ teaspoon of Sriracha sauce, 1 teaspoon of sesame oil, and the peanut butter. Season with pink Himalayan salt and pepper. 7. Serve the chicken skewers with a small dish of the peanut sauce.

Per Serving:
calories: 586 | fat: 29g | protein: 75g | carbs: 6g | net carbs: 5g | fiber: 1g

Chicken Meatballs with Green Cabbage

Prep time: 15 minutes | Cook time: 4 minutes | Serves 4

1 pound (454 g) ground chicken	black pepper, divided
¼ cup heavy (whipping) cream	¼ teaspoon ground allspice
2 teaspoons salt, divided	4 to 6 cups thickly chopped green cabbage
½ teaspoon ground caraway seeds	½ cup coconut milk
1½ teaspoons freshly ground	2 tablespoons unsalted butter

1. To make the meatballs, put the chicken in a bowl. Add the cream, 1 teaspoon of salt, the caraway, ½ teaspoon of pepper, and the allspice. Mix thoroughly. Refrigerate the mixture for 30 minutes. Once the mixture has cooled, it is easier to form the meatballs. 2. Using a small scoop, form the chicken mixture into small-to medium-size meatballs. Place half the meatballs in the inner cooking pot of your Instant Pot and cover them with half the cabbage. Place the remaining meatballs on top of the cabbage, then cover them with the rest of the cabbage. 3. Pour in the milk, place pats of the butter here and there, and sprinkle with the remaining 1 teaspoon of salt and 1 teaspoon of pepper. 4. Lock the lid into place. Select Manual and adjust the pressure to High. Cook for 4 minutes. When the cooking is complete, quick-release the pressure. Unlock the lid. Serve the meatballs on top of the cabbage.

Per Serving:
calories: 338 | fat: 23g | protein: 23g | carbs: 7g | net carbs: 4g | fiber: 3g

Tuscan Chicken Drumsticks

Prep time: 15 minutes | Cook time: 12 minutes | Serves 4

4 chicken drumsticks	1 cup heavy cream
1 cup chopped spinach	1 teaspoon cayenne pepper
1 teaspoon minced garlic	1 ounce (28 g) sun-dried
1 teaspoon ground paprika	tomatoes, chopped

1. Put all ingredients in the instant pot. 2. Close and seal the lid. 3. Cook the meal on Manual mode (High Pressure) for 12 minutes. 4. Then allow the natural pressure release for 10 minutes. 5. Serve the chicken with hot sauce from the instant pot.

Per Serving:
calories: 188 | fat: 14g | protein: 14g | carbs: 2g | net carbs: 1g | fiber: 1g

Easy Turkey Tenderloin

Prep time: 20 minutes | Cook time: 30 minutes | Serves 4

Olive oil	black pepper
½ teaspoon paprika	Pinch cayenne pepper
½ teaspoon garlic powder	1½ pounds (680 g) turkey
½ teaspoon salt	breast tenderloin
½ teaspoon freshly ground	

1. Spray the air fryer basket lightly with olive oil. 2. In a small bowl, combine the paprika, garlic powder, salt, black pepper, and cayenne pepper. Rub the mixture all over the turkey. 3. Place the turkey in the air fryer basket and lightly spray with olive oil. 4. Air fry at 370ºF (188ºC) for 15 minutes. Flip the turkey over and lightly spray with olive oil. Air fry until the internal temperature reaches at least 170ºF (77ºC) for an additional 10 to 15 minutes. 5. Let the turkey rest for 10 minutes before slicing and serving.

Per Serving:
calories: 196 | fat: 3g | protein: 40g | carbs: 1g | fiber: 0g | sodium: 483mg

Harissa-Rubbed Cornish Game Hens

Prep time: 30 minutes | Cook time: 21 minutes | Serves 4

Harissa:	1 teaspoon kosher salt
½ cup olive oil	½ to 1 teaspoon cayenne pepper
6 cloves garlic, minced	Hens:
2 tablespoons smoked paprika	½ cup yogurt
1 tablespoon ground coriander	2 Cornish game hens, any
1 tablespoon ground cumin	giblets removed, split in half
1 teaspoon ground caraway	lengthwise

1. For the harissa: In a medium microwave-safe bowl, combine the oil, garlic, paprika, coriander, cumin, caraway, salt, and cayenne. Microwave on high for 1 minute, stirring halfway through the cooking time. (You can also heat this on the stovetop until the oil is hot and bubbling. Or, if you must use your air fryer for everything, cook it in the air fryer at 350ºF (177ºC) for 5 to 6 minutes, or until the paste is heated through.) 2. For the hens: In a small bowl, combine 1 to 2 tablespoons harissa and the yogurt. Whisk until well combined. Place the hen halves in a resealable plastic bag and pour the marinade over. Seal the bag and massage until all of the pieces are thoroughly coated. Marinate at room temperature for 30 minutes or in the refrigerator for up to 24 hours. 3. Arrange the hen halves in a single layer in the air fryer basket. (If you have a smaller air fryer, you may have to cook this in two batches.) Set the air fryer to 400ºF (204ºC) for 20 minutes. Use a meat thermometer to ensure the game hens have reached an internal temperature of 165ºF (74ºC).

Per Serving:
calories: 421 | fat: 33g | protein: 26g | carbs: 6g | fiber: 2g | sodium: 683mg

Shredded Chicken

Prep time: 5 minutes | Cook time: 14 minutes | Serves 4

½ teaspoon salt	2 (6-ounce / 170-g) boneless,
½ teaspoon pepper	skinless chicken breasts
½ teaspoon dried oregano	1 tablespoon coconut oil
½ teaspoon dried basil	1 cup water
½ teaspoon garlic powder	

1. In a small bowl, combine the salt, pepper, oregano, basil, and garlic powder. Rub this mix over both sides of the chicken. 2. Set your Instant Pot to Sauté and heat the coconut oil until sizzling. 3. Add the chicken and sear for 3 to 4 minutes until golden on both sides. 4. Remove the chicken and set aside. 5. Pour the water into the Instant Pot and use a wooden spoon or rubber spatula to make sure no seasoning is stuck to bottom of pot. 6. Add the trivet to the Instant Pot and place the chicken on top. 7. Secure the lid. Select the Manual mode and set the cooking time for 10 minutes at High Pressure. 8. Once cooking is complete, do a natural pressure release for 5 minutes, then release any remaining pressure. Carefully open the lid. 9. Remove the chicken and shred, then serve.

Per Serving:
calories: 135 | fat: 5g | protein: 20g | carbs: 0g | net carbs: 0g | fiber: 0g

Parmesan-Crusted Chicken

Prep time: 15 minutes | Cook time: 13 minutes | Serves 2

1 tomato, sliced	1 teaspoon butter
8 ounces (227 g) chicken fillets	4 tablespoons water, for
2 ounces (57 g) Parmesan,	sprinkling
sliced	1 cup water, for cooking

1. Pour water and insert the steamer rack in the instant pot. 2. Then grease the baking mold with butter. 3. Slice the chicken fillets into halves and put them in the mold. 4. Sprinkle the chicken with water and top with tomato and Parmesan. 5. Cover the baking mold with foil and place it on the rack. 6. Close and seal the lid. 7. Cook the meal in Manual mode for 13 minutes. Then allow the natural pressure release for 10 minutes.

Per Serving:
calories: 329 | fat: 16g | protein: 42g | carbs: 2g | net carbs: 2g | fiber: 0g

Turkey with Mushroom Gravy

Prep time: 10 minutes | Cook time: 45 minutes | Serves 4

1 (2-pound / 907-g) piece of turkey breast
½ teaspoon pink Himalayan sea salt, plus more for seasoning
¼ teaspoon freshly ground black pepper, plus more for seasoning
4 tablespoons (½ stick) butter
2 cups sliced fresh mushrooms
½ medium onion, chopped
1 cup chicken broth
¼ cup sour cream

1. Preheat the oven to 450ºF (235ºC). 2. Slice the turkey breast into 4 cutlets that are roughly 2 inches thick. 3. Place the cutlets in an 8-inch square baking dish and season lightly with a little salt and pepper. Bake for 30 minutes. 4. In a medium saucepan, melt the butter over medium heat. Add the mushrooms and onion and cook for 3 to 5 minutes, until the onion is almost translucent. 5. Add the broth, sour cream, ½ teaspoon of salt, and ¼ teaspoon of pepper to the pan. Stir to form a sauce, then simmer over low heat for about 5 minutes, until it reaches your desired thickness. Keep warm. 6. When the turkey is almost finished baking, pour the gravy over it and bake for an additional 5 to 10 minutes, until the gravy is bubbling. Serve.

Per Serving:
calories: 499 | fat: 30g | protein: 51g | carbs: 3g | net carbs: 2g | fiber: 1g

Chicken Alfredo

Prep time: 5 minutes | Cook time: 20 minutes | Serves 2

2 teaspoons extra-virgin olive oil, divided
8 ounces (227 g) boneless, skinless chicken thighs, cubed
2 tablespoons butter
½ teaspoon minced garlic
½ cup heavy (whipping) cream
⅔ cup grated Parmesan cheese
¼ cup shredded low-moisture
mozzarella cheese
Pinch of red pepper flakes
Pink Himalayan sea salt
Freshly ground black pepper
1 (7-ounce / 198-g) package shirataki noodles, drained, or 7 ounces / 198 g zoodles (spiralized zucchini)

1. In a small sauté pan or skillet, heat 1 teaspoon of olive oil over medium heat and cook the chicken for 10 to 12 minutes, until cooked through. 2. In a medium saucepan, melt the butter over medium heat. Add the garlic and cook for 1 to 2 minutes, until slightly browned. Add the cream and bring to a simmer. 3. Slowly add the Parmesan and mozzarella while stirring. The cheese should melt into the sauce. 4. Reduce the heat, add the chicken, and heat through, without allowing the sauce to boil. Season with the salt and pepper. 5. In the same skillet as you cooked the chicken, add the remaining 1 teaspoon of olive oil and drop in the shirataki noodles. Cook the noodles over medium heat for 2 to 3 minutes, until heated through. 6. Spoon the noodles onto 2 serving plates and top with the sauce.

Per Serving:
calories: 810 | fat: 70g | protein: 36g | carbs: 11g | net carbs: 9g | fiber: 2g

Chicken with Tomatoes and Spinach

Prep time: 5 minutes | Cook time: 18 minutes | Serves 4

4 boneless, skinless chicken breasts (about 2 pounds / 907 g)
2½ ounces (71 g) sun-dried tomatoes, coarsely chopped (about 2 tablespoons)
¼ cup chicken broth
2 tablespoons creamy, no-sugar-added balsamic vinegar dressing
1 tablespoon whole-grain mustard
2 cloves garlic, minced
1 teaspoon salt
8 ounces (227 g) fresh spinach
¼ cup sour cream
1 ounce (28 g) cream cheese, softened

1. Place the chicken breasts in the Instant Pot. Add the tomatoes, broth, and dressing. 2. Close the lid and seal the vent. Cook on High Pressure for 10 minutes. Quick release the steam. Press Cancel. 3. Remove the chicken from the pot and place on a plate. Cover with aluminum foil to keep warm while you make the sauce. 4. Turn the pot to Sauté mode. Whisk in the mustard, garlic, and salt and then add the spinach. Stir the spinach continuously until it is completely cooked down, 2 to 3 minutes. The spinach will absorb the sauce but will release it again as it continues to cook down. 5. Once the spinach is completely wilted, add the sour cream and cream cheese. Whisk until completed incorporated. 6. Let the sauce simmer to thicken and reduce by about one-third, about 5 minutes. Stir occasionally to prevent burning. Press Cancel. 7. Pour the sauce over the chicken. Serve.

Per Serving:
calories: 357 | fat: 13g | protein: 52g | carbs: 7g | net carbs: 5g | fiber: 2g

Chicken Bacon Burgers

Prep time: 10 minutes | Cook time: 25 minutes | Serves 6

1 pound ground chicken
8 bacon slices, chopped
¼ cup ground almonds
1 teaspoon chopped fresh basil
¼ teaspoon sea salt
Pinch freshly ground black
pepper
2 tablespoons coconut oil
4 large lettuce leaves
1 avocado, peeled, pitted, and sliced

1. Preheat the oven to 350°F. Line a baking sheet with parchment paper and set aside. 2. In a medium bowl, combine the chicken, bacon, ground almonds, basil, salt, and pepper until well mixed. 3. Form the mixture into 6 equal patties. 4. Place a large skillet over medium-high heat and add the coconut oil. 5. Pan sear the chicken patties until brown on both sides, about 6 minutes in total. 6. Place the browned patties on the baking sheet and bake until completely cooked through, about 15 minutes. 7. Serve on the lettuce leaves, topped with the avocado slices.

Per Serving:
calories: 374 | fat: 33g | protein: 18g | carbs: 3g | net carbs: 1g | fiber: 2g

Chili Lime Turkey Burgers

Prep time: 10 minutes | Cook time: 3 minutes | Serves 4

Burgers:

2 pounds (907 g) ground turkey

1½ ounces (43 g) diced red onion

2 cloves garlic, minced

1½ teaspoons minced cilantro

1½ teaspoons salt

1 teaspoon Mexican chili powder

Juice and zest of 1 lime

½ cup water

Dipping Sauce:

½ cup sour cream

4 teaspoons sriracha

1 tablespoon chopped cilantro, plus more for garnish

1 teaspoon lime juice

1. Make the burgers: In a large bowl, add the turkey, onion, garlic, cilantro, salt, chili powder, and lime juice and zest. Use a wooden spoon to mix until the ingredients are well distributed. 2. Divide the meat into four 8-ounce / 227-g balls. Use a kitchen scale to measure for accuracy. Pat the meat into thick patties, about 1 inch thick. 3. Add the water and trivet to the Instant Pot. Place the turkey patties on top of the trivet, overlapping if necessary. 4. Close the lid and seal the vent. Cook on High Pressure for 3 minutes. Quick release the steam. 5. Remove the patties from the pot. 6. Make the dipping sauce: In a small bowl, whisk together the sour cream, sriracha, cilantro, and lime juice. 7. Top each patty with 2 tablespoons of the sauce and garnish with fresh cilantro.

Per Serving:

calories: 417 | fat: 25g | protein: 44g | carbs: 5g | net carbs: 4g | fiber: 1g

Crack Chicken Breasts

Prep time: 5 minutes | Cook time: 15 minutes | Serves 2

½ pound (227 g) boneless, skinless chicken breasts

2 ounces (57 g) cream cheese, softened

½ cup grass-fed bone broth

¼ cup tablespoons keto-friendly ranch dressing

½ cup shredded full-fat Cheddar cheese

3 slices bacon, cooked and chopped into small pieces

1. Combine all the ingredients except the Cheddar cheese and bacon in the Instant Pot. 2. Secure the lid. Select the Manual mode and set the cooking time for 15 minutes at High Pressure. 3. Once cooking is complete, do a quick pressure release. Carefully open the lid. 4. Add the Cheddar cheese and bacon and stir well, then serve.

Per Serving:

calories: 549 | fat: 45.7g | protein: 32.4g | carbs: 2.4g | net carbs: 2.4g | fiber: 0g

Chicken and Grape Tomatoes

Prep time: 15 minutes | Cook time: 8 hours | Serves 2

1 pint grape tomatoes

4 garlic cloves, smashed

Zest of 1 lemon

1 teaspoon extra-virgin olive oil

2 bone-in, skinless chicken thighs, about 8 ounces (227 g) each

1 teaspoon fresh thyme

½ teaspoon fresh rosemary

⅛ teaspoon sea salt

Freshly ground black pepper

1. Put the tomatoes, garlic, lemon zest, and olive oil in the slow cooker. Gently stir to mix. 2. Place the chicken thighs over the tomato mixture and season them with the thyme, rosemary, salt, and a few grinds of black pepper. 3. Cover and cook on low for 8 hours.

Per Serving:

calories: 284 | fat: 10g | protein: 40g | carbs: 9g | net carbs: 7g | sugars: 5g | fiber: 2g | sodium: 366mg | cholesterol: 182mg

Chapter 5 Fish and Seafood

Italian Salmon

Prep time: 10 minutes | Cook time: 4 minutes | Serves 2

10 ounces (283 g) salmon fillet
1 teaspoon Italian seasoning
1 cup water

1. Pour water and insert the trivet in the instant pot. 2. Then rub the salmon fillet with Italian seasoning and wrap in the foil. 3. Place the wrapped fish on the trivet and close the lid. 4. Cook the meal on Manual mode (High Pressure) for 4 minutes. 5. Make a quick pressure release and remove the fish from the foil. 6. Cut it into servings.

Per Serving:
calories: 195 | fat: 10g | protein: 27g | carbs: 0g | net carbs: 0g | fiber: 0g

Classic Fish Sticks with Tartar Sauce

Prep time: 10 minutes | Cook time: 12 to 15 minutes | Serves 4

1½ pounds (680 g) cod fillets, cut into 1-inch strips
1 teaspoon salt
½ teaspoon freshly ground black pepper
2 eggs
¾ cup almond flour
¼ cup grated Parmesan cheese
Tartar Sauce:
½ cup sour cream
½ cup mayonnaise
3 tablespoons chopped dill pickle
2 tablespoons capers, drained and chopped
½ teaspoon dried dill
1 tablespoon dill pickle liquid (optional)

1. Preheat the air fryer to 400ºF (204ºC). 2. Season the cod with the salt and black pepper; set aside. 3. In a shallow bowl, lightly beat the eggs. In a second shallow bowl, combine the almond flour and Parmesan cheese. Stir until thoroughly combined. 4. Working with a few pieces at a time, dip the fish into the egg mixture followed by the flour mixture. Press lightly to ensure an even coating. 5. Working in batches if necessary, arrange the fish in a single layer in the air fryer basket and spray lightly with olive oil. Pausing halfway through the cooking time to turn the fish, air fry for 12 to 15 minutes, until the fish flakes easily with a fork. Let sit in the basket for a few minutes before serving with the tartar sauce. 6. To make the tartar sauce: In a small bowl, combine the sour cream, mayonnaise, pickle, capers, and dill. If you prefer a thinner sauce, stir in the pickle liquid.

Per Serving:
calories: 382 | fat: 23g | protein: 36g | carbs: 7g | net carbs: 5g | fiber: 2g

Sheet-Pan Shrimp

Prep time: 15 minutes | Cook time: 10 minutes | Serves 4

8 tablespoons (1 stick) butter, melted
4 ounces (113 g) cream cheese, at room temperature
1 teaspoon garlic salt
1 pound (454 g) shrimp, any size, peeled, deveined, tails off, patted dry
Juice of 1 lemon
2 scallions, thinly sliced

1. Preheat the oven to 400ºF (205ºC). Line a rimmed baking sheet with parchment paper and set aside. 2. In a medium bowl, mix together the melted butter, cream cheese, and garlic salt until well combined. 3. Drop the shrimp into the butter mixture and fold gently to coat all the shrimp. 4. Pour the shrimp mixture onto the prepared baking sheet and spread out the shrimp so none overlap. 5. Bake for 8 to 10 minutes. 6. Squeeze the lemon juice across the top of the shrimp, garnish with the scallions, and serve immediately.

Per Serving:
¼ recipe: calories: 420 | fat: 35g | protein: 25g | carbs: 3g | net carbs: 3g | fiber: 0g

Shrimp Ceviche Salad

Prep time: 15 minutes | Cook time: 0 minutes | Serves 4

1 pound (454 g) fresh shrimp, peeled and deveined
1 small red or yellow bell pepper, cut into ½-inch chunks
½ English cucumber, peeled and cut into ½-inch chunks
½ small red onion, cut into thin slivers
¼ cup chopped fresh cilantro or flat-leaf Italian parsley
⅓ cup freshly squeezed lime juice
2 tablespoons freshly squeezed lemon juice
2 tablespoons freshly squeezed clementine juice or orange juice
½ cup extra-virgin olive oil
1 teaspoon salt
½ teaspoon freshly ground black pepper
2 ripe avocados, peeled, pitted, and cut into ½-inch chunks

1. Cut the shrimp in half lengthwise. In a large glass bowl, combine the shrimp, bell pepper, cucumber, onion, and cilantro. 2. In a small bowl, whisk together the lime, lemon, and clementine juices, olive oil, salt, and pepper. Pour the mixture over the shrimp and veggies and toss to coat. Cover and refrigerate for at least 2 hours, or up to 8 hours. Give the mixture a toss every 30 minutes for the first 2 hours to make sure all the shrimp "cook" in the juices. 3. Add the cut avocado just before serving and toss to combine.

Per Serving:
calories: 520 | fat: 42g | protein: 26g | carbs: 14g | fiber: 8g | sodium: 593mg

Cod with Parsley Pistou

Prep time: 15 minutes | Cook time: 10 minutes | Serves 4

1 cup packed roughly chopped fresh flat-leaf Italian parsley	½ teaspoon freshly ground black pepper
1 to 2 small garlic cloves, minced	1 cup extra-virgin olive oil, divided
Zest and juice of 1 lemon	1 pound (454 g) cod fillets, cut into 4 equal-sized pieces
1 teaspoon salt	

1. In a food processor, combine the parsley, garlic, lemon zest and juice, salt, and pepper. Pulse to chop well. 2. While the food processor is running, slowly stream in ¾ cup olive oil until well combined. Set aside. 3. In a large skillet, heat the remaining ¼ cup olive oil over medium-high heat. Add the cod fillets, cover, and cook 4 to 5 minutes on each side, or until cooked through. Thicker fillets may require a bit more cooking time. Remove from the heat and keep warm. 4. Add the pistou to the skillet and heat over medium-low heat. Return the cooked fish to the skillet, flipping to coat in the sauce. Serve warm, covered with pistou.
Per Serving:
calories: 580 | fat: 55g | protein: 21g | carbs: 2g | fiber: 1g | sodium: 591mg

Salmon with Provolone Cheese

Prep time: 5 minutes | Cook time: 15 minutes | Serves 4

1 pound (454 g) salmon fillet, chopped	grated
	1 teaspoon avocado oil
2 ounces (57 g) Provolone,	¼ teaspoon ground paprika

1. Sprinkle the salmon fillets with avocado oil and put in the air fryer. 2. Then sprinkle the fish with ground paprika and top with Provolone cheese. 3. Cook the fish at 360ºF (182ºC) for 15 minutes.
Per Serving:
calories: 204 | fat: 10g | protein: 27g | carbs: 0g | fiber: 0g | sodium: 209mg

Rosemary Baked Haddock

Prep time: 7 minutes | Cook time: 10 minutes | Serves 2

2 eggs, beaten	¾ teaspoon dried rosemary
12 ounces (340 g) haddock fillet, chopped	2 ounces (57 g) Parmesan, grated
1 tablespoon cream cheese	1 teaspoon butter

1. Whisk the beaten eggs until homogenous. Add the cream cheese, dried rosemary, and dill. 2. Grease the springform with the butter and place the haddock inside. 3. Pour the egg mixture over the fish and add sprinkle with Parmesan. 4. Set the Manual mode (High Pressure) and cook for 5 minutes. Then make a natural release pressure for 5 minutes.
Per Serving:
calories: 380 | fat: 16g | protein: 56g | carbs: 18g | net carbs: 18g | fiber: 0g

Coconut Crab Patties

Prep time: 5 minutes | Cook time: 6 minutes | Serves 8

2 tablespoons coconut oil	2 teaspoons Dijon mustard
1 tablespoon lemon juice	1 egg, beaten
1cup lump crab meat	1½ tablespoons coconut flour

1. In a bowl to the crabmeat, add all the ingredients, except for the oil; mix well to combine. Make patties out of the mixture. Melt the coconut oil in a skillet over medium heat. Add the crab patties and cook for about 2-3 minutes per side.
Per Serving:
calories: 209 | fat: 13g | protein: 17g | carbs: 6g | net carbs: 4g | fiber: 2g

Cajun Salmon

Prep time: 5 minutes | Cook time: 7 minutes | Serves 2

2 (4-ounce / 113-g) salmon fillets, skin removed	pepper
	½ teaspoon garlic powder
2 tablespoons unsalted butter, melted	1 teaspoon paprika
	¼ teaspoon ground black
⅛ teaspoon ground cayenne	pepper

1. Brush each fillet with butter. 2. Combine remaining ingredients in a small bowl and then rub onto fish. Place fillets into the air fryer basket. 3. Adjust the temperature to 390ºF (199ºC) and air fry for 7 minutes. 4. When fully cooked, internal temperature will be 145ºF (63ºC). Serve immediately.
Per Serving:
calories: 213 | fat: 12g | protein: 24g | carbs: 1g | net carbs: 0g | fiber: 1g

Simple Fish Curry

Prep time: 10 minutes | Cook time: 25 minutes | Serves 4

2 tablespoons coconut oil	2 cups coconut milk
1½ tablespoons grated fresh ginger	16 ounces firm white fish, cut into 1-inch chunks
2 teaspoons minced garlic	1 cup shredded kale
1 tablespoon curry powder	2 tablespoons chopped cilantro
½ teaspoon ground cumin	

1. Place a large saucepan over medium heat and melt the coconut oil. 2. Sauté the ginger and garlic until lightly browned, about 2 minutes. 3. Stir in the curry powder and cumin and sauté until very fragrant, about 2 minutes. 4. Stir in the coconut milk and bring the liquid to a boil. 5. Reduce the heat to low and simmer for about 5 minutes to infuse the milk with the spices. 6. Add the fish and cook until the fish is cooked through, about 10 minutes. 7. Stir in the kale and cilantro and simmer until wilted, about 2 minutes. 8. Serve.
Per Serving:
calories: 416 | fat: 31g | protein: 26g | carbs: 5g | net carbs: 4g | fiber: 1g

Herbed Coconut Milk Steamed Mussels

Prep time: 10 minutes | Cook time: 15 minutes | Serves 4

2 tablespoons coconut oil	1½ pounds fresh mussels,
½ sweet onion, chopped	scrubbed and debearded
2 teaspoons minced garlic	1 scallion, finely chopped
1 teaspoon grated fresh ginger	2 tablespoons chopped fresh
½ teaspoon turmeric	cilantro
1 cup coconut milk	1 tablespoon chopped fresh
Juice of 1 lime	thyme

1. Sauté the aromatics. In a large skillet, warm the coconut oil. Add the onion, garlic, ginger, and turmeric and sauté until they've softened, about 3 minutes. 2. Add the liquid. Stir in the coconut milk and lime juice and bring the mixture to a boil. 3. Steam the mussels. Add the mussels to the skillet, cover, and steam until the shells are open, about 10 minutes. Take the skillet off the heat and throw out any unopened mussels. 4. Add the herbs. Stir in the scallion, cilantro, and thyme. 5. Serve. Divide the mussels and the sauce between four bowls and serve them immediately.
Per Serving:
calories: 319 | fat: 23g | protein: 23g | carbs: 8g | net carbs: 6g | fiber: 2g

Mascarpone Tilapia with Nutmeg

Prep time: 10 minutes | Cook time: 20 minutes | Serves 2

10 ounces (283 g) tilapia	1 teaspoon ground nutmeg
½ cup mascarpone	1 tablespoon olive oil
1 garlic clove, diced	½ teaspoon salt

1. Pour olive oil in the instant pot. 2. Add diced garlic and sauté it for 4 minutes. 3. Add tilapia and sprinkle it with ground nutmeg. Sauté the fish for 3 minutes per side. 4. Add mascarpone and close the lid. 5. Sauté tilapia for 10 minutes.
Per Serving:
calories: 293 | fat: 17g | protein: 33g | carbs: 3g | net carbs: 2g | fiber: 1g

Mahi-Mahi Fillets with Peppers

Prep time: 10 minutes | Cook time: 3 minutes | Serves 3

2 sprigs fresh rosemary	melted
2 sprigs dill, tarragon	Sea salt and ground black
1 sprig fresh thyme	pepper, to taste
1 cup water	1 serrano pepper, seeded and
1 lemon, sliced	sliced
3 mahi-mahi fillets	1 green bell pepper, sliced
2 tablespoons coconut oil,	1 red bell pepper, sliced

1. Add the herbs, water, and lemon slices to the Instant Pot and insert a steamer basket. 2. Arrange the mahi-mahi fillets in the steamer basket. 3. Drizzle the melted coconut oil over the top and season with the salt and black pepper. 4. Lock the lid. Select the Manual mode and set the cooking time for 3 minutes at Low

Pressure. 5. When the timer beeps, perform a natural pressure release for 10 minutes, then release any remaining pressure. Carefully remove the lid. 6. Place the peppers on top. Select the Sauté mode and let it simmer for another 1 minute. 7. Serve immediately.
Per Serving:
calories: 454 | fat: 14.7g | protein: 76.4g | carbs: 4.1g | net carbs: 3.5g | fiber: 0.6g

Salmon Cakes

Prep time: 10 minutes | Cook time: 15 minutes | Serves 4

1 (16-ounce / 454-g) can pink	3 tablespoons mayonnaise
salmon, drained and bones	1 teaspoon garlic salt
removed	1 teaspoon freshly ground black
¼ cup almond flour	pepper
¼ cup crushed pork rinds	2 tablespoons extra-virgin olive
2 scallions, diced	oil
1 large egg	

1. Line a plate with paper towels and set aside. 2. In a bowl, combine the salmon, almond flour, pork rinds, scallions, egg, mayonnaise, garlic salt, and pepper, and mix together well, using your hands or a spatula. 3. Form 8 small patties or 4 large patties. If the patties seem too dry, add a little more mayonnaise. If they seem too wet, add a little more almond flour or pork rinds. 4. In a skillet over medium heat, heat the oil. Cook the patties for 4 to 5 minutes on each side, until crispy. Larger patties may need to cook a little longer. 5. Transfer the patties to the lined plate to drain.
Per Serving:
2 small patties: calories: 313 | fat: 21g | protein: 26g | carbs: 5g | net carbs: 5g | fiber: 0g

Trout Casserole

Prep time: 5 minutes | Cook time: 10 minutes | Serves 3

1½ cups water	more to taste
1½ tablespoons olive oil	⅓ teaspoon black pepper
3 plum tomatoes, sliced	Salt, to taste
½ teaspoon dried oregano	1 bay leaf
1 teaspoon dried basil	1 cup shredded Pepper Jack
3 trout fillets	cheese
½ teaspoon cayenne pepper, or	

1. Pour the water into your Instant Pot and insert a trivet. 2. Grease a baking dish with the olive oil. Add the tomatoes slices to the baking dish and sprinkle with the oregano and basil. 3. Add the fish fillets and season with the cayenne pepper, black pepper, and salt. Add the bay leaf. Lower the baking dish onto the trivet. 4. Lock the lid. Select the Manual mode and set the cooking time for 10 minutes at High Pressure. 5. When the timer beeps, perform a quick pressure release. Carefully remove the lid. 6. Scatter the Pepper Jack cheese on top, lock the lid, and allow the cheese to melt. 7. Serve warm.
Per Serving:
calories: 361 | fat: 23.5g | protein: 25.2g | carbs: 12.1g | net carbs: 11.3g | fiber: 0.8g

Lobster Pie

Prep time: 15 minutes | Cook time: 35 minutes | Serves 6

FILLING:
¼ cup (52 g) coconut oil
2 cups (160 g) chopped green onions, green parts only
2½ cups (450 g) chopped cooked lobster meat
¼ cup (60 ml) full-fat coconut milk
¼ cup (18 g) chopped fresh dill
½ teaspoon finely ground gray sea salt

TOPPING:
3 cups (475 g) roughly chopped turnips, steamed
¼ cup (60 ml) full-fat coconut milk
2 tablespoons coconut oil
½ teaspoon finely ground gray sea salt
¼ teaspoon ground black pepper
3 large egg yolks

1. Preheat the oven to 400°F (205°C). 2. Make the filling: Place ¼ cup (52 g) of coconut oil and the green onions in a large frying pan over medium heat. Sauté the onions in the oil for 5 minutes. Add the lobster meat, ¼ cup coconut milk, dill, and ½ teaspoon salt and sauté for another 2 minutes. Transfer the mixture to a shallow 1½-quart (1.4-L) casserole dish. 3. Make the topping: Place the steamed turnips, ¼ cup (60 ml) coconut milk, 2 tablespoons coconut oil, ¼ teaspoon salt, and the pepper in a blender or food processor or the bowl of a stand mixer. Pulse or whip until mashed but with a bit of chunkiness remaining. Add the egg yolks and mix until just combined. 4. Spread the mashed turnips evenly over the lobster mixture in the casserole dish. Using a fork, fluff the turnip topping until little peaks form. 5. Bake for 25 minutes, or until the top turns light golden. Remove from the oven and serve!

Per Serving:
calories: 301 | fat: 21g | protein: 18g | carbs: 10g | net carbs: 8g | fiber: 3g

Shrimp and Avocado Lettuce Cups

Prep time: 10 minutes | Cook time: 5 minutes | Serves 2

1 tablespoon ghee
½ pound shrimp (I use defrosted Trader Joe's Frozen Medium Cooked Shrimp, which are peeled and deveined, with tail off)
½ cup halved grape tomatoes

½ avocado, sliced
Pink Himalayan salt
Freshly ground black pepper
4 butter lettuce leaves, rinsed and patted dry
1 tablespoon Spicy Red Pepper Miso Mayo

1. In a medium skillet over medium-high heat, heat the ghee. Add the shrimp and cook. (I use cooked shrimp, so they take only about 1 minute to heat through, and I flip them halfway through cooking. Uncooked shrimp take about 2 minutes to cook.) Season with pink Himalayan salt and pepper. Shrimp are cooked when they turn pink and opaque. 2. Season the tomatoes and avocado with pink Himalayan salt and pepper. 3. Divide the lettuce cups between two plates. Fill each cup with shrimp, tomatoes, and avocado. Drizzle the mayo sauce on top and serve.

Per Serving:
calories: 326 | fat: 11g | protein: 33g | carbs: 7g | net carbs: 4g | fiber: 3g

Basil Alfredo Sea Bass

Prep time: 15 minutes | Cook time: 30 minutes | Serves 4

Sea Bass:
4 (6-ounce / 170-g) sea bass pieces
2 tablespoons olive oil
Pesto:
1 cup tightly packed fresh basil leaves
¼ cup grated Parmesan cheese
3 tablespoons pine nuts, or walnuts
1 tablespoon water
½ teaspoon salt

Freshly ground black pepper, to taste
3 tablespoons olive oil
Alfredo Sauce:
2 tablespoons butter
1 tablespoon olive oil
1 garlic clove, minced
1 cup heavy (whipping) cream
¾ cup Parmesan cheese
Salt, to taste
Freshly ground black pepper, to taste

Make the Sea Bass 1. Preheat the oven to 375ºF (190ºC). 2. Rub the sea bass with the olive oil and place it in a baking dish or on a rimmed baking sheet. Bake for 20 to 25 minutes or until the fish is completely opaque and the flesh flakes easily with a fork. Make the Pesto 1. In a blender or food processor (I prefer a blender because I like this very finely chopped/blended), combine the basil, Parmesan, pine nuts, water, and salt. Season with pepper. 2. With the blender running, stream the olive oil in. Set aside. Make the Alfredo Sauce 1. In a small saucepan over medium heat, melt the butter and olive oil together. 2. Stir in the garlic and cream. Bring to a low simmer and cook for 5 to 7 minutes until thickened. 3. Slowly add the Parmesan, stirring well to mix as it melts. Continue to stir until smooth. Season with salt and pepper. Set aside. 4. In a small bowl, stir together ½ cup of pesto and ½ cup of Alfredo sauce. Spoon over the fish before serving. Refrigerate leftovers in an airtight container for up to 4 days.

Per Serving:
calories: 768 | fat: 64g | protein: 45g | carbs: 4g | net carbs: 4g | fiber: 0g

Fish Taco Bowl

Prep time: 10 minutes | Cook time: 12 minutes | Serves 4

½ teaspoon salt
¼ teaspoon garlic powder
¼ teaspoon ground cumin
4 (4-ounce / 113-g) cod fillets
4 cups finely shredded green cabbage

⅓ cup mayonnaise
¼ teaspoon ground black pepper
¼ cup chopped pickled jalapeños

1. Sprinkle salt, garlic powder, and cumin over cod and place into ungreased air fryer basket. Adjust the temperature to 350ºF (177ºC) and air fry for 12 minutes, turning fillets halfway through cooking. Cod will flake easily and have an internal temperature of at least 145ºF (63ºC) when done. 2. In a large bowl, toss cabbage with mayonnaise, pepper, and jalapeños until fully coated. Serve cod warm over cabbage slaw on four medium plates.

Per Serving:
calories: 161 | fat: 7g | protein: 19g | carbs: 5g | net carbs: 3g | fiber: 2g

Creamy Hoki with Almond Bread Crust

Prep time: 10 minutes | Cook time: 35 minutes | Serves 4

1 cup flaked smoked hoki, bones removed	2 cups sour cream
1 cup cubed hoki fillets, cubed	1 tablespoon chopped parsley
4 eggs	1 cup pork rinds, crushed
1 cup water	1 cup grated cheddar cheese
3 tablespoons almond flour	Salt and black pepper to taste
1 onion, sliced	2 tablespoons butter

1. Preheat the oven to 360ºF and lightly grease a baking dish with cooking spray. 2. Then, boil the eggs in water in a pot over medium heat to be well done for 10 minutes, run the eggs under cold water and peel the shells. After, place on a cutting board and chop them. 3. Melt the butter in a saucepan over medium heat and sauté the onion for 4 minutes. Turn the heat off and stir in the almond flour to form a roux. Turn the heat back on and cook the roux to be golden brown and stir in the cream until the mixture is smooth. Season with salt and black pepper, and stir in the parsley. 4. Spread the smoked and cubed fish in the baking dish, sprinkle the eggs on top, and spoon the sauce over. In a bowl, mix the pork rinds with the cheddar cheese, and sprinkle it over the sauce. 5. Bake the casserole in the oven for 20 minutes until the top is golden and the sauce and cheese are bubbly. Remove the bake after and serve with a steamed green vegetable mix.

Per Serving:
calories: 411 | fat: 31g | protein: 27g | carbs: 6g | net carbs: 4g | fiber: 2g

Aromatic Monkfish Stew

Prep time: 5 minutes | Cook time: 6 minutes | Serves 6

Juice of 1 lemon	½ teaspoon mixed peppercorns
1 tablespoon fresh basil	¼ teaspoon turmeric powder
1 tablespoon fresh parsley	¼ teaspoon ground cumin
1 tablespoon olive oil	Sea salt and ground black
1 teaspoon garlic, minced	pepper, to taste
1½ pounds (680 g) monkfish	2 cups fish stock
1 tablespoon butter	½ cup water
1 bell pepper, chopped	¼ cup dry white wine
1 onion, sliced	2 bay leaves
½ teaspoon cayenne pepper	1 ripe tomato, crushed

1. Stir together the lemon juice, basil, parsley, olive oil, and garlic in a ceramic dish. Add the monkfish and marinate for 30 minutes. 2. Set your Instant Pot to Sauté. Add and melt the butter. Once hot, cook the bell pepper and onion until fragrant. 3. Stir in the remaining ingredients. 4. Lock the lid. Select the Manual mode and set the cooking time for 6 minutes at High Pressure. 5. When the timer beeps, perform a quick pressure release. Carefully remove the lid. 6. Discard the bay leaves and divide your stew into serving bowls. Serve hot.

Per Serving:
calories: 153 | fat: 6.9g | protein: 18.9g | carbs: 3.8g | net carbs: 3.0g | fiber: 0.8g

Paprika Shrimp

Prep time: 5 minutes | Cook time: 6 minutes | Serves 2

8 ounces (227 g) medium shelled and deveined shrimp	1 teaspoon paprika
2 tablespoons salted butter, melted	½ teaspoon garlic powder
	¼ teaspoon onion powder
	½ teaspoon Old Bay seasoning

1. Toss all ingredients together in a large bowl. Place shrimp into the air fryer basket. 2. Adjust the temperature to 400ºF (204ºC) and set the timer for 6 minutes. 3. Turn the shrimp halfway through the cooking time to ensure even cooking. Serve immediately.
Per Serving:
calories: 155 | fat: 9g | protein: 16g | carbs: 3g | net carbs: 2g | fiber: 1g

Ahi Tuna Steaks

Prep time: 5 minutes | Cook time: 14 minutes | Serves 2

2 (6-ounce / 170-g) ahi tuna steaks	3 tablespoons everything bagel seasoning
2 tablespoons olive oil	

1. Drizzle both sides of each steak with olive oil. Place seasoning on a medium plate and press each side of tuna steaks into seasoning to form a thick layer. 2. Place steaks into ungreased air fryer basket. Adjust the temperature to 400ºF (204ºC) and air fry for 14 minutes, turning steaks halfway through cooking. Steaks will be done when internal temperature is at least 145ºF (63ºC) for well-done. Serve warm.

Per Serving:
calories: 305 | fat: 14g | protein: 42g | carbs: 0g | fiber: 0g | sodium: 377mg

Tuna-Stuffed Tomatoes

Prep time: 5 minutes | Cook time: 5 minutes | Serves 2

2 medium beefsteak tomatoes, tops removed, seeded, membranes removed	2 tablespoons mayonnaise
	¼ teaspoon salt
2 (2.6-ounce / 74-g) pouches tuna packed in water, drained	¼ teaspoon ground black pepper
1 medium stalk celery, trimmed and chopped	2 teaspoons coconut oil
	¼ cup shredded mild Cheddar cheese

1. Scoop pulp out of each tomato, leaving ½-inch shell. 2. In a medium bowl, mix tuna, celery, mayonnaise, salt, and pepper. Drizzle with coconut oil. Spoon ½ mixture into each tomato and top each with 2 tablespoons Cheddar. 3. Place tomatoes into ungreased air fryer basket. Adjust the temperature to 320ºF (160ºC) and air fry for 5 minutes. Cheese will be melted when done. Serve warm.

Per Serving:
calories: 232 | fat: 15g | protein: 20g | carbs: 6g | net carbs: 4g | fiber: 2g

Poke Salad Bowls

Prep time: 15 minutes | Cook time: 0 minutes | Makes 2 bowls

¼ cup gluten-free soy sauce

2 tablespoons sesame oil

1 teaspoon chili garlic sauce

2 cups salad greens

¼ pound (113 g) ahi tuna, diced

¼ pound (113 g) snow crab leg meat, chopped

½ large cucumber, diced

1 large carrot, julienned or peeled into ribbons

½ avocado, sliced

Sliced scallion, green parts only, for garnish

Sesame seeds, for garnish

3 tablespoons pickled ginger, for garnish (optional)

1. In a large bowl, whisk together the soy sauce, sesame oil, and chili garlic sauce. 2. Add the salad greens and toss to combine. Transfer the greens to two bowls. 3. To the bowl you just tossed the salad in, add the tuna, crab meat, cucumber, and carrot and toss again. Top the greens with the seafood and veggie mixture. 4. Add the sliced avocado and garnish with scallion, sesame seeds, and pickled ginger (if using). Serve immediately.

Per Serving:
calories: 578 | fat: 30g | protein: 59g | carbs: 18g | net carbs: 12g | fiber: 6g

Perch Fillets with Red Curry

Prep time: 5 minutes | Cook time: 6 minutes | Serves 4

1 cup water

2 sprigs rosemary

1 large-sized lemon, sliced

1 pound (454 g) perch fillets

1 teaspoon cayenne pepper

Sea salt and ground black pepper, to taste

1 tablespoon red curry paste

1 tablespoons butter

1. Add the water, rosemary, and lemon slices to the Instant Pot and insert a trivet. 2. Season the perch fillets with the cayenne pepper, salt, and black pepper. Spread the red curry paste and butter over the fillets. 3. Arrange the fish fillets on the trivet. 4. Lock the lid. Select the Manual mode and set the cooking time for 6 minutes at Low Pressure. 5. When the timer beeps, perform a quick pressure release. Carefully remove the lid. Serve with your favorite keto sides.

Per Serving:
calories: 142 | fat: 4.3g | protein: 22.5g | carbs: 3.2g | net carbs: 1.6g | fiber: 1.6g

Shrimp Fry

Prep time: 5 minutes | Cook time: 20 minutes | Serves 4

¼ cup (55 g) coconut oil

1 pound (455 g) medium shrimp, peeled, deveined, and tails removed

12 ounces (340 g) smoked sausage (chicken, pork, beef—

anything goes), cubed

5 asparagus spears, woody ends snapped off, thinly sliced

4 ounces (115 g) cremini mushrooms, sliced

1 medium zucchini, cubed

1 tablespoon paprika

2 teaspoons garlic powder

1 teaspoon onion powder

1 teaspoon dried thyme leaves

½ teaspoon finely ground sea salt

¼ teaspoon ground black pepper

Pinch of cayenne pepper (optional)

Handful of fresh parsley leaves, chopped, for serving

1. Melt the oil in a large frying pan over medium heat. 2. Add the remaining ingredients, except the parsley. Toss to coat in the oil, then cover and cook for 15 to 20 minutes, until the asparagus is tender and the shrimp has turned pink. 3. Divide the mixture among 4 serving plates, sprinkle with parsley, and serve.

Per Serving:
calories: 574 | fat: 40g | protein: 45g | carbs: 8g | net carbs: 6g | fiber: 2g

Cod Fillet with Olives

Prep time: 15 minutes | Cook time: 10 minutes | Serves 2

8 ounces (227 g) cod fillet

¼ cup sliced olives

1 teaspoon olive oil

¼ teaspoon salt

1 cup water, for cooking

1. Pour water and insert the steamer rack in the instant pot. 2. Then cut the cod fillet into 2 servings and sprinkle with salt and olive oil. 3. Then place the fish on the foil and top with the sliced olives. Wrap the fish and transfer it in the steamer rack. 4. Close and seal the lid. Cook the fish on Manual mode (High Pressure) for 10 minutes. 5. Allow the natural pressure release for 5 minutes.

Per Serving:
calories: 130 | fat: 5g | protein: 20g | carbs: 1g | net carbs: 1g | fiber: 0g

Salmon Steaks with Garlicky Yogurt

Prep time: 2 minutes | Cook time: 4 minutes | Serves 4

1 cup water

2 tablespoons olive oil

4 salmon steaks

Coarse sea salt and ground black pepper, to taste

Garlicky Yogurt:

1 (8-ounce / 227-g) container full-fat Greek yogurt

2 cloves garlic, minced

2 tablespoons mayonnaise

⅓ teaspoon Dijon mustard

1. Pour the water into the Instant Pot and insert a trivet. 2. Rub the olive oil into the fish and sprinkle with the salt and black pepper on all sides. Put the fish on the trivet. 3. Lock the lid. Select the Manual mode and set the cooking time for 4 minutes at High Pressure. 4. When the timer beeps, perform a quick pressure release. Carefully remove the lid. 5. Meanwhile, stir together all the ingredients for the garlicky yogurt in a bowl. 6. Serve the salmon steaks alongside the garlicky yogurt.

Per Serving:
calories: 128 | fat: 11.2g | protein: 2.5g | carbs:4.9g | net carbs: 4.7g | fiber: 0.2g

Chilean Sea Bass with Olive Relish

Prep time: 10 minutes | Cook time: 10 minutes | Serves 2

Olive oil spray

2 (6-ounce / 170-g) Chilean sea bass fillets or other firm-fleshed white fish

3 tablespoons extra-virgin olive oil

½ teaspoon ground cumin

½ teaspoon kosher salt

½ teaspoon black pepper

⅓ cup pitted green olives, diced

¼ cup finely diced onion

1 teaspoon chopped capers

1. Spray the air fryer basket with the olive oil spray. Drizzle the fillets with the olive oil and sprinkle with the cumin, salt, and pepper. Place the fish in the air fryer basket. Set the air fryer to 325ºF (163ºC) for 10 minutes, or until the fish flakes easily with a fork. 2. Meanwhile, in a small bowl, stir together the olives, onion, and capers. 3. Serve the fish topped with the relish.

Per Serving:
calories: 379 | fat: 26g | protein: 32g | carbs: 3g | fiber: 1g | sodium: 581mg

Sesame-Crusted Tuna Steak

Prep time: 5 minutes | Cook time: 8 minutes | Serves 2

2 (6-ounce / 170-g) tuna steaks

1 tablespoon coconut oil, melted

½ teaspoon garlic powder

2 teaspoons white sesame seeds

2 teaspoons black sesame seeds

1. Brush each tuna steak with coconut oil and sprinkle with garlic powder. 2. In a large bowl, mix sesame seeds and then press each tuna steak into them, covering the steak as completely as possible. Place tuna steaks into the air fryer basket. 3. Adjust the temperature to 400ºF (204ºC) and air fry for 8 minutes. 4. Flip the steaks halfway through the cooking time. Steaks will be well-done at 145ºF (63ºC) internal temperature. Serve warm.

Per Serving:
calories: 281 | fat: 11g | protein: 43g | carbs: 1g | fiber: 1g | sodium: 80mg

Savory Shrimp

Prep time: 5 minutes | Cook time: 8 to 10 minutes | Serves 4

1 pound (454 g) fresh large shrimp, peeled and deveined

1 tablespoon avocado oil

2 teaspoons minced garlic, divided

½ teaspoon red pepper flakes

Sea salt and freshly ground black pepper, to taste

2 tablespoons unsalted butter, melted

2 tablespoons chopped fresh parsley

1. Place the shrimp in a large bowl and toss with the avocado oil, 1 teaspoon of minced garlic, and red pepper flakes. Season with salt and pepper. 2. Set the air fryer to 350ºF (177ºC). Arrange the shrimp in a single layer in the air fryer basket, working in batches if necessary. Cook for 6 minutes. Flip the shrimp and cook for 2 to 4 minutes more, until the internal temperature of the shrimp reaches 120ºF (49ºC). (The time it takes to cook will depend on the size of the shrimp.) 3. While the shrimp are cooking, melt the butter in a small saucepan over medium heat and stir in the remaining 1 teaspoon of garlic. 4. Transfer the cooked shrimp to a large bowl, add the garlic butter, and toss well. Top with the parsley and serve warm.

Per Serving:
calories: 182 | fat: 10g | protein: 23g | carbs: 1g | sugars: 0g | fiber: 0g | sodium: 127mg

Curried Fish Stew

Prep time: 10 minutes | Cook time: 20 minutes | Serves 6

1 tablespoon olive oil

1 medium onion, chopped

3 garlic cloves, minced

1 tablespoon tomato paste

2 tablespoons curry powder

1 head cauliflower, chopped

2 cups fish broth, or vegetable broth

1½ pounds (680 g) firm whitefish (cod or halibut),

cubed

1 teaspoon ground cayenne pepper (more or less depending on your taste)

Salt, to taste

Freshly ground black pepper, to taste

1 (13½-ounce / 383-g) can full-fat coconut milk

1. In a large saucepan over medium heat, heat the olive oil. 2. Add the onion and garlic. Sauté for 5 to 7 minutes until the onion is softened and translucent. 3. Stir in the tomato paste, curry powder, and cauliflower. Cook for 1 to 2 minutes. 4. While stirring, slowly add the broth. Bring to a simmer and add the fish. Cook for 10 to 15 minutes or until the fish is opaque. Season with the cayenne and some salt and pepper. 5. Stir in the coconut milk. Simmer on low until ready to serve. Refrigerate leftovers in an airtight container for up to 4 days.

Per Serving:
calories: 373 | fat: 21g | protein: 33g | carbs: 13g | net carbs: 8g | fiber: 5g

Red Cabbage Tilapia Taco Bowl

Prep time: 15 minutes | Cook time: 10 minutes | Serves 4

2 cups cauli rice

2 teaspoons ghee

4 tilapia fillets, cut into cubes

¼ teaspoon taco seasoning

Salt and chili pepper to taste

¼ head red cabbage, shredded

1 ripe avocado, pitted and chopped

1. Sprinkle cauli rice in a bowl with a little water and microwave for 3 minutes. Fluff after with a fork and set aside. Melt ghee in a skillet over medium heat, rub the tilapia with the taco seasoning, salt, and chili pepper, and fry until brown on all sides, for about 8 minutes in total. 2. Transfer to a plate and set aside. In 4 serving bowls, share the cauli rice, cabbage, fish, and avocado. Serve with chipotle lime sour cream dressing.

Per Serving:
calories: 315 | fat: 23g | protein: 21g | carbs: 6g | net carbs: 3g | fiber: 3g

Simply Broiled or Air-Fried Salmon

Prep time: 5 minutes | Cook time: 30 minutes | Serves 2 to 4

1 tablespoon olive, avocado, or macadamia nut oil	pepper, to taste
1 pound (454 g) salmon fillet or steak (with or without skin), cut into 2 to 4 equal pieces	Dried herbs and spices of your choice (optional)
Salt and freshly ground black	Steamed or roasted asparagus or spaghetti squash, for serving

1. Preheat the broiler. Line a broiling pan with aluminum foil and grease with the oil. If air-frying, line the air fryer basket with foil and grease with the oil. 2. Season the salmon with salt, pepper, and any other herbs and spices you'd like. Then lay it in the broiling pan (skin-side down, if applicable) or place it in the air-fryer basket. 3. Broil the salmon in the oven for about 30 minutes, checking for doneness (it should form a crisp crust) after about 20 minutes, or cook in the air fryer at 400ºF (205ºC) for 25 to 30 minutes. To crisp up skin in the broiler, flip the salmon when there are about 5 minutes left of cooking. 4. Serve the salmon with steamed or roasted vegetables.

Per Serving:
calories: 258 | fat: 18g | protein: 24g | carbs: 0g | net carbs: 0g | fiber: 0g

Steamed Lobster Tails with Thyme

Prep time: 10 minutes | Cook time: 4 minutes | Serves 4

4 lobster tails	1 teaspoon dried thyme
1 tablespoon butter, softened	1 cup water

1. Pour water and insert the steamer rack in the instant pot. 2. Put the lobster tails on the rack and close the lid. 3. Cook the meal on Manual mode (High Pressure) for 4 minutes. Make a quick pressure release. 4. After this, mix up butter and dried thyme. Peel the lobsters and rub them with thyme butter.

Per Serving:
calories: 126 | fat: 3g | protein: 24g | carbs: 0g | net carbs: 0g | fiber: 0g

Lemon Salmon with Tomatoes

Prep time: 7 minutes | Cook time: 21 minutes | Serves 4

1 tablespoon unsalted butter	garnish
3 cloves garlic, minced	¼ teaspoon ground black pepper
¼ cup lemon juice	
1¼ cups fresh or canned diced tomatoes	4 (6-ounce / 170-g) skinless salmon fillets
1 tablespoon chopped fresh flat-leaf parsley, plus more for	1 teaspoon fine sea salt
	Lemon wedges, for garnish

1. Add the butter to your Instant Pot and select the Sauté mode. Once melted, add the garlic (if using) and sauté for 1 minute. 2. Add the roasted garlic, lemon juice, tomatoes, parsley, and pepper.

Let simmer for 5 minutes, or until the liquid has reduced a bit. 3. Meanwhile, rinse the salmon and pat dry with a paper towel. Sprinkle on all sides with the salt. 4. Using a spatula, push the reduced sauce to one side of the pot and place the salmon on the other side. Spoon the sauce over the salmon. 5. Sauté uncovered for another 15 minutes, or until the salmon flakes easily with a fork. The timing will depend on the thickness of the fillets. 6. Transfer the salmon to a serving plate. Serve with the sauce and garnish with the parsley and lemon wedges.

Per Serving:
calories: 248 | fat: 9.7g | protein: 34.8g | carbs: 5.1g | net carbs: 4.1g | fiber: 1.0g

Crab-Stuffed Avocado Boats

Prep time: 5 minutes | Cook time: 7 minutes | Serves 4

2 medium avocados, halved and pitted	¼ teaspoon Old Bay seasoning
8 ounces (227 g) cooked crab meat	2 tablespoons peeled and diced yellow onion
	2 tablespoons mayonnaise

1. Scoop out avocado flesh in each avocado half, leaving ½ inch around edges to form a shell. Chop scooped-out avocado. 2. In a medium bowl, combine crab meat, Old Bay seasoning, onion, mayonnaise, and chopped avocado. Place ¼ mixture into each avocado shell. 3. Place avocado boats into ungreased air fryer basket. Adjust the temperature to 350ºF (177ºC) and air fry for 7 minutes. Avocado will be browned on the top and mixture will be bubbling when done. Serve warm.

Per Serving:
calories: 226 | fat: 17g | protein: 12g | carbs: 10g | sugars: 1g | fiber: 7g | sodium: 239mg

Lemon and Dill Salmon Kabobs

Prep time: 10 minutes | Cook time: 15 minutes | Serves 8

1 tablespoon fresh dill	⅛ teaspoon ground cayenne
¼ cup olive oil	1 pound salmon, cubed
¼ cup lemon juice	1 medium zucchini, sliced into
¼ teaspoon salt	¼" rounds
¼ teaspoon black pepper	

1 Soak wooden skewers in water for at least 5 minutes in a shallow dish to prevent them from burning on grill. 2 In a medium bowl, combine dill, oil, lemon juice, salt, pepper, and cayenne. 3 Toss salmon cubes with marinade and stir to coat completely. Let marinate 10 minutes while prepping grill. 4 Clean and grease outdoor grill grate. Preheat outdoor grill to medium heat for 5 minutes. 5 Skewer salmon and zucchini on eight skewers using alternating pattern. Brush with remaining marinade. 6 Grill kabobs ½" apart, turning regularly until fully cooked, about 15 minutes total cooking time.

Per Serving:
calories: 137 | fat: 8g | protein: 12g | carbs: 1g | net carbs: 1g | fiber: 0g

Garam Masala Fish

Prep time: 10 minutes | Cook time: 10 minutes | Serves 4

2 tablespoons sesame oil

½ teaspoon cumin seeds

½ cup chopped leeks

1 teaspoon ginger-garlic paste

1 pound (454 g) cod fillets, boneless and sliced

2 ripe tomatoes, chopped

1½ tablespoons fresh lemon juice

½ teaspoon garam masala

½ teaspoon turmeric powder

1 tablespoon chopped fresh dill leaves

1 tablespoon chopped fresh curry leaves

1 tablespoon chopped fresh parsley leaves

Coarse sea salt, to taste

½ teaspoon smoked cayenne pepper

¼ teaspoon ground black pepper, or more to taste

1. Set the Instant Pot to Sauté. Add and heat the sesame oil until hot. Sauté the cumin seeds for 30 seconds. 2. Add the leeks and cook for another 2 minutes until translucent. Add the ginger-garlic paste and cook for an additional 40 seconds. 3. Stir in the remaining ingredients. 4. Lock the lid. Select the Manual mode and set the cooking time for 6 minutes at Low Pressure. 5. When the timer beeps, perform a quick pressure release. Carefully remove the lid. 6. Serve immediately.

Per Serving:
calories: 166 | fat: 7.8g | protein: 18.4g | carbs: 5.9g | net carbs: 3.9g | fiber: 2.0g

Tuna Salad with Tomatoes and Peppers

Prep time: 10 minutes | Cook time: 4 minutes | Serves 4

1½ cups water

1 pound (454 g) tuna steaks

1 green bell pepper, sliced

1 red bell pepper, sliced

2 Roma tomatoes, sliced

1 head lettuce

1 red onion, chopped

2 tablespoons Kalamata olives, pitted and halved

2 tablespoons extra-virgin olive oil

2 tablespoons balsamic vinegar

½ teaspoon chili flakes

Sea salt, to taste

1. Add the water to the Instant Pot and insert a steamer basket. 2. Arrange the tuna steaks in the basket. Put the bell peppers and tomato slices on top. 3. Lock the lid. Select the Manual mode and set the cooking time for 4 minutes at High Pressure. 4. When the timer beeps, perform a quick pressure release. Carefully remove the lid. 5. Flake the fish with a fork. 6. Divide the lettuce leaves among 4 serving plates to make a bed for your salad. Add the onion and olives. Drizzle with the olive oil and balsamic vinegar. 7. Season with the chili flakes and salt. Place the prepared fish, tomatoes, and bell peppers on top. 8. Serve immediately.

Per Serving:
calories: 170 | fat: 4.8g | protein: 23.9g | carbs: 7.6g | net carbs: 6.0g | fiber: 1.6g

Rainbow Salmon Kebabs

Prep time: 10 minutes | Cook time: 8 minutes | Serves 2

6 ounces (170 g) boneless, skinless salmon, cut into 1-inch cubes

¼ medium red onion, peeled and cut into 1-inch pieces

½ medium yellow bell pepper, seeded and cut into 1-inch

pieces

½ medium zucchini, trimmed and cut into ½-inch slices

1 tablespoon olive oil

½ teaspoon salt

¼ teaspoon ground black pepper

1. Using one (6-inch) skewer, skewer 1 piece salmon, then 1 piece onion, 1 piece bell pepper, and finally 1 piece zucchini. Repeat this pattern with additional skewers to make four kebabs total. Drizzle with olive oil and sprinkle with salt and black pepper. 2. Place kebabs into ungreased air fryer basket. Adjust the temperature to 400°F (204°C) and air fry for 8 minutes, turning kebabs halfway through cooking. Salmon will easily flake and have an internal temperature of at least 145°F (63°C) when done; vegetables will be tender. Serve warm.

Per Serving:
calories: 195 | fat: 11g | protein: 19g | carbs: 6g | fiber: 2g | sodium: 651mg

Rosemary-Lemon Snapper Baked in Parchment

Prep time: 15 minutes | Cook time: 15 minutes | Serves 4

1¼ pounds (567 g) fresh red snapper fillet, cut into two equal pieces

2 lemons, thinly sliced

6 to 8 sprigs fresh rosemary, stems removed or 1 to 2

tablespoons dried rosemary

½ cup extra-virgin olive oil

6 garlic cloves, thinly sliced

1 teaspoon salt

½ teaspoon freshly ground black pepper

1. Preheat the oven to 425°F(220°C). 2. Place two large sheets of parchment (about twice the size of each piece of fish) on the counter. Place 1 piece of fish in the center of each sheet. 3. Top the fish pieces with lemon slices and rosemary leaves. 4. In a small bowl, combine the olive oil, garlic, salt, and pepper. Drizzle the oil over each piece of fish. 5. Top each piece of fish with a second large sheet of parchment and starting on a long side, fold the paper up to about 1 inch from the fish. Repeat on the remaining sides, going in a clockwise direction. Fold in each corner once to secure. 6. Place both parchment pouches on a baking sheet and bake until the fish is cooked through, 10 to 12 minutes.

Per Serving:
calories: 399 | fat: 29g | protein: 30g | carbs: 5g | fiber: 1g | sodium: 584mg

Chapter 6 Vegetarian Mains

Vegetable Vodka Sauce Bake

Prep time: 10 minutes | Cook time: 30 minutes | Serves 4

3 tablespoons melted grass-fed butter, divided
4 cups mushrooms, halved
4 cups cooked cauliflower florets
1½ cups purchased vodka sauce
¾ cup heavy (whipping) cream
½ cup grated Asiago cheese
Sea salt, for seasoning
Freshly ground black pepper, for seasoning
1 cup shredded provolone cheese
2 tablespoons chopped fresh oregano

1. Preheat the oven. Set the oven temperature to 350°F and use 1 tablespoon of the melted butter to grease a 9-by-13-inch baking dish. 2. Mix the vegetables. In a large bowl, combine the mushrooms, cauliflower, vodka sauce, cream, Asiago, and the remaining 2 tablespoons of butter. Season the vegetables with salt and pepper. 3. Bake. Transfer the vegetable mixture to the baking dish and top it with the provolone cheese. Bake for 30 to 35 minutes until it's bubbly and heated through. 4. Serve. Divide the mixture between four plates and top with the oregano.

Per Serving:
calories: 537 | fat: 45g | protein: 19g | carbs: 14g | net carbs: 8g | fiber: 19g

Crustless Spanakopita

Prep time: 15 minutes | Cook time: 45 minutes | Serves 6

12 tablespoons extra-virgin olive oil, divided
1 small yellow onion, diced
1 (32-ounce / 907-g) bag frozen chopped spinach, thawed, fully drained, and patted dry (about 4 cups)
4 garlic cloves, minced
½ teaspoon salt
½ teaspoon freshly ground black pepper
1 cup whole-milk ricotta cheese
4 large eggs
¾ cup crumbled traditional feta cheese
¼ cup pine nuts

1. Preheat the oven to 375°F (190°C). 2. In a large skillet, heat 4 tablespoons olive oil over medium-high heat. Add the onion and sauté until softened, 6 to 8 minutes. 3. Add the spinach, garlic, salt, and pepper and sauté another 5 minutes. Remove from the heat and allow to cool slightly. 4. In a medium bowl, whisk together the ricotta and eggs. Add to the cooled spinach and stir to combine. 5. Pour 4 tablespoons olive oil in the bottom of a 9-by-13-inch glass baking dish and swirl to coat the bottom and sides. Add the spinach-ricotta mixture and spread into an even layer. 6. Bake for 20 minutes or until the mixture begins to set. Remove from the oven and crumble the feta evenly across the top of the spinach. Add the pine nuts and drizzle with the remaining 4 tablespoons olive oil. Return to the oven and bake for an additional 15 to 20 minutes, or until the spinach is fully set and the top is starting to turn golden brown. Allow to cool slightly before cutting to serve.

Per Serving:
calories: 497 | fat: 44g | protein: 18g | carbs: 11g | fiber: 5g | sodium: 561mg

Pesto Spinach Flatbread

Prep time: 10 minutes | Cook time: 8 minutes | Serves 4

1 cup blanched finely ground almond flour
2 ounces (57 g) cream cheese
2 cups shredded Mozzarella
cheese
1 cup chopped fresh spinach leaves
2 tablespoons basil pesto

1. Place flour, cream cheese, and Mozzarella in a large microwave-safe bowl and microwave on high 45 seconds, then stir. 2. Fold in spinach and microwave an additional 15 seconds. Stir until a soft dough ball forms. 3. Cut two pieces of parchment paper to fit air fryer basket. Separate dough into two sections and press each out on ungreased parchment to create 6-inch rounds. 4. Spread 1 tablespoon pesto over each flatbread and place rounds on parchment into ungreased air fryer basket. Adjust the temperature to 350°F (177°C) and air fry for 8 minutes, turning crusts halfway through cooking. Flatbread will be golden when done. 5. Let cool 5 minutes before slicing and serving.

Per Serving:
calories: 387 | fat: 28g | protein: 28g | carbs: 10g | fiber: 5g | sodium: 556mg

Crustless Spinach Cheese Pie

Prep time: 10 minutes | Cook time: 20 minutes | Serves 4

6 large eggs
¼ cup heavy whipping cream
1 cup frozen chopped spinach, drained
1 cup shredded sharp Cheddar cheese
¼ cup diced yellow onion

1. In a medium bowl, whisk eggs and add cream. Add remaining ingredients to bowl. 2. Pour into a round baking dish. Place into the air fryer basket. 3. Adjust the temperature to 320°F (160°C) and bake for 20 minutes. 4. Eggs will be firm and slightly browned when cooked. Serve immediately.

Per Serving:
calories: 263 | fat: 20g | protein: 18g | carbs: 4g | fiber: 1g | sodium: 321mg

Crispy Tofu

Prep time: 30 minutes | Cook time: 15 to 20 minutes | Serves 4

1 (16-ounce / 454-g) block extra-firm tofu	1 tablespoon chili-garlic sauce
2 tablespoons coconut aminos	1½ teaspoons black sesame seeds
1 tablespoon toasted sesame oil	1 scallion, thinly sliced
1 tablespoon olive oil	

1. Press the tofu for at least 15 minutes by wrapping it in paper towels and setting a heavy pan on top so that the moisture drains. 2. Slice the tofu into bite-size cubes and transfer to a bowl. Drizzle with the coconut aminos, sesame oil, olive oil, and chili-garlic sauce. Cover and refrigerate for 1 hour or up to overnight. 3. Preheat the air fryer to 400ºF (204ºC). 4. Arrange the tofu in a single layer in the air fryer basket. Pausing to shake the pan halfway through the cooking time, air fry for 15 to 20 minutes until crisp. Serve with any juices that accumulate in the bottom of the air fryer, sprinkled with the sesame seeds and sliced scallion.

Per Serving:
calories: 173 | fat: 14g | protein: 12g | carbs: 3g | fiber: 1g | sodium: 49mg

Zucchini Roll Manicotti

Prep time: 15 minutes | Cook time: 30 minutes | Serves 4

Olive oil cooking spray	cheese
4 zucchini	1 tablespoon chopped fresh oregano
2 tablespoons good-quality olive oil	Sea salt, for seasoning
1 red bell pepper, diced	Freshly ground black pepper, for seasoning
½ onion, minced	2 cups low-carb marinara sauce, divided
2 teaspoons minced garlic	½ cup grated Parmesan cheese
1 cup goat cheese	
1 cup shredded mozzarella	

1. Preheat the oven. Set the oven temperature to 375°F. Lightly grease a 9-by-13-inch baking dish with olive oil cooking spray. 2. Prepare the zucchini. Cut the zucchini lengthwise into ⅛-inch-thick slices and set them aside. 3. Make the filling. In a medium skillet over medium-high heat, warm the olive oil. Add the red bell pepper, onion, and garlic and sauté until they've softened, about 4 minutes. Remove the skillet from the heat and transfer the vegetables to a medium bowl. Stir the goat cheese, mozzarella, and oregano into the vegetables. Season it all with salt and pepper. 4. Assemble the manicotti. Spread 1 cup of the marinara sauce in the bottom of the baking dish. Lay a zucchini slice on a clean cutting board and place a couple tablespoons of filling at one end. Roll the slice up and place it in the baking dish, seam-side down. Repeat with the remaining zucchini slices. Spoon the remaining sauce over the rolls and top with the Parmesan. 5. Bake. Bake the rolls for 30 to 35 minutes until the zucchini is tender and the cheese is golden. 6. Serve. Spoon the rolls onto four plates and serve them hot.

Per Serving:
calories: 342 | fat: 24g | protein: 20g | carbs: 14g | net carbs: 11g | fiber: 3g

Stuffed Eggplant

Prep time: 20 minutes | Cook time: 1 hour | Serves 2 to 4

1 small eggplant, halved lengthwise	extra-firm tofu (optional)
3 tablespoons olive, avocado, or macadamia nut oil	3 tablespoons chopped fresh basil leaves
1 onion, diced	Salt and freshly ground black pepper, to taste
12 asparagus spears or green beans, diced	¼ cup water
1 red bell pepper, diced	2 eggs
1 large tomato, chopped	Chopped fresh parsley, for garnish (optional)
2 garlic cloves, minced	Shredded cheese, for garnish (optional)
½ block (8 ounces / 227 g)	

1. Preheat the oven to 350ºF (180ºC). 2. Scoop out the flesh from the halved eggplant and chop it into cubes. Reserve the eggplant skin. 3. In a sauté pan with a lid, heat the oil over medium-high heat. Add the eggplant, onion, asparagus, bell pepper, tomato, garlic, and tofu (if using) and stir. Stir in the basil, season with salt and pepper, and cook for about 5 minutes. 4. Add the water, cover the pan, reduce the heat to medium, and cook for about 15 minutes longer. 5. Put the eggplant "boats" (the reserved skin) on a baking sheet. Scoop some of the cooked eggplant mixture into each boat (you may have some filling left over, which is fine—you can roast it alongside the eggplant). 6. Crack an egg into each eggplant boat, on top of the filling, then bake for about 40 minutes, or until desired doneness. 7. Remove the eggplant from the oven and, if desired, sprinkle parsley and cheese over the top. Let the cheese melt and cool for about 5 minutes, then serve them up!

Per Serving:
calories: 380 | fat: 26g | protein: 12g | carbs: 25g | net carbs: 15g | fiber: 10g

Broccoli Crust Pizza

Prep time: 15 minutes | Cook time: 12 minutes | Serves 4

3 cups riced broccoli, steamed and drained well	3 tablespoons low-carb Alfredo sauce
1 large egg	½ cup shredded Mozzarella cheese
½ cup grated vegetarian Parmesan cheese	

1. In a large bowl, mix broccoli, egg, and Parmesan. 2. Cut a piece of parchment to fit your air fryer basket. Press out the pizza mixture to fit on the parchment, working in two batches if necessary. Place into the air fryer basket. 3. Adjust the temperature to 370ºF (188ºC) and air fry for 5 minutes. 4. The crust should be firm enough to flip. If not, add 2 additional minutes. Flip crust. 5. Top with Alfredo sauce and Mozzarella. Return to the air fryer basket and cook an additional 7 minutes or until cheese is golden and bubbling. Serve warm.

Per Serving:
calories: 87 | fat: 2g | protein: 11g | carbs: 5g | fiber: 1g | sodium: 253mg

Vegetable Burgers

Prep time: 10 minutes | Cook time: 12 minutes | Serves 4

8 ounces (227 g) cremini mushrooms	yellow onion
2 large egg yolks	1 clove garlic, peeled and finely minced
½ medium zucchini, trimmed and chopped	½ teaspoon salt
¼ cup peeled and chopped	¼ teaspoon ground black pepper

1. Place all ingredients into a food processor and pulse twenty times until finely chopped and combined. 2. Separate mixture into four equal sections and press each into a burger shape. Place burgers into ungreased air fryer basket. Adjust the temperature to 375°F (191°C) and air fry for 12 minutes, turning burgers halfway through cooking. Burgers will be browned and firm when done. 3. Place burgers on a large plate and let cool 5 minutes before serving.

Per Serving:
calories: 50 | fat: 3g | protein: 3g | carbs: 4g | fiber: 1g | sodium: 299mg

Zucchini Lasagna

Prep time: 15 minutes | Cook time: 1 hour | Serves 8

½ cup extra-virgin olive oil, divided	1 teaspoon garlic powder
4 to 5 medium zucchini squash	½ teaspoon freshly ground black pepper
1 teaspoon salt	2 cups shredded fresh whole-milk mozzarella cheese
8 ounces (227 g) frozen spinach, thawed and well drained (about 1 cup)	1¾ cups shredded Parmesan cheese
2 cups whole-milk ricotta cheese	½ (24-ounce / 680-g) jar low-sugar marinara sauce (less than 5 grams sugar)
¼ cup chopped fresh basil or 2 teaspoons dried basil	

1. Preheat the oven to 425°F (220°C). 2. Line two baking sheets with parchment paper or aluminum foil and drizzle each with 2 tablespoons olive oil, spreading evenly. 3. Slice the zucchini lengthwise into ¼-inch-thick long slices and place on the prepared baking sheet in a single layer. Sprinkle with ½ teaspoon salt per sheet. Bake until softened, but not mushy, 15 to 18 minutes. Remove from the oven and allow to cool slightly before assembling the lasagna. 4. Reduce the oven temperature to 375°F (190°C). 5. While the zucchini cooks, prep the filling. In a large bowl, combine the spinach, ricotta, basil, garlic powder, and pepper. In a small bowl, mix together the mozzarella and Parmesan cheeses. In a medium bowl, combine the marinara sauce and remaining ¼ cup olive oil and stir to fully incorporate the oil into sauce. 6. To assemble the lasagna, spoon a third of the marinara sauce mixture into the bottom of a 9-by-13-inch glass baking dish and spread evenly. Place 1 layer of softened zucchini slices to fully cover the sauce, then add a third of the ricotta-spinach mixture and spread evenly on top of the zucchini. Sprinkle a third of the mozzarella-Parmesan mixture on top of the ricotta. Repeat with 2 more cycles of these layers: marinara, zucchini, ricotta-spinach, then cheese

blend. 7. Bake until the cheese is bubbly and melted, 30 to 35 minutes. Turn the broiler to low and broil until the top is golden brown, about 5 minutes. Remove from the oven and allow to cool slightly before slicing.

Per Serving:
calories: 473 | fat: 36g | protein: 23g | carbs: 17g | fiber: 3g | sodium: 868mg

Pesto Vegetable Skewers

Prep time: 30 minutes | Cook time: 8 minutes | Makes 8 skewers

1 medium zucchini, trimmed and cut into ½-inch slices	squares
½ medium yellow onion, peeled and cut into 1-inch squares	16 whole cremini mushrooms
1 medium red bell pepper, seeded and cut into 1-inch	⅓ cup basil pesto
	½ teaspoon salt
	¼ teaspoon ground black pepper

1. Divide zucchini slices, onion, and bell pepper into eight even portions. Place on 6-inch skewers for a total of eight kebabs. Add 2 mushrooms to each skewer and brush kebabs generously with pesto. 2. Sprinkle each kebab with salt and black pepper on all sides, then place into ungreased air fryer basket. Adjust the temperature to 375°F (191°C) and air fry for 8 minutes, turning kebabs halfway through cooking. Vegetables will be browned at the edges and tender-crisp when done. Serve warm.

Per Serving:
calories: 75 | fat: 6g | protein: 3g | carbs: 4g | fiber: 1g | sodium: 243mg

Asparagus and Fennel Frittata

Prep time: 10 minutes | Cook time: 30 minutes | Serves 4

1 teaspoon coconut or regular butter, plus more for greasing	½ cup full-fat regular milk or coconut milk
8 asparagus spears, diced	1 tomato, sliced
½ cup diced fennel	1 teaspoon salt
½ cup mushrooms, sliced (optional)	½ teaspoon freshly ground black pepper
8 eggs	Grated cheese (optional)

1. Preheat the oven to 350°F (180°C). Grease a pie dish with butter. 2. Melt 1 teaspoon of butter in a shallow skillet over medium-high heat and sauté the asparagus, fennel, and mushrooms (if using) for about 5 minutes, or until fork-tender. 3. Transfer the vegetables to the prepared pie dish. 4. Crack the eggs into a mixing bowl and pour in the milk. Whisk together until fully combined. 5. Pour the egg mixture over the vegetables in the pie dish, season with salt and pepper, and carefully and lightly mix everything together. Lay the tomato slices on top. 6. Bake the frittata for about 30 minutes. 7. Remove from the oven and let cool for 5 to 10 minutes. Slice into wedges and sprinkle with grated cheese, if desired.

Per Serving:
calories: 188 | fat: 12g | protein: 14g | carbs: 6g | net carbs: 4g | fiber: 2g

Spinach-Artichoke Stuffed Mushrooms

Prep time: 10 minutes | Cook time: 10 to 14 minutes | Serves 4

2 tablespoons olive oil
4 large portobello mushrooms, stems removed and gills scraped out
½ teaspoon salt
¼ teaspoon freshly ground pepper
4 ounces (113 g) goat cheese,

crumbled
½ cup chopped marinated artichoke hearts
1 cup frozen spinach, thawed and squeezed dry
½ cup grated Parmesan cheese
2 tablespoons chopped fresh parsley

1. Preheat the air fryer to 400°F (204°C). 2. Rub the olive oil over the portobello mushrooms until thoroughly coated. Sprinkle both sides with the salt and black pepper. Place top-side down on a clean work surface. 3. In a small bowl, combine the goat cheese, artichoke hearts, and spinach. Mash with the back of a fork until thoroughly combined. Divide the cheese mixture among the mushrooms and sprinkle with the Parmesan cheese. 4. Air fry for 10 to 14 minutes until the mushrooms are tender and the cheese has begun to brown. Top with the fresh parsley just before serving.

Per Serving:
calories: 284 | fat: 21g | protein: 16g | carbs: 10g | fiber: 4g | sodium: 686mg

Greek Vegetable Briam

Prep time: 10 minutes | Cook time: 30 minutes | Serves 4

⅓ cup good-quality olive oil, divided
1 onion, thinly sliced
1 tablespoon minced garlic
¾ small eggplant, diced
2 zucchini, diced
2 cups chopped cauliflower
1 red bell pepper, diced
2 cups diced tomatoes

2 tablespoons chopped fresh parsley
2 tablespoons chopped fresh oregano
Sea salt, for seasoning
Freshly ground black pepper, for seasoning
1½ cups crumbled feta cheese
¼ cup pumpkin seeds

1. Preheat the oven. Set the oven to broil and lightly grease a 9-by-13-inch casserole dish with olive oil. 2. Sauté the aromatics. In a medium stockpot over medium heat, warm 3 tablespoons of the olive oil. Add the onion and garlic and sauté until they've softened, about 3 minutes. 3. Sauté the vegetables. Stir in the eggplant and cook for 5 minutes, stirring occasionally. Add the zucchini, cauliflower, and red bell pepper and cook for 5 minutes. Stir in the tomatoes, parsley, and oregano and cook, giving it a stir from time to time, until the vegetables are tender, about 10 minutes. Season it with salt and pepper. 4. Broil. Transfer the vegetable mixture to the casserole dish and top with the crumbled feta. Broil for about 4 minutes until the cheese is golden. 5. Serve. Divide the casserole between four plates and top it with the pumpkin seeds. Drizzle with the remaining olive oil.

Per Serving:
calories: 356 | fat: 28g | protein: 11g | carbs: 18g | net carbs: 11g | fiber: 7g

Caprese Eggplant Stacks

Prep time: 5 minutes | Cook time: 12 minutes | Serves 4

1 medium eggplant, cut into ¼-inch slices
2 large tomatoes, cut into ¼-inch slices
4 ounces (113 g) fresh

Mozzarella, cut into ½-ounce / 14-g slices
2 tablespoons olive oil
¼ cup fresh basil, sliced

1. In a baking dish, place four slices of eggplant on the bottom. Place a slice of tomato on top of each eggplant round, then Mozzarella, then eggplant. Repeat as necessary. 2. Drizzle with olive oil. Cover dish with foil and place dish into the air fryer basket. 3. Adjust the temperature to 350°F (177°C) and bake for 12 minutes. 4. When done, eggplant will be tender. Garnish with fresh basil to serve.

Per Serving:
calories: 97 | fat: 7g | protein: 2g | carbs: 8g | fiber: 4g | sodium: 11mg

Fettuccine Alfredo (2 Variations)

Prep time: 5 minutes | Cook time: 10 minutes | Serves 4 to 6

For Both Variations:
2 (7-ounce / 198-g) packages shirataki noodles or 5 cups spaghetti squash or hearts of palm noodles
1 tablespoon chopped fresh parsley, chives, or basil, for serving (optional)
For the Dairy Variation:
2 tablespoons grass-fed butter or ghee
2 teaspoons garlic powder or 2 small garlic cloves, minced
1½ cups grass-fed heavy (whipping) cream

1 cup grated Parmesan cheese
Salt and freshly ground black pepper, to taste
For the Vegan Variation:
2 tablespoons butter-flavored coconut oil
2 teaspoons garlic powder or 2 small garlic cloves, minced
1½ cups heavy coconut cream (shake the can well before measuring)
4 tablespoons nutritional yeast
Salt and freshly ground black pepper, to taste

1. If you're making the dairy version, melt the butter in a skillet over medium heat, add the garlic, and stir together. Add the cream and cheese, season with salt and pepper, and whisk everything together. Cook for about 10 minutes, or until the cheese is melted. 2. If you're making the vegan version, melt the coconut oil in a skillet over medium heat, add the garlic, and stir together. Add the coconut cream and nutritional yeast, season with salt and pepper, and whisk everything together. Cook for about 10 minutes. 3. Add the noodles to the skillet and cook, stirring, for 1 minute to coat in the sauce. 4. Dish up in bowls and sprinkle with chopped parsley, chives, or basil, if desired.

Per Serving:
calories: 510 | fat: 46g | protein: 12g | carbs: 12g | net carbs: 10g | fiber: 2g

Cauliflower Tikka Masala

Prep time: 10 minutes | Cook time: 20 minutes | Serves 4

FOR THE CAULIFLOWER
1 head cauliflower, cut into small florets
1 tablespoon coconut oil, melted
1 teaspoon ground cumin
½ teaspoon ground coriander
FOR THE SAUCE
2 tablespoons coconut oil
½ onion, chopped

1 tablespoon minced garlic
1 tablespoon grated ginger
2 tablespoons garam masala
1 tablespoon tomato paste
½ teaspoon salt
1 cup crushed tomatoes
1 cup heavy (whipping) cream
1 tablespoon chopped fresh cilantro

TO MAKE THE CAULIFLOWER 1. Preheat the oven. Set the oven temperature to 425°F. Line a baking sheet with aluminum foil. 2. Prepare the cauliflower. In a large bowl, toss the cauliflower with the coconut oil, cumin, and coriander. Spread the cauliflower on the baking sheet in a single layer and bake it for 20 minutes, until the cauliflower is tender. TO MAKE THE SAUCE 1. Sauté the vegetables. While the cauliflower is baking, in a large skillet over medium-high heat, warm the coconut oil. Add the onion, garlic, and ginger and sauté until they've softened, about 3 minutes. 2. Finish the sauce. Stir in the garam masala, tomato paste, and salt until the vegetables are coated. Stir in the crushed tomatoes and bring to a boil, then reduce the heat to low and simmer the sauce for 10 minutes, stirring it often. Remove the skillet from the heat and stir in the cream and cilantro. 3. Assemble and serve. Add the cauliflower to the sauce, stirring to combine everything. Divide the mixture between four bowls and serve it hot.
Per Serving:
calories: 372 | fat: 32g | protein: 8g | carbs: 17g | net carbs: 10g | fiber: 7g

Three-Cheese Zucchini Boats

Prep time: 15 minutes | Cook time: 20 minutes | Serves 2

2 medium zucchini
1 tablespoon avocado oil
¼ cup low-carb, no-sugar-added pasta sauce
¼ cup full-fat ricotta cheese
¼ cup shredded Mozzarella

cheese
¼ teaspoon dried oregano
¼ teaspoon garlic powder
½ teaspoon dried parsley
2 tablespoons grated vegetarian Parmesan cheese

1. Cut off 1 inch from the top and bottom of each zucchini. Slice zucchini in half lengthwise and use a spoon to scoop out a bit of the inside, making room for filling. Brush with oil and spoon 2 tablespoons pasta sauce into each shell. 2. In a medium bowl, mix ricotta, Mozzarella, oregano, garlic powder, and parsley. Spoon the mixture into each zucchini shell. Place stuffed zucchini shells into the air fryer basket. 3. Adjust the temperature to 350°F (177°C) and air fry for 20 minutes. 4. To remove from the basket, use tongs or a spatula and carefully lift out. Top with Parmesan. Serve immediately.
Per Serving:
calories: 208 | fat: 14g | protein: 12g | carbs: 11g | fiber: 3g | sodium: 247mg

Moroccan Vegetable Tagine

Prep time: 20 minutes | Cook time: 1 hour | Serves 6

½ cup extra-virgin olive oil
2 medium yellow onions, sliced
6 celery stalks, sliced into ¼-inch crescents
6 garlic cloves, minced
1 teaspoon ground cumin
1 teaspoon ginger powder
1 teaspoon salt
½ teaspoon paprika
½ teaspoon ground cinnamon
¼ teaspoon freshly ground black pepper
2 cups vegetable stock
1 medium eggplant, cut into 1-inch cubes

2 medium zucchini, cut into ½-inch-thick semicircles
2 cups cauliflower florets
1 (13¾-ounce / 390-g) can artichoke hearts, drained and quartered
1 cup halved and pitted green olives
½ cup chopped fresh flat-leaf parsley, for garnish
½ cup chopped fresh cilantro leaves, for garnish
Greek yogurt, for garnish (optional)

1. In a large, thick soup pot or Dutch oven, heat the olive oil over medium-high heat. Add the onion and celery and sauté until softened, 6 to 8 minutes. Add the garlic, cumin, ginger, salt, paprika, cinnamon, and pepper and sauté for another 2 minutes. 2. Add the stock and bring to a boil. Reduce the heat to low and add the eggplant, zucchini, and cauliflower. Simmer on low heat, covered, until the vegetables are tender, 30 to 35 minutes. Add the artichoke hearts and olives, cover, and simmer for another 15 minutes. 3. Serve garnished with parsley, cilantro, and Greek yogurt (if using).
Per Serving:
calories: 265 | fat: 21g | protein: 5g | carbs: 19g | fiber: 9g | sodium: 858mg

Stuffed Portobellos

Prep time: 10 minutes | Cook time: 8 minutes | Serves 4

3 ounces (85 g) cream cheese, softened
½ medium zucchini, trimmed and chopped
¼ cup seeded and chopped red bell pepper
1½ cups chopped fresh spinach

leaves
4 large portobello mushrooms, stems removed
2 tablespoons coconut oil, melted
½ teaspoon salt

1. In a medium bowl, mix cream cheese, zucchini, pepper, and spinach. 2. Drizzle mushrooms with coconut oil and sprinkle with salt. Scoop ¼ zucchini mixture into each mushroom. 3. Place mushrooms into ungreased air fryer basket. Adjust the temperature to 400°F (204°C) and air fry for 8 minutes. Portobellos will be tender and tops will be browned when done. Serve warm.
Per Serving:
calories: 151 | fat: 13g | protein: 4g | carbs: 6g | fiber: 2g | sodium: 427mg

Cauliflower Rice-Stuffed Peppers

Prep time: 10 minutes | Cook time: 15 minutes | Serves 4

2 cups uncooked cauliflower rice	cheese
¾ cup drained canned petite diced tomatoes	¼ teaspoon salt
2 tablespoons olive oil	¼ teaspoon ground black pepper
1 cup shredded Mozzarella	4 medium green bell peppers, tops removed, seeded

1. In a large bowl, mix all ingredients except bell peppers. Scoop mixture evenly into peppers. 2. Place peppers into ungreased air fryer basket. Adjust the temperature to 350ºF (177ºC) and air fry for 15 minutes. Peppers will be tender and cheese will be melted when done. Serve warm.

Per Serving:
calories: 144 | fat: 7g | protein: 11g | carbs: 11g | fiber: 5g | sodium: 380mg

Mediterranean Pan Pizza

Prep time: 5 minutes | Cook time: 8 minutes | Serves 2

1 cup shredded Mozzarella cheese	leaves
¼ medium red bell pepper, seeded and chopped	2 tablespoons chopped black olives
½ cup chopped fresh spinach	2 tablespoons crumbled feta cheese

1. Sprinkle Mozzarella into an ungreased round nonstick baking dish in an even layer. Add remaining ingredients on top. 2. Place dish into air fryer basket. Adjust the temperature to 350ºF (177ºC) and bake for 8 minutes, checking halfway through to avoid burning. Top of pizza will be golden brown and the cheese melted when done. 3. Remove dish from fryer and let cool 5 minutes before slicing and serving.

Per Serving:
calories: 108 | fat: 1g | protein: 20g | carbs: 5g | fiber: 3g | sodium: 521mg

Vegetarian Chili with Avocado and Sour Cream

Prep time: 10 minutes | Cook time: 25 minutes | Serves 8

2 tablespoons good-quality olive oil	1 teaspoon ground cumin
½ onion, finely chopped	4 cups canned diced tomatoes
1 red bell pepper, diced	2 cups pecans, chopped
2 jalapeño peppers, chopped	1 cup sour cream
1 tablespoon minced garlic	1 avocado, diced
2 tablespoons chili powder	2 tablespoons chopped fresh cilantro

1. Sauté the vegetables. In a large pot over medium-high heat, warm the olive oil. Add the onion, red bell pepper, jalapeño peppers, and garlic and sauté until they've softened, about 4 minutes. Stir in the chili powder and cumin, stirring to coat the vegetables with the spices. 2. Cook the chili. Stir in the tomatoes and pecans and bring the chili to a boil, then reduce the heat to low and simmer until the vegetables are soft and the flavors mellow, about 20 minutes. 3. Serve. Ladle the chili into bowls and serve it with the sour cream, avocado, and cilantro.

Per Serving:
calories: 332 | fat: 32g | protein: 5g | carbs: 11g | net carbs: 5g | fiber: 6g

Herbed Ricotta-Stuffed Mushrooms

Prep time: 10 minutes | Cook time: 30 minutes | Serves 4

6 tablespoons extra-virgin olive oil, divided	(such as basil, parsley, rosemary, oregano, or thyme)
4 portobello mushroom caps, cleaned and gills removed	2 garlic cloves, finely minced
1 cup whole-milk ricotta cheese	½ teaspoon salt
⅓ cup chopped fresh herbs	¼ teaspoon freshly ground black pepper

1. Preheat the oven to 400ºF (205ºC). 2. Line a baking sheet with parchment or foil and drizzle with 2 tablespoons olive oil, spreading evenly. Place the mushroom caps on the baking sheet, gill-side up. 3. In a medium bowl, mix together the ricotta, herbs, 2 tablespoons olive oil, garlic, salt, and pepper. Stuff each mushroom cap with one-quarter of the cheese mixture, pressing down if needed. Drizzle with remaining 2 tablespoons olive oil and bake until golden brown and the mushrooms are soft, 30 to 35 minutes, depending on the size of the mushrooms.

Per Serving:
calories: 308 | fat: 29g | protein: 9g | carbs: 6g | fiber: 1g | sodium: 351mg

Greek Stuffed Eggplant

Prep time: 15 minutes | Cook time: 20 minutes | Serves 2

1 large eggplant	1 cup fresh spinach
2 tablespoons unsalted butter	2 tablespoons diced red bell pepper
¼ medium yellow onion, diced	½ cup crumbled feta
¼ cup chopped artichoke hearts	

1. Slice eggplant in half lengthwise and scoop out flesh, leaving enough inside for shell to remain intact. Take eggplant that was scooped out, chop it, and set aside. 2. In a medium skillet over medium heat, add butter and onion. Sauté until onions begin to soften, about 3 to 5 minutes. Add chopped eggplant, artichokes, spinach, and bell pepper. Continue cooking 5 minutes until peppers soften and spinach wilts. Remove from the heat and gently fold in the feta. 3. Place filling into each eggplant shell and place into the air fryer basket. 4. Adjust the temperature to 320ºF (160ºC) and air fry for 20 minutes. 5. Eggplant will be tender when done. Serve warm.

Per Serving:
calories: 259 | fat: 16.32g | protein: 9.81g | carbs: 22.16g | sugars: 12.44g | fiber: 10.1g | sodium: 386mg

Crispy Cabbage Steaks

Prep time: 5 minutes | Cook time: 10 minutes | Serves 4

1 small head green cabbage, cored and cut into ½-inch-thick slices	2 tablespoons olive oil
	1 clove garlic, peeled and finely minced
¼ teaspoon salt	½ teaspoon dried thyme
¼ teaspoon ground black pepper	½ teaspoon dried parsley

1. Sprinkle each side of cabbage with salt and pepper, then place into ungreased air fryer basket, working in batches if needed. 2. Drizzle each side of cabbage with olive oil, then sprinkle with remaining ingredients on both sides. Adjust the temperature to 350°F (177°C) and air fry for 10 minutes, turning "steaks" halfway through cooking. 3. Cabbage will be browned at the edges and tender when done. Serve warm.

Per Serving:
calories: 63 | fat: 7g | protein: 0g | carbs: 1g | fiber: 0g | sodium: 155mg

Parmesan Artichokes

Prep time: 10 minutes | Cook time: 10 minutes | Serves 4

2 medium artichokes, trimmed and quartered, center removed	Parmesan cheese
2 tablespoons coconut oil	¼ cup blanched finely ground almond flour
1 large egg, beaten	½ teaspoon crushed red pepper flakes
½ cup grated vegetarian	

1. In a large bowl, toss artichokes in coconut oil and then dip each piece into the egg. 2. Mix the Parmesan and almond flour in a large bowl. Add artichoke pieces and toss to cover as completely as possible, sprinkle with pepper flakes. Place into the air fryer basket. 3. Adjust the temperature to 400°F (204°C) and air fry for 10 minutes. 4. Toss the basket two times during cooking. Serve warm.

Per Serving:
calories: 207 | fat: 13g | protein: 10g | carbs: 15g | fiber: 5g | sodium: 211mg

Cheesy Garden Veggie Crustless Quiche

Prep time: 5 minutes | Cook time: 25 minutes | Serves 4

1 tablespoon grass-fed butter, divided	chopped
6 eggs	1 scallion, white and green parts, chopped
¾ cup heavy (whipping) cream	1 cup shredded fresh spinach
3 ounces goat cheese, divided	10 cherry tomatoes, cut in half
½ cup sliced mushrooms,	

1. Preheat the oven. Set the oven temperature to 350°F. Grease a 9-inch pie plate with ½ teaspoon of the butter and set it aside. 2. Mix the quiche base. In a medium bowl, whisk the eggs, cream, and 2 ounces of the cheese until it's all well blended. Set it aside. 3. Sauté the vegetables. In a small skillet over medium-high heat, melt the remaining butter. Add the mushrooms and scallion and sauté them until they've softened, about 2 minutes. Add the spinach and sauté until it's wilted, about 2 minutes. 4. Assemble and bake. Spread the vegetable mixture in the bottom of the pie plate and pour the egg-and-cream mixture over the vegetables. Scatter the cherry tomatoes and the remaining 1 ounce of goat cheese on top. Bake for 20 to 25 minutes until the quiche is cooked through, puffed, and lightly browned. 5. Serve. Cut the quiche into wedges and divide it between four plates. Serve it warm or cold.

Per Serving:
calories: 355 | fat: 30g | protein: 18g | carbs: 5g | net carbs: 4g | fiber: 1g

Cheese Stuffed Zucchini

Prep time: 20 minutes | Cook time: 8 minutes | Serves 4

1 large zucchini, cut into four pieces	parsley, roughly chopped
	1 heaping tablespoon coriander, minced
2 tablespoons olive oil	
1 cup Ricotta cheese, room temperature	2 ounces (57 g) Cheddar cheese, preferably freshly grated
2 tablespoons scallions, chopped	1 teaspoon celery seeds
	½ teaspoon salt
1 heaping tablespoon fresh	½ teaspoon garlic pepper

1. Cook your zucchini in the air fryer basket for approximately 10 minutes at 350°F (177°C). Check for doneness and cook for 2-3 minutes longer if needed. 2. Meanwhile, make the stuffing by mixing the other items. 3. When your zucchini is thoroughly cooked, open them up. Divide the stuffing among all zucchini pieces and bake an additional 5 minutes.

Per Serving:
calories: 242 | fat: 20g | protein: 12g | carbs: 5g | fiber: 1g | sodium: 443mg

Cheesy Cauliflower Pizza Crust

Prep time: 15 minutes | Cook time: 11 minutes | Serves 2

1 (12-ounce / 340-g) steamer bag cauliflower	2 tablespoons blanched finely ground almond flour
½ cup shredded sharp Cheddar cheese	1 teaspoon Italian blend seasoning
1 large egg	

1. Cook cauliflower according to package instructions. Remove from bag and place into cheesecloth or paper towel to remove excess water. Place cauliflower into a large bowl. 2. Add cheese, egg, almond flour, and Italian seasoning to the bowl and mix well. 3. Cut a piece of parchment to fit your air fryer basket. Press cauliflower into 6-inch round circle. Place into the air fryer basket. 4. Adjust the temperature to 360°F (182°C) and air fry for 11 minutes. 5. After 7 minutes, flip the pizza crust. 6. Add preferred toppings to pizza. Place back into air fryer basket and cook an additional 4 minutes or until fully cooked and golden. Serve immediately.

Per Serving:
calories: 251 | fat: 17g | protein: 15g | carbs: 12g | fiber: 5g | sodium: 375mg

Cauliflower Steak with Gremolata

Prep time: 15 minutes | Cook time: 25 minutes | Serves 4

2 tablespoons olive oil

1 tablespoon Italian seasoning

1 large head cauliflower, outer leaves removed and sliced lengthwise through the core into thick "steaks"

Salt and freshly ground black pepper, to taste

¼ cup Parmesan cheese

Gremolata:

1 bunch Italian parsley (about 1 cup packed)

2 cloves garlic

Zest of 1 small lemon, plus 1 to 2 teaspoons lemon juice

½ cup olive oil

Salt and pepper, to taste

1. Preheat the air fryer to 400°F (204°C). 2. In a small bowl, combine the olive oil and Italian seasoning. Brush both sides of each cauliflower "steak" generously with the oil. Season to taste with salt and black pepper. 3. Working in batches if necessary, arrange the cauliflower in a single layer in the air fryer basket. Pausing halfway through the cooking time to turn the "steaks," air fry for 15 to 20 minutes until the cauliflower is tender and the edges begin to brown. Sprinkle with the Parmesan and air fry for 5 minutes longer. 4. To make the gremolata: In a food processor fitted with a metal blade, combine the parsley, garlic, and lemon zest and juice. With the motor running, add the olive oil in a steady stream until the mixture forms a bright green sauce. Season to taste with salt and black pepper. Serve the cauliflower steaks with the gremolata spooned over the top.

Per Serving:
calories: 336 | fat: 30g | protein: 7g | carbs: 15g | fiber: 5g | sodium: 340mg

Green Vegetable Stir-Fry with Tofu

Prep time: 15 minutes | Cook time: 15 minutes | Serves 2

3 tablespoons avocado oil, divided

1 cup Brussels sprouts, halved

½ onion, diced

½ leek, white and light green parts diced

½ head green cabbage, diced

¼ cup water, plus more if needed

½ cup kale, coarsely chopped

1 cup spinach, coarsely chopped

8 ounces (227 g) tofu, diced

2 teaspoons garlic powder

Salt and freshly ground black pepper, to taste

½ avocado, pitted, peeled, and diced

MCT oil (optional)

1. In a large skillet with a lid (or a wok if you have one), heat 2 tablespoons of avocado oil over medium-high heat. Add the Brussels sprouts, onion, leek, and cabbage and stir together. Add the water, cover, lower the heat to medium, and cook for about 5 minutes. 2. Toss in the kale and spinach and cook for 3 minutes, stirring constantly, until the onion, leek, and cabbage are caramelized. 3. Add the tofu to the stir-fry, then season with the garlic, salt, pepper, and the remaining tablespoon of avocado oil. 4. Turn the heat back up to medium-high and cook for about 10 minutes, stirring constantly, until the tofu is nice and caramelized on all sides. If you experience any burning, turn down the heat and add 2 to 3 tablespoons of water. 5. Divide the stir-fry between two plates and sprinkle with diced avocado. Feel free to drizzle algae oil or MCT oil over the top for a little extra fat.

Per Serving:
calories: 473 | fat: 33g | protein: 17g | carbs: 27g | net carbs: 15g | fiber: 12g

Eggplant Parmesan

Prep time: 15 minutes | Cook time: 17 minutes | Serves 4

1 medium eggplant, ends trimmed, sliced into ½-inch rounds

¼ teaspoon salt

2 tablespoons coconut oil

½ cup grated Parmesan cheese

1 ounce (28 g) 100% cheese crisps, finely crushed

½ cup low-carb marinara sauce

½ cup shredded Mozzarella cheese

1. Sprinkle eggplant rounds with salt on both sides and wrap in a kitchen towel for 30 minutes. Press to remove excess water, then drizzle rounds with coconut oil on both sides. 2. In a medium bowl, mix Parmesan and cheese crisps. Press each eggplant slice into mixture to coat both sides. 3. Place rounds into ungreased air fryer basket. Adjust the temperature to 350°F (177°C) and air fry for 15 minutes, turning rounds halfway through cooking. They will be crispy around the edges when done. 4. Spoon marinara over rounds and sprinkle with Mozzarella. Continue cooking an additional 2 minutes at 350°F (177°C) until cheese is melted. Serve warm.

Per Serving:
calories: 208 | fat: 13g | protein: 12g | carbs: 13g | fiber: 5g | sodium: 531mg

Chapter 7 Salads

Spinach Salad with Smoked Salmon and Avocado

Prep time: 15 minutes | Cook time: 0 minutes | Serves 4

For the Dressing:
½ cup good-quality olive oil
¼ cup white balsamic vinegar
¼ cup chopped fresh dill
1 teaspoon lemon zest
Sea salt, for seasoning
Freshly ground black pepper, for seasoning
For the Salad:

6 cups fresh spinach, thoroughly washed and dried
1 pound smoked salmon, chopped
1 avocado, diced
½ red onion, chopped
½ cup crumbled goat cheese
¼ cup chopped pecans, divided

Make the Dressing: 1. Mix the dressing. In a small bowl, whisk together the olive oil, vinegar, dill, and lemon zest. 2. Season. Season the dressing with salt and pepper and set it aside. Make the Salad: 1. Mix the salad. In a large bowl, toss together the spinach, salmon, avocado, and red onion until everything is well combined. Add the dressing to the salad and toss to coat all the ingredients with dressing. 2. Assemble the salad. Divide the salad evenly between four plates. Top each salad with goat cheese and pecans and serve.
Per Serving:
calories: 540 | fat: 45g | protein: 26g | carbs: 9g | net carbs: 5g | fiber: 4g

Roasted Vegetable Salad

Prep time: 15 minutes | Cook time: 45 minutes | Serves 4

½ eggplant, diced
1 medium bulb fennel, diced
12 asparagus spears, diced
1 zucchini, diced
12 Brussels sprouts, halved
1 cup cubed fresh pumpkin
1 medium red or white onion, diced
4 tablespoons avocado oil
1 teaspoon minced garlic or garlic powder

1 teaspoon dried oregano or marjoram (or both)
1 teaspoon dried thyme
Salt and freshly ground black pepper, to taste
2 cups mixed greens (or any salad greens of choice)
Freshly grated Parmesan cheese, for serving (optional)
16 ounces (454 g) steak or black cod, for serving (optional)

1. Preheat the oven to 450ºF (235ºC). 2. In a mixing bowl, combine the eggplant, fennel, asparagus, zucchini, Brussels sprouts, pumpkin, and onion. Pour in the avocado oil, add the garlic, oregano or marjoram, and thyme, and season with salt and pepper. Mix together until the vegetables are well coated. 3. Spread the vegetables in an even layer on a baking sheet and roast for 35 to 45 minutes, checking occasionally and stirring every 15 to 20 minutes. (Your oven may be very powerful, so feel free to take the veggies out sooner than 35 minutes if they are browned to your liking.) 4. Divide the greens among four plates and evenly distribute the roasted vegetables on top. Sprinkle with freshly grated cheese and serve with steak or cod, if desired.
Per Serving:
calories: 227 | fat: 15g | protein: 4g | carbs: 19g | net carbs: 12g | fiber: 7g

Raw Tabouli

Prep time: 5 minutes | Cook time: 0 minutes | serves 4

4 cups cauliflower rice
4 cups chopped fresh parsley
1 cup finely diced tomato
½ cup finely diced yellow onion
2 cups finely diced cucumber

½ cup chopped fresh mint
Juice of 3 lemons
½ cup cold-pressed olive oil
Sea salt
Freshly ground black pepper

1. In a medium bowl, stir together the cauliflower rice, parsley, tomato, onion, cucumber, and mint. 2. Dress with the lemon juice and olive oil, and season with salt and pepper. 3. Place the tabouli in the refrigerator to chill for up to 1 hour to allow the flavors to combine, then serve.
Per Serving:
calories: 317 | fat: 28g | protein: 5g | carbs: 17g | net carbs: 11g | fiber: 6g

Bigass Salad

Prep time: 5 minutes | Cook time: 0 minutes | Serves 1

3 to 4 cups lettuce or mixed greens
1 to 2 cups sliced veggies
¼ cup shredded Cheddar cheese (optional)
1 can (5 ounces / 142 g) tuna

packed in water, drained
¼ cup nuts (walnuts, pecans, almonds)
2 tablespoons sunflower or pumpkin seeds
2 tablespoons olive oil

1. In a large, shallow bowl, layer lettuce, veggies, and cheese in that order. Flake the tuna over the top. 2. When you are ready to eat, sprinkle the nuts and seeds over the top, and drizzle with the olive oil.
Per Serving:
calories: 843 | fat: 63g | protein: 54g | carbs: 24g | net carbs: 10g | fiber: 14g

Salmon and Spinach Cobb Salad

Prep time: 5 minutes | Cook time: 25 minutes | Serves 2

4 bacon slices

2 large eggs

2 (6-ounce) salmon fillets

Pink Himalayan salt

Freshly ground black pepper

1 tablespoon ghee, if needed

1 avocado, sliced

6 ounces organic baby spinach

¼ cup crumbled blue cheese

1 tablespoon olive oil

1. In a medium skillet over medium-high heat, cook the bacon on both sides until crispy, about 8 minutes. Transfer the bacon to a paper towel–lined plate. 2. Bring a small saucepan filled with water to a boil over high heat. Put the eggs on to softboil, turn the heat down to medium-high, and cook for about 6 minutes. 3. Meanwhile, pat the salmon fillets on both sides with a paper towel to remove excess moisture. Season both sides with pink Himalayan salt and pepper. 4. With the bacon grease still in the skillet, add the salmon. If you need more grease in the pan, add some ghee to the bacon grease. 5. Cook the salmon on medium-high heat for 5 minutes on each side, or until it reaches your preferred degree of doneness. (I like it medium-rare.) 6. Meanwhile, transfer the bacon to a cutting board and chop it. Peel the softboiled eggs. Season the avocado with pink Himalayan salt and pepper. 7. Divide the spinach, bacon, and avocado between two plates. 8. Carefully halve the softboiled eggs and place them on the salads. Sprinkle the blue cheese crumbles over the salads. 9. Top with the salmon, drizzle the salads with the olive oil, and serve.

Per Serving:
calories: 623 | fat: 43g | protein: 54g | carbs: 12g | net carbs: 5g | fiber: 7g

Massaged Kale Salad with Goat Cheese

Prep time: 10 minutes | Cook time: 5 minutes | Serves 6

1 bunch curly kale (green or purple)

1 medium lemon

1 teaspoon kosher salt

3 tablespoons extra-virgin olive oil

1 tablespoon walnut oil

1 tablespoon balsamic vinegar

Freshly ground black pepper, to taste

11 ounces (312 g) goat cheese (1 large log), crumbled

½ cup raw pine nuts

1 large avocado, cubed

1. Use a sharp knife to remove the thick stem from each kale leaf. Cut or tear the leaves into small, bite-size pieces. Place in a large bowl. Squeeze the juice from the lemon over the kale and sprinkle in the salt. With both hands, massage the kale by squeezing, kneading, and rolling it between your hands. Do this for about 1 minute. Be aggressive! You can't hurt the kale. 2. In a small jar with a lid, combine both oils, the vinegar, and a few grinds of black pepper. Secure the lid and shake well. 3. Pour the dressing over the kale and toss. Add the goat cheese and toss again. 4. Heat a small skillet over medium-low heat. Add the pine nuts to the dry skillet and cook, stirring frequently, until lightly browned. 5. Add the warm nuts to the salad and toss well. The nuts will slightly melt the goat cheese. Top with the avocado and serve.

Per Serving:
calories: 402 | fat: 35g | protein: 15g | carbs: 9g | net carbs: 6g | fiber: 3g

Cheeseburger Salad

Prep time: 10 minutes | Cook time: 10 minutes | Serves 2

1 tablespoon ghee

1 pound ground beef

Pink Himalayan salt

Freshly ground black pepper

½ cup finely chopped dill pickles

2 cups chopped romaine

½ cup shredded Cheddar cheese

2 tablespoons ranch salad dressing (I use Primal Kitchen Ranch)

1. In a medium skillet over medium-high heat, heat the ghee. 2. When the ghee is hot, add the ground beef, breaking it up into smaller pieces with a spoon. Stir, cooking until the beef is browned, about 10 minutes. Season with pink Himalayan salt and pepper. 3. Put the pickles in a large bowl, and add the romaine and cheese. 4. Using a slotted spoon, transfer the browned beef from the skillet to the bowl. 5. Top the salad with the dressing, and toss to thoroughly coat. 6. Divide into two bowls and serve.

Per Serving:
calories: 662 | fat: 50g | protein: 47g | carbs: 6g | net carbs: 4g | fiber: 2g

Japanese Hibachi House Salad

Prep time: 5 minutes | Cook time: 0 minutes | serves 6

1-inch knob fresh ginger, peeled and chopped

½ medium carrot

½ celery stalk

Juice of 2 limes

¼ cup liquid aminos

1 teaspoon sesame oil

3 drops liquid stevia

2 heads romaine lettuce, chopped

1 small tomato, diced

½ cup sliced mushrooms

⅓ cup shredded carrots

⅓ cup diced red onion

2 tablespoons sesame seeds

1. In a high-powered blender, combine the ginger, carrot, celery, lime juice, aminos, sesame oil, and liquid stevia to create the dressing. 2. Divide the lettuce among 6 bowls and top each bowl with a generous portion of dressing. Garnish with the tomato, mushrooms, shredded carrots, onion, and sesame seeds.

Per Serving:
calories: 65 | fat: 3g | protein: 4g | carbs: 8g | net carbs: 4g | fiber: 4g

Antipasto Salad

Prep time: 10 minutes | Cook time: 0 minutes | Serves 4

1 (12-oz/340-g) jar roasted red peppers, drained and roughly chopped

1 (6½-oz/185-g) jar marinated artichoke quarters, drained and roughly chopped

1 (4-oz/113-g) can sliced cremini mushrooms, drained

4 ounces (115 g) salami, sliced

3 tablespoons capers, drained

¾ cup (210 ml) vinaigrette of choice

1. Place all the ingredients in a large mixing bowl. Toss to coat, then serve.

Per Serving:
calories: 433 | fat: 39g | protein: 7g | carbs: 14g | net carbs: 9g | fiber: 4g

Southern Fauxtato Salad

Prep time: 20 minutes | Cook time: 10 minutes | serves 6 to 8

2 (10-ounce) bags frozen cauliflower florets	1 cup mayonnaise
3 hard-boiled eggs, peeled and chopped	½ cup dill relish
¼ cup chopped onions	1 tablespoon prepared yellow mustard
1 rib celery, chopped	1 drop liquid stevia
	Salt and ground black pepper

1. Cook the cauliflower according to the package directions. Drain the excess water and set aside to cool. 2. In a large mixing bowl, mix together the eggs, onions, celery, mayonnaise, relish, mustard, and stevia. Stir in the cauliflower until well combined. Season to taste with salt and pepper. 3. Refrigerate the salad for at least 2 hours before serving. Leftovers can be stored in an airtight container in the refrigerator for up to 5 days.

Per Serving:
calories: 333 | fat: 35g | protein: 5g | carbs: 6g | net carbs: 3g | fiber: 3g

Mixed Green Salad with BLT Deviled Eggs and Bacon Vinaigrette

Prep time: 15 minutes | Cook time: 15 minutes | Serves 6

12 large eggs	½ cup mayonnaise, homemade or store-bought
4 slices bacon, cut into ¼-inch dice	2 teaspoons prepared yellow mustard
2 tablespoons diced onions	½ teaspoon fine sea salt
3 tablespoons plus 2 teaspoons coconut vinegar or red wine vinegar, divided	6 cherry tomatoes, quartered
1 teaspoon Dijon mustard	6 cups mixed greens, plus a few tablespoons finely chopped greens for garnish
3 tablespoons MCT oil or extra-virgin olive oil	Sliced fresh chives, for garnish

1. Place the eggs in a large saucepan and cover with cold water. Bring to a boil, then immediately cover the pan and remove it from the heat. Allow the eggs to cook in the hot water for 11 minutes. 2. Meanwhile, make the bacon vinaigrette: Cook the diced bacon in a skillet over medium heat until crispy, about 5 minutes. Remove the bacon from the pan, leaving the drippings in the skillet. Add the onions, 3 tablespoons of the vinegar, and the Dijon mustard. Cook over medium heat until the onions soften, about 2 minutes. While stirring with a whisk, slowly add the oil to the pan. Whisk well to combine. Set aside. 3. To make the deviled eggs: After the eggs cook for 11 minutes, drain the hot water and rinse the eggs with very cold water for a minute or two to stop the cooking process. Peel the eggs and cut them in half lengthwise. Remove the yolks and place them in a bowl (or food processor). Mash the yolks with a fork (or in a food processor) until they are the texture of very fine crumbles. Add the mayonnaise, remaining 2 teaspoons of vinegar, yellow mustard, and salt. Fill the egg white halves with the yolk mixture. Top each deviled egg with a cherry tomato quarter and sprinkle with the crispy bacon, chopped lettuce, and sliced chives. 4. Dress the rest of the lettuce with the bacon vinaigrette, divide among six plates, and place four deviled eggs on each plate. 5. If not serving immediately, do not dress the lettuce with the vinaigrette until just before serving. Store the vinaigrette in an airtight jar in the fridge for up to 5 days. Keep leftover deviled eggs in an airtight container in the fridge for up to 3 days.

Per Serving:
calories: 418 | fat: 37g | protein: 17g | carbs: 4g | net carbs: 3g | fiber: 1g

Berry Avocado Salad

Prep time: 10 minutes | Cook time: 0 minutes | Serves 4

DRESSING:	skinned, pitted, and cubed (12 ounces/340 g flesh) 12 strawberries, cut into quarters or eighths (depending on size)
2 tablespoons extra-virgin olive oil or refined avocado oil	
1½ teaspoons fresh lime juice	
1½ teaspoons chili powder	½ packed cup (30 g) fresh parsley, chopped
1 small clove garlic, minced	
2 drops liquid stevia	1 packed tablespoon fresh cilantro leaves, chopped
Finely ground gray sea salt, to taste	
SALAD:	1 tablespoon finely diced white onion
2 large Hass avocados,	

1. Place the ingredients for the dressing in a large bowl and whisk to combine. Add the salad ingredients and toss gently to coat. 2. Divide the salad among 4 bowls and serve immediately.

Per Serving:
calories: 259 | fat: 22g | protein: 4g | carbs: 13g | net carbs: 3g | fiber: 10g

Taverna-Style Greek Salad

Prep time: 20 minutes | Cook time: 0 minutes | Serves 4

4 to 5 medium tomatoes, roughly chopped	1 teaspoon dried oregano or fresh herbs of your choice, such as parsley, cilantro, chives, or basil, divided
1 large cucumber, peeled and roughly chopped	
1 medium green bell pepper, sliced	½ cup extra-virgin olive oil, divided
1 small red onion, sliced	1 pack feta cheese
16 pitted Kalamata olives	Optional: salt, pepper, and fresh oregano, for garnish
¼ cup capers, or more olives	

1. Place the vegetables in a large serving bowl. Add the olives, capers, feta, half of the dried oregano and half of the olive oil. Mix to combine. Place the whole piece of feta cheese on top, sprinkle with the remaining dried oregano, and drizzle with the remaining olive oil. Season to taste and serve immediately, or store in the fridge for up to 1 day.

Per Serving:
calories: 320 | fat: 31g | protein: 3g | carbs: 11g | fiber: 4g | sodium: 445mg

Greek Salad with Avocado

Prep time: 10 minutes | Cook time: 0 minutes | Serves 4

Salad:
3 Roma (plum) tomatoes, seeded and chopped
1 medium cucumber, peeled and cut into ½-inch pieces
1 green bell pepper, cored, seeded, and cut into ½-inch strips
1 cup pitted Kalamata olives
1 medium avocado, cut into ½-inch cubes
½ cup crumbled feta cheese
¼ medium red onion, thinly sliced

Dressing:
¼ cup extra-virgin olive oil
2 tablespoons red wine vinegar
1 tablespoon chopped fresh parsley
1 garlic clove, minced
1 teaspoon dried oregano
1 teaspoon freshly squeezed lemon juice
½ teaspoon pink Himalayan sea salt
¼ teaspoon freshly ground black pepper

1. To make the salad: In a large bowl, combine the tomatoes, cucumber, bell pepper, olives, avocado, feta, and red onion. 2. To make the dressing: In a small bowl, combine the olive oil, vinegar, parsley, garlic, oregano, lemon juice, salt, and pepper. 3. Toss the salad ingredients until well coated with the dressing.

Per Serving:
calories: 334 | fat: 31g | protein: 6g | carbs: 12g | net carbs: 6g | fiber: 6g

Kale Salad with Spicy Lime-Tahini Dressing

Prep time: 15 minutes | Cook time: 0 minutes | Serves 4

DRESSING:
½ cup (120 ml) avocado oil
¼ cup (60 ml) lime juice
¼ cup (60 ml) tahini
2 cloves garlic, minced
1 jalapeño pepper, seeded and finely diced
Handful of fresh cilantro leaves, chopped
½ teaspoon ground cumin
½ teaspoon finely ground sea salt

¼ teaspoon red pepper flakes
SALAD:
6 cups (360 g) destemmed kale leaves, roughly chopped
12 radishes, thinly sliced
1 green bell pepper, sliced
1 medium Hass avocado, peeled, pitted, and cubed (about 4 oz/110 g of flesh)
¼ cup (30 g) hulled pumpkin seeds

1. Make the dressing: Place the dressing ingredients in a medium-sized bowl and whisk to combine. Set aside. 2. Make the salad: Rinse the kale under hot water for about 30 seconds to soften it and make it easier to digest. Dry the kale well, then place it in a large salad bowl. Add the remaining salad ingredients and toss to combine. 3. Divide the salad evenly among 4 bowls. Drizzle each bowl with ¼ cup (60 ml) of the dressing and serve.

Per Serving:
calories: 517 | fat: 47g | protein: 11g | carbs: 21g | net carbs: 12g | fiber: 9g

Curried Okra Salad

Prep time: 15 minutes | Cook time: 15 minutes | Serves 4

FRIED OKRA:
¼ cup (55 g) plus 2 tablespoons coconut oil, divided
15 ounces (420 g) okra, trimmed and quartered lengthwise
SALAD:
¾ packed cup (60 g) fresh cilantro leaves, chopped
1 large tomato (about 2½ ounces/70 g), diced

½ small red onion, sliced (optional)
DRESSING:
⅓ cup (80 ml) extra-virgin olive oil, unrefined canola oil, or refined avocado oil
2 tablespoons fresh lemon juice
2 teaspoons curry powder
¼ teaspoon finely ground gray sea salt
2 drops liquid stevia

1. Melt ¼ cup (55 g) of the coconut oil in a large frying pan over medium-high heat. Place half of the okra in the pan and fry for 6 to 8 minutes, until the pieces are browned. Transfer the browned okra pieces to a clean plate, add the remaining 2 tablespoons of oil to the pan, and repeat with the remaining okra. 2. Meanwhile, place the ingredients for the salad in a large bowl. After all the okra is browned, transfer it to the bowl with the salad. 3. In a separate small bowl, whisk together the ingredients for the dressing, then drizzle the dressing over the salad and toss to coat. Divide among 4 salad bowls and serve.

Per Serving:
calories: 390 | fat: 38g | protein: 3g | carbs: 9g | net carbs: 5g | fiber: 5g

Basic Chicken Salad in Lettuce Cups

Prep time: 10 minutes | Cook time: 0 minutes | Serves 2

8 ounces (227 g) cooked chicken breast, diced (if using store-bought, make sure it's sugar-free)
½ red bell pepper, diced
¼ cup diced jicama
1 celery stalk, diced
2 tablespoons Primal Kitchen avocado oil mayonnaise
1 teaspoon Dijon mustard
4 slices cooked bacon, chopped

Splash freshly squeezed lemon juice
1 teaspoon fresh dill
Salt and freshly ground black pepper, to taste
4 romaine or butter lettuce leaves
1 tablespoon sliced almonds (optional)
Chopped fresh parsley, for serving (optional)

1. In a mixing bowl, toss together the chicken, bell pepper, jicama, and celery. 2. Add the mayonnaise, mustard, bacon, and lemon juice, then sprinkle in the dill, season with salt and pepper, and stir everything together. 3. Arrange the lettuce leaves on plates and scoop in the chicken salad mixture. 4. Sprinkling almonds and parsley on top before serving is completely optional but gives these cups a little extra flavor and a nutritional boost!

Per Serving:
calories: 454 | fat: 30g | protein: 36g | carbs: 8g | net carbs: 6g | fiber: 2g

Warm Bacon Broccoli Salad

Prep time: 15 minutes | Cook time: 5 minutes | Makes 2 salads

2 cups fresh spinach leaves	¼ red onion, thinly sliced
¼ cup avocado oil	Salt and freshly ground black
¼ cup red wine vinegar	pepper, to taste
1 tablespoon Dijon mustard	2 or 3 cooked bacon slices, cut
½ cup broccoli florets	widthwise into strips
1 tablespoon olive oil	

1. Place the spinach in a large bowl. Set aside. 2. In a small bowl, whisk the avocado oil, vinegar, and mustard. Set aside. 3. In a large skillet over medium-low heat, gently sauté the broccoli in the olive oil for about 4 minutes. Add the warm broccoli to the spinach, letting the broccoli slightly wilt the spinach leaves. 4. Add the red onion to the skillet. Give the dressing another whisk, add it to the bacon and spinach, and toss everything to coat. Season with salt and pepper. Top with the bacon strips and divide between two salad bowls.

Per Serving:
1 salad: calories: 400 | fat: 40g | protein: 6g | carbs: 4g | net carbs: 2g | fiber: 2g

Zucchini Pasta Salad

Prep time: 5 minutes | Cook time: 0 minutes | Serves 4

4 medium zucchinis, spiral sliced	½ cup (75 g) pine nuts
12 ounces (340 g) pitted black olives, cut in half lengthwise	¼ cup plus 2 tablespoons (55 g) sesame seeds
1 pint (290 g) cherry tomatoes, cut in half lengthwise	⅔ cup (160 ml) creamy Italian dressing or other creamy salad dressing of choice

1. Place all the ingredients in a large mixing bowl. Toss to coat, then divide evenly between 4 serving plates or bowls.

Per Serving:
calories: 562 | fat: 53g | protein: 9g | carbs: 22g | net carbs: 14g | fiber: 9g

Chopped Bitter Greens Salad

Prep time: 10 minutes | Cook time: 0 minutes | Serves 2

1 ounce (28 g) arugula	½ cup fresh cilantro
½ cup shredded red cabbage	½ cup dandelion greens
½ cup shredded green cabbage	2 tablespoons olive oil
1 head endive, trimmed and chopped into bite-size pieces	1 tablespoon lemon-flavored Nordic Naturals Omega-3 Oil
½ head radicchio, chopped into bite-size pieces	1 teaspoon Dijon mustard
½ cup fresh Italian parsley leaves	1 teaspoon apple cider vinegar
	1 can sardines, for serving (optional)

1. In a large salad bowl, combine the arugula, red and green cabbage, endive, radicchio, parsley, cilantro, and dandelion greens. 2. In a small mixing bowl, combine the olive oil, omega-3 oil, mustard, and vinegar and whisk together until well mixed. 3. Pour the dressing over the greens in the salad bowl and toss with salad tongs. Serve with sardines, if desired.

Per Serving:
calories: 288 | fat: 28g | protein: 2g | carbs: 7g | net carbs: 4g | fiber: 3g

Buffalo Chicken Salad

Prep time: 10 minutes | Cook time: 20 minutes | Serves 6

Buffalo Chicken:	Salad:
1 cup hot sauce	12 cups chopped romaine lettuce or spinach
1 tablespoon garlic powder	6 ounces (170 g) blue cheese or feta, crumbled
1 pound (454 g) boneless, skinless chicken thighs	6 tablespoons ranch dressing
2 tablespoons butter, cubed	

Make the Buffalo Chicken 1. Preheat the oven to 350ºF (180ºC). 2. In a glass baking dish, whisk together the hot sauce and garlic powder. Add the chicken and coat with the sauce. Top with the butter and bake for 15 to 20 minutes until the chicken is cooked through. 3. Let cool and then shred with a fork. 4. Store a few portions of the buffalo chicken in the refrigerator for an easy lunch or dinner during the week, and freeze the remaining portions. Make One Serving of Salad 5. Combine 2 cups of lettuce or spinach, 1 ounce (28 g) of cheese, and 1 tablespoon of dressing. Top with 1 portion of chicken.

Per Serving:
1 salad: calories: 407 | fat: 31g | protein: 26g | carbs: 6g | net carbs: 4g | fiber: 2g

Orange-Tarragon Chicken Salad Wrap

Prep time: 15 minutes | Cook time: 0 minutes | Serves 4

½ cup plain whole-milk Greek yogurt	black pepper
2 tablespoons Dijon mustard	2 cups cooked shredded chicken
2 tablespoons extra-virgin olive oil	½ cup slivered almonds
	4 to 8 large Bibb lettuce leaves, tough stem removed
2 tablespoons chopped fresh tarragon or 1 teaspoon dried tarragon	2 small ripe avocados, peeled and thinly sliced
½ teaspoon salt	Zest of 1 clementine, or ½ small orange (about 1 tablespoon)
¼ teaspoon freshly ground	

1. In a medium bowl, combine the yogurt, mustard, olive oil, tarragon, orange zest, salt, and pepper and whisk until creamy. 2. Add the shredded chicken and almonds and stir to coat. 3. To assemble the wraps, place about ½ cup chicken salad mixture in the center of each lettuce leaf and top with sliced avocados.

Per Serving:
calories: 491 | fat: 38g | protein: 28g | carbs: 14g | fiber: 9g | sodium: 454mg

Chopped Salad in Jars

Prep time: 8 minutes | Cook time: 0 minutes | Serves 4

½ cup ranch dressing	1 cup diced celery
1 cup diced tomatoes	4 hard-boiled eggs, chopped
1 cup diced cucumber	(omit for egg-free)
1 cup coarsely chopped	4 slices bacon, diced and
radicchio or romaine lettuce	cooked until crispy

1. Have on hand four pint-sized mason jars. Place 2 tablespoons of ranch dressing in the bottom of each jar. Top with a quarter of the diced tomatoes. Then add the rest of the salad ingredients to the jars in the order listed, dividing the ingredients equally among the jars.
Per Serving:
calories: 382 | fat: 31g | protein: 18g | carbs: 8g | net carbs: 5g | fiber: 3g

Big Greek Spinach Salad

Prep time: 5 minutes | Cook time: 0 minutes | serves 4

½ cup cold-pressed olive oil	½ cup cherry tomatoes, halved
Juice of 1 lemon	½ green bell pepper, sliced
1 tablespoon dried mint	¼ small red onion, thinly sliced
1 tablespoon dried oregano	¼ cup coarsely chopped fresh
Sea salt	mint
Freshly ground black pepper	5 cups fresh spinach, chopped
1 cup cubed, drained, firm	1 head romaine lettuce, chopped
sprouted tofu	⅓ cup sliced olives
1 medium cucumber, sliced	¼ cup pine nuts

1. In a medium mixing bowl, whisk together the olive oil, lemon juice, mint, and oregano, and season with salt and pepper. 2. Toss the tofu in the dressing and set aside to marinate. 3. In a separate medium bowl, toss together the cucumber, tomatoes, bell pepper, onion, and mint. 4. Add the spinach, lettuce, and olives. 5. Add the dressed tofu. Toss salad again. 6. Serve the salad in small bowls, garnished with the olives and pine nuts.
Per Serving:
calories: 406 | fat: 38g | protein: 10g | carbs: 13g | net carbs: 7g | fiber: 6g

Marinated Bok Choy Salad

Prep time: 20 minutes | Cook time: 0 minutes | Serves 6

DRESSING:	ginger root, minced
⅓ cup (80 ml) extra-virgin olive	2 teaspoons prepared yellow
oil or refined avocado oil	mustard
3 tablespoons MCT oil	¼ teaspoon finely ground gray
3 tablespoons apple cider	sea salt
vinegar	¼ teaspoon ground black
2 tablespoons coconut aminos	pepper
4 small cloves garlic, minced	2 drops liquid stevia
1 (2-inch/5-cm) piece fresh	SALAD:

8 cups (900 g) chopped bok choy (about 1 large head)   ⅓ cup (40 g) sliced raw almonds, divided

1. Combine the ingredients for the dressing in a large bowl. 2. Add the bok choy and ¼ cup (30 g) of the sliced almonds. Toss to coat. Cover the bowl and place in the fridge for at least 12 hours, but not longer than 3 days. 3. When ready to serve, divide the salad among 6 bowls and sprinkle each salad with the remaining sliced almonds.
Per Serving:
calories: 234 | fat: 21g | protein: 4g | carbs: 7g | net carbs: 5g | fiber: 2g

Spinach Salad with Hot Bacon Dressing

Prep time: 10 minutes | Cook time: 0 minutes | serves 1

1 loosely packed cup baby	2 tablespoons hot bacon
spinach leaves	drippings
1 hard-boiled egg, peeled and	2 tablespoons white vinegar
chopped	1 tablespoon extra-virgin olive
2 slices bacon, cooked and cut	oil
into small pieces	1 tablespoon granular erythritol
¼ cup raw pecan halves	1 teaspoon Dijon mustard
6 fresh blackberries	Salt and ground black pepper
DRESSING:	

1. Place the spinach leaves in a salad bowl. Top with the egg, bacon, pecans, and blackberries. 2. Prepare the dressing: In a small bowl, whisk together the bacon drippings, vinegar, olive oil, erythritol, and mustard. Season to taste with salt and pepper. Drizzle the dressing over the salad and serve immediately.
Per Serving:
calories: 366 | fat: 36g | protein: 9g | carbs: 4g | net carbs: 2g | fiber: 2g

Burger in a Bowl

Prep time: 10 minutes | Cook time: 10 minutes | Serves 2

1 pound (454 g) ground beef	2 tablespoons yellow mustard
(80/20)	1 tablespoon dill relish
¼ teaspoon pink Himalayan sea	1 (8-ounce / 227-g) bag
salt	shredded lettuce
¼ teaspoon freshly ground	½ cup sliced red onion
black pepper	½ cup chopped ripe tomato
¼ cup mayonnaise	1 dill pickle, sliced
2 tablespoons sugar-free	¼ cup shredded Cheddar cheese
ketchup	

1. In a medium sauté pan or skillet, brown the ground beef, stirring, for 7 to 10 minutes. Season with the salt and pepper, then drain the meat, if desired. 2. In a small bowl, combine the mayonnaise, ketchup, mustard, and relish. 3. Fill a large bowl with the shredded lettuce. Top with the beef, red onion, tomato, dill pickle, and cheese. Drizzle the dressing over top and serve.
Per Serving:
calories: 867 | fat: 72g | protein: 45g | carbs: 9g | net carbs: 6g | fiber: 3g

Skirt Steak Cobb Salad

Prep time: 15 minutes | Cook time: 10 minutes | Serves 2

8 ounces skirt steak

Pink Himalayan salt

Freshly ground black pepper

1 tablespoon butter

2 romaine hearts or 2 cups chopped romaine

½ cup halved grape tomatoes

¼ cup crumbled blue cheese

¼ cup pecans

1 tablespoon olive oil

1. Heat a large skillet over high heat. 2. Pat the steak dry with a paper towel, and season both sides with pink Himalayan salt and pepper. 3. Add the butter to the skillet. When it melts, put the steak in the skillet. 4. Sear the steak for about 3 minutes on each side, for medium-rare. 5. Transfer the steak to a cutting board and let it rest for at least 5 minutes. 6. Meanwhile, divide the romaine between two plates, and top with the grape tomato halves, blue cheese, and pecans. Drizzle with the olive oil. 7. Slice the skirt steak across the grain, top the salads with it, and serve.

Per Serving:

calories: 451 | fat: 36g | protein: 30g | carbs: 7g | net carbs: 5g | fiber: 3g

Herbaceous Salad

Prep time: 10 minutes | Cook time: 0 minutes | Serves 8

Dressing:

¼ cup coconut vinegar or white wine vinegar

2 teaspoons Swerve confectioners'-style sweetener or equivalent amount of liquid or powdered sweetener

2 teaspoons Dijon mustard

½ teaspoon fine sea salt

½ teaspoon freshly ground black pepper

½ cup MCT oil or extra-virgin olive oil

Salad:

3 cups fresh basil leaves (preferably purple basil)

3 cups fresh flat-leaf parsley leaves

2 cups arugula leaves

½ cup fresh tarragon leaves

½ cup chopped fresh chives

1. To make the dressing: Place the vinegar, sweetener, mustard, salt, and pepper in a small food processor or blender and pulse until blended. With the machine running, slowly add the oil until the mixture is well combined and velvety. Set aside. 2. In a large bowl, combine the basil, parsley, arugula, tarragon, and chives. Add the dressing and toss to coat. Best served fresh.

Per Serving:

calories: 147 | fat: 14g | protein: 2g | carbs: 3g | net carbs: 2g | fiber: 1g

Chapter 8 Stews and Soups

Shrimp Chowder

Prep time: 10 minutes | Cook time: 40 minutes | Serves 6

¼ cup (60 ml) refined avocado oil or melted ghee (if tolerated)

1⅔ cups (140 g) diced mushrooms

⅓ cup (55 g) diced yellow onions

10½ ounces (300 g) small raw shrimp, shelled and deveined

1 can (13½-ounce/400-ml) full-fat coconut milk

⅓ cup (80 ml) chicken bone broth

2 tablespoons apple cider vinegar

1 teaspoon onion powder

1 teaspoon paprika

1 bay leaf

¾ teaspoon finely ground gray sea salt

½ teaspoon dried oregano leaves

¼ teaspoon ground black pepper

12 radishes (about 6 ounces/170 g), cubed

1 medium zucchini (about 7 ounces/200 g), cubed

1. Heat the avocado oil in a large saucepan on medium for a couple of minutes, then add the mushrooms and onions. Sauté for 8 to 10 minutes, until the onions are translucent and mushrooms are beginning to brown. 2. Add the remaining ingredients, except the radishes and zucchini. Cover and bring to a boil, then reduce the heat to low and simmer for 20 minutes. 3. After 20 minutes, add the radishes and zucchini. Continue to cook for 10 minutes, until the vegetables are fork-tender. 4. Remove the bay leaf, divide among 6 small soup bowls, and enjoy.

Per Serving:
calories: 301 | fat: 23g | protein: 14g | carbs: 7g | net carbs: 5g | fiber: 2g

Broccoli Cheddar Pancetta Soup

Prep time: 15 minutes | Cook time: 30 minutes | Serves 6

2 ounces (57 g) pancetta, diced

2 tablespoons butter or ghee

¼ medium onion, finely chopped (about ½ cup)

3 garlic cloves, minced

3 cups bone broth

½ cup heavy (whipping) cream

2 cups broccoli florets, chopped into bite-size pieces

1 teaspoon garlic powder

1 teaspoon onion powder

1 teaspoon paprika

1 teaspoon salt

½ teaspoon freshly ground black pepper

Pinch cayenne pepper

½ tablespoon gelatin (or ½ teaspoon xanthan or guar gum), for thickening

2 cups shredded sharp Cheddar cheese

1. In a large pot over medium heat, cook the pancetta, stirring often, until crisp. Remove the pancetta pieces to a paper towel using a slotted spoon, leaving as much grease as possible in the pot. 2. Add the butter, onion, and garlic to the pot and sauté for 5 minutes. 3. Add the bone broth, cream, broccoli, garlic, onion, paprika, salt, pepper, and cayenne to the pot and stir well. Sprinkle in the gelatin and stir until well incorporated. Bring to a boil. 4. Once boiling, reduce the heat to low and simmer for 10 to 15 minutes, stirring occasionally. 5. Then, with the heat on low, gradually add the cheese, ½ cup at a time, stirring constantly. Once all of the cheese has been added, remove the pot from the heat. Sprinkle the pancetta pieces over the top and serve. 6. To store, divide the soup into glass jars and freeze for easy meals throughout the coming weeks and months. Make sure to only fill the jars three-quarters full because the liquid will expand as it freezes.

Per Serving:
1½ cups: calories: 311 | fat: 29g | protein: 17g | carbs: 5g | net carbs: 4g | fiber: 1g

Cauliflower Rice and Chicken Thigh Soup

Prep time: 15 minutes | Cook time: 13 minutes | Serves 5

2 cups cauliflower florets

1 pound (454 g) boneless, skinless chicken thighs

4½ cups chicken broth

½ yellow onion, chopped

2 garlic cloves, minced

1 tablespoon unflavored gelatin powder

2 teaspoons sea salt

½ teaspoon ground black

pepper

½ cup sliced zucchini

⅓ cup sliced turnips

1 teaspoon dried parsley

3 celery stalks, chopped

1 teaspoon ground turmeric

½ teaspoon dried marjoram

1 teaspoon dried thyme

½ teaspoon dried oregano

1. Add the cauliflower florets to a food processor and pulse until a ricelike consistency is achieved. Set aside. 2. Add the chicken thighs, chicken broth, onions, garlic, gelatin powder, sea salt, and black pepper to the pot. Gently stir to combine. 3. Lock the lid. Select Manual mode and set cooking time for 10 minutes on High Pressure. 4. When cooking is complete, quick release the pressure and open the lid. 5. Transfer the chicken thighs to a cutting board. Chop the chicken into bite-sized pieces and then return the chopped chicken to the pot. 6. Add the cauliflower rice, zucchini, turnips, parsley, celery, turmeric, marjoram, thyme, and oregano to the pot. Stir to combine. 7. Lock the lid. Select Manual mode and set cooking time for 3 minutes on High Pressure. 8. When cooking is complete, quick release the pressure. 9. Open the lid. Ladle the soup into serving bowls. Serve hot.

Per Serving:
calories: 247 | fat: 10.4g | protein: 30.2g | carbs: 8.3g | net carbs: 6.1g | fiber: 2.2g

Cauliflower Soup

Prep time: 10 minutes | Cook time: 6 minutes | Serves 4

2 cups chopped cauliflower	2 cups beef broth
2 tablespoons fresh cilantro	3 ounces (85 g) Provolone
1 cup coconut cream	cheese, chopped

1. Put cauliflower, cilantro, coconut cream, beef broth, and cheese in the Instant Pot. Stir to mix well. 2. Select Manual mode and set cooking time for 6 minutes on High Pressure. 3. When timer beeps, allow a natural pressure release for 4 minutes, then release any remaining pressure. Open the lid. 4. Blend the soup and ladle in bowls to serve.

Per Serving:
calories: 244 | fat: 21g | protein: 10g | carbs: 7g | net carbs: 4g | fiber: 3g

Broccoli Cheddar Soup

Prep time: 5 minutes | Cook time: 10 minutes | Serves 4

2 tablespoons butter	1 cup chopped broccoli
⅛ cup onion, diced	1 tablespoon cream cheese,
½ teaspoon garlic powder	softened
½ teaspoon salt	¼ cup heavy cream
¼ teaspoon pepper	1 cup shredded Cheddar cheese
2 cups chicken broth	

1. Press the Sauté button and add butter to Instant Pot. Add onion and sauté until translucent. Press the Cancel button and add garlic powder, salt, pepper, broth, and broccoli to pot. 2. Click lid closed. Press the Soup button and set time for 5 minutes. When timer beeps, stir in heavy cream, cream cheese, and Cheddar.

Per Serving:
calories: 250 | fat: 20g | protein: 9g | carbs: 4g | net carbs: 3g | fiber: 1g

Creamy Mushroom Soup

Prep time: 10 minutes | Cook time: 30 minutes | Serves 4

2 slices bacon, cut into ¼-inch dice	homemade or store-bought
	1 teaspoon fine sea salt
2 tablespoons minced shallots or onions	½ teaspoon freshly ground black pepper
1 teaspoon minced garlic	2 large eggs
1 pound (454 g) button mushrooms, cleaned and quartered or sliced	2 tablespoons lemon juice
	For Garnish:
	Fresh thyme leaves
1 teaspoon dried thyme leaves	MCT oil or extra-virgin olive
2 cups chicken bone broth,	oil, for drizzling

1. Place the diced bacon in a stockpot and sauté over medium heat until crispy, about 3 minutes. Remove the bacon from the pan, but leave the drippings. Add the shallots and garlic to the pan with the drippings and sauté over medium heat for about 3 minutes, until softened and aromatic. 2. Add the mushrooms and dried thyme and sauté over medium heat until the mushrooms are golden brown, about 10 minutes. Add the broth, salt, and pepper and bring to boil. 3. Whisk the eggs and lemon juice in a medium bowl. While whisking, very slowly pour in ½ cup of the hot soup (if you add the hot soup too quickly, the eggs will curdle). Slowly whisk another cup of the hot soup into the egg mixture. 4. Pour the hot egg mixture into the pot while stirring. Add the cooked bacon, then reduce the heat and simmer for 10 minutes, stirring constantly. The soup will thicken slightly as it cooks. Remove from the heat. Garnish with fresh thyme and drizzle with MCT oil before serving. 5. This soup is best served fresh but can be stored in an airtight container in the fridge for up to 3 days. To reheat, place in a saucepan over medium-low heat until warmed, stirring constantly to keep the eggs from curdling.

Per Serving:
calories: 185 | fat: 13g | protein: 11g | carbs: 6g | net carbs: 4g | fiber: 2g

Thai Tum Yum Soup

Prep time: 10 minutes | Cook time: 20 minutes | serves 8

8 cups vegetable broth	½ yellow onion, coarsely
1-inch knob fresh ginger, peeled and diced	chopped
	1 cup coarsely chopped broccoli
2 garlic cloves, diced	1 cup coarsely chopped
1 teaspoon galangal	cauliflower
2 kefir lime leaves	1 cup chopped fresh cilantro,
1 cup coconut cream	for garnish
1 cup sliced mushrooms	1 lime, cut into wedges, for
1 Roma tomato, coarsely chopped	garnish

1. In a large stockpot over medium heat, bring the broth to a simmer with the ginger, garlic, galangal, and lime leaves. 2. Pour in the coconut cream, followed by the mushrooms, tomato, onion, broccoli, and cauliflower. Simmer until tender. 3. Remove the pot from the heat and serve the soup garnished with the cilantro and a lime slice.

Per Serving:
calories: 97 | fat: 7g | protein: 1g | carbs: 9g | net carbs: 6g | fiber: 3g

Salmon and Tomatillos Stew

Prep time: 15 minutes | Cook time: 12 minutes | Serves 2

10 ounces (283 g) salmon fillet, chopped	1 cup coconut cream
	1 teaspoon ground paprika
2 tomatillos, chopped	½ teaspoon salt
½ teaspoon ground turmeric	

1. Put all ingredients in the Instant Pot. Stir to mix well. 2. Close the lid. Select Manual mode and set cooking time for 12 minutes on Low Pressure. 3. When timer beeps, use a quick pressure release. Open the lid. 4. Serve warm.

Per Serving:
calories: 479 | fat: 37.9g | protein: 30.8g | carbs: 9.6g | net carbs: 5.8g | fiber: 3.8g

Broccoli and Bacon Cheese Soup

Prep time: 6 minutes | Cook time: 10 minutes | Serves 6

3 tablespoons butter

2 stalks celery, diced

½ yellow onion, diced

3 garlic cloves, minced

3½ cups chicken stock

4 cups chopped fresh broccoli florets

3 ounces (85 g) block-style cream cheese, softened and cubed

½ teaspoon ground nutmeg

½ teaspoon sea salt

1 teaspoon ground black pepper

3 cups shredded Cheddar cheese

½ cup shredded Monterey Jack cheese

2 cups heavy cream

4 slices cooked bacon, crumbled

1 tablespoon finely chopped chives

1. Select Sauté mode. Once the Instant Pot is hot, add the butter and heat until the butter is melted. 2. Add the celery, onions, and garlic. Continue sautéing for 5 minutes or until the vegetables are softened. 3. Add the chicken stock and broccoli florets to the pot. Bring the liquid to a boil. 4. Lock the lid,. Select Manual mode and set cooking time for 5 minutes on High Pressure. 5. When cooking is complete, allow the pressure to release naturally for 10 minutes and then release the remaining pressure. 6. Open the lid and add the cream cheese, nutmeg, sea salt, and black pepper. Stir to combine. 7. Select Sauté mode. Bring the soup to a boil and then slowly stir in the Cheddar and Jack cheeses. Once the cheese has melted, stir in the heavy cream. 8. Ladle the soup into serving bowls and top with bacon and chives. Serve hot.

Per Serving:
calories: 681 | fat: 59.0g | protein: 27.4g | carbs: 11.6g | net carbs: 10.3g | fiber: 1.3g

Thai Shrimp and Mushroom Soup

Prep time: 15 minutes | Cook time: 10 minutes | Serves 6

2 tablespoons unsalted butter, divided

½ pound (227 g) medium uncooked shrimp, shelled and deveined

½ medium yellow onion, diced

2 cloves garlic, minced

1 cup sliced fresh white mushrooms

1 tablespoon freshly grated ginger root

4 cups chicken broth

2 tablespoons fish sauce

2½ teaspoons red curry paste

2 tablespoons lime juice

1 stalk lemongrass, outer stalk removed, crushed, and finely chopped

2 tablespoons coconut aminos

1 teaspoon sea salt

½ teaspoon ground black pepper

13.5 ounces (383 g) can unsweetened, full-fat coconut milk

3 tablespoons chopped fresh cilantro

1. Select the Instant Pot on Sauté mode. Add 1 tablespoon butter. 2. Once the butter is melted, add the shrimp and sauté for 3 minutes or until opaque. Transfer the shrimp to a medium bowl. Set aside. 3. Add the remaining butter to the pot. Once the butter is melted, add the onions and garlic and sauté for 2 minutes or until the garlic

is fragrant and the onions are softened. 4. Add the mushrooms, ginger root, chicken broth, fish sauce, red curry paste, lime juice, lemongrass, coconut aminos, sea salt, and black pepper to the pot. Stir to combine. 5. Lock the lid. Select Manual mode and set cooking time for 5 minutes on High Pressure. 6. When cooking is complete, allow the pressure to release naturally for 5 minutes, then release the remaining pressure. 7. Open the lid. Stir in the cooked shrimp and coconut milk. 8. Select Sauté mode. Bring the soup to a boil and then press Keep Warm / Cancel. Let the soup rest in the pot for 2 minutes. 9. Ladle the soup into bowls and sprinkle the cilantro over top. Serve hot.

Per Serving:
calories: 237 | fat: 20.0g | protein: 9.1g | carbs: 8.5g | net carbs: 6.3g | fiber: 2.2g

Garlicky Chicken Soup

Prep time: 5 minutes | Cook time: 20 minutes | Serves 6

10 roasted garlic cloves

½ medium onion, diced

4 tablespoons butter

4 cups chicken broth

½ teaspoon salt

¼ teaspoon pepper

1 teaspoon thyme

1 pound (454 g) boneless, skinless chicken thighs, cubed

½ cup heavy cream

2 ounces (57 g) cream cheese

1. In small bowl, mash roasted garlic into paste. Press the Sauté button and add garlic, onion, and butter to Instant Pot. Sauté for 2 to 3 minutes until onion begins to soften. Press the Cancel button. 2. Add Chicken Broth, salt, pepper, thyme, and chicken to Instant Pot. Click lid closed. Press the Manual button and adjust time for 20 minutes. 3. When timer beeps, quick-release the pressure. Stir in heavy cream and cream cheese until smooth. Serve warm.

Per Serving:
calories: 291 | fat: 21g | protein: 17g | carbs: 4g | net carbs: 3g | fiber: 1g

Salsa Verde Chicken Soup

Prep time: 5 minutes | Cook time: 10 minutes | Serves 4

½ cup salsa verde

2 cups cooked and shredded chicken

2 cups chicken broth

1 cup shredded cheddar cheese

4 ounces cream cheese

½ tsp chili powder

½ tsp ground cumin

½ tsp fresh cilantro, chopped

Salt and black pepper, to taste

1. Combine the cream cheese, salsa verde, and broth, in a food processor; pulse until smooth. Transfer the mixture to a pot and place over medium heat. Cook until hot, but do not bring to a boil. Add chicken, chili powder, and cumin and cook for about 3-5 minutes, or until it is heated through. 2. Stir in cheddar cheese and season with salt and pepper to taste. If it is very thick, add a few tablespoons of water and boil for 1-3 more minutes. Serve hot in bowls sprinkled with fresh cilantro.

Per Serving:
calories: 346 | fat: 23g | protein: 25g | carbs: 4g | net carbs: 3g | fiber: 1g

Broccoli and Red Feta Soup

Prep time: 10 minutes | Cook time: 25 minutes | Serves 4

1 cup broccoli, chopped	4 cups beef broth
½ cup coconut cream	1 teaspoon chili flakes
1 teaspoon unsweetened tomato purée	6 ounces (170 g) feta, crumbled

1. Put broccoli, coconut cream, tomato purée, and beef broth in the Instant Pot. Sprinkle with chili flakes and stir to mix well. 2. Close the lid and select Manual mode. Set cooking time for 8 minutes on High Pressure. 3. When timer beeps, make a quick pressure release and open the lid. 4. Add the feta cheese and stir the soup on Sauté mode for 5 minutes or until the cheese melt. 5. Serve immediately.

Per Serving:
calories: 229 | fat: 17.7g | protein: 12.3g | carbs: 6.1g | net carbs: 4.8g | fiber: 1.3g

Beef and Okra Stew

Prep time: 15 minutes | Cook time: 25 minutes | Serves 3

8 ounces (227 g) beef sirloin, chopped	1 tablespoon avocado oil
¼ teaspoon cumin seeds	¼ cup coconut cream
1 teaspoon dried basil	1 cup water
	6 ounces (170 g) okra, chopped

1. Sprinkle the beef sirloin with cumin seeds and dried basil and put in the Instant Pot. 2. Add avocado oil and roast the meat on Sauté mode for 5 minutes. Flip occasionally. 3. Add coconut cream, water, and okra. 4. Close the lid and select Manual mode. Set cooking time for 25 minutes on High Pressure. 5. When timer beeps, use a natural pressure release for 10 minutes, the release any remaining pressure. Open the lid. 6. Serve warm.

Per Serving:
calories: 216 | fat: 10.2g | protein: 24.6g | carbs: 5.7g | net carbs: 3.2g | fiber: 2.5g

Cauliflower & Blue Cheese Soup

Prep time: 15 minutes | Cook time: 20 minutes | Serves 5

2 tablespoons extra-virgin avocado oil	whipping cream
1 small red onion, diced	Salt and black pepper, to taste
1 medium celery stalk, sliced	1 cup crumbled goat's or sheep's blue cheese, such as Roquefort
1 medium cauliflower, cut into small florets	2 tablespoons chopped fresh chives
2 cups vegetable or chicken stock	5 tablespoons extra-virgin olive oil
¼ cup goat's cream or heavy	

1. Heat a medium saucepan greased with the avocado oil over medium heat. Sweat the onion and celery for 3 to 5 minutes, until soft and fragrant. Add the cauliflower florets and cook for 5 minutes. Add the vegetable stock and bring to a boil. Cook for about 10 minutes, or until the cauliflower is tender. Remove from

the heat and let cool for a few minutes. 2. Add the cream. Use an immersion blender, or pour into a blender, to process until smooth and creamy. Season with salt and pepper to taste. Divide the soup between serving bowls and top with the crumbled blue cheese, chives, and olive oil. To store, let cool and refrigerate in a sealed container for up to 5 days.

Per Serving:
calories: 337 | fat: 30g | protein: 10g | carbs: 9g | fiber: 3g | sodium: 383mg

Cabbage Soup

Prep time: 20 minutes | Cook time: 30 minutes | Serves 6

1 tablespoon olive oil	2 tablespoons tomato paste
3 garlic cloves, minced	2 (32-ounce / 907-g) cartons chicken broth
1 onion, diced	
3 carrots, diced	1 large head cabbage, chopped
1 celery stalk, diced	1 teaspoon dried oregano
½ green bell pepper, diced	1 teaspoon dried thyme
Salt and freshly ground black pepper, to taste	Grated Parmesan cheese, for topping
1 cup chopped kale	

1. In a large saucepan over medium heat, heat the olive oil. 2. Add the garlic and onion. Sauté for 5 minutes. 3. Add the carrots and celery. Cook for 5 to 7 minutes until softened. 4. Add the bell pepper and stir well to combine. Cook for 5 to 7 minutes more. Season with salt and pepper and add the kale. 5. Stir in the tomato paste until well combined. 6. Pour in the chicken broth and bring the soup to a gentle boil. 7. Add the cabbage, oregano, and thyme. Season with more salt and pepper. Reduce the heat to low, cover the pan, and simmer for 15 minutes (a little longer if you have the time). Ladle into bowls and top with Parmesan before serving.

Per Serving:
calories: 156 | fat: 5g | protein: 10g | carbs: 23g | net carbs: 16g | fiber: 7g

Cream of Mushroom Soup

Prep time: 10 minutes | Cook time: 10 minutes | Serves 4

1 pound (454 g) sliced button mushrooms	2 cups chicken broth
3 tablespoons butter	½ teaspoon salt
2 tablespoons diced onion	¼ teaspoon pepper
2 cloves garlic, minced	½ cup heavy cream
	¼ teaspoon xanthan gum

1. Press the Sauté button and then press the Adjust button to set heat to Less. Add mushrooms, butter, and onion to pot. Sauté for 5 to 8 minutes or until onions and mushrooms begin to brown. Add garlic and sauté until fragrant. Press the Cancel button. 2. Add broth, salt, and pepper. Click lid closed. Press the Manual button and adjust time for 3 minutes. When timer beeps, quick-release the pressure. Stir in heavy cream and xanthan gum. Allow a few minutes to thicken and serve warm.

Per Serving:
calories: 220 | fat: 19g | protein: 5g | carbs: 6g | net carbs: 5g | fiber: 1g

Broccoli-Cheese Soup

Prep time: 5 minutes | Cook time: 20 minutes | Serves 4

2 tablespoons butter	Pink Himalayan salt
1 cup broccoli florets, finely chopped	Freshly ground black pepper
1 cup heavy (whipping) cream	1 cup shredded cheese, some reserved for topping (I use sharp Cheddar)
1 cup chicken or vegetable broth	

1. In a medium saucepan over medium heat, melt the butter. 2. Add the broccoli and sauté in the butter for about 5 minutes, until tender. 3. Add the cream and the chicken broth, stirring constantly. Season with pink Himalayan salt and pepper. Cook, stirring occasionally, for 10 to 15 minutes, until the soup has thickened. 4. Turn down the heat to low, and begin adding the shredded cheese. Reserve a small handful of cheese for topping the bowls of soup. (Do not add all the cheese at once, or it may clump up.) Add small amounts, slowly, while stirring constantly. 5. Pour the soup into four bowls, top each with half of the reserved cheese, and serve.

Per Serving:
calories: 383 | fat: 37g | protein: 10g | carbs: 4g | net carbs: 4g | fiber: 0g

Mexican Chicken Soup

Prep time: 5 minutes | Cook time: 20 minutes | Serves 4

¼ cup (60 ml) avocado oil	vinegar
1 small white onion, diced	1 teaspoon ground cumin
2 cloves garlic, minced	1 teaspoon dried oregano leaves
1 red bell pepper, diced	1 teaspoon paprika
1 pound (455 g) boneless, skinless chicken breasts, thinly sliced	¾ teaspoon finely ground sea salt
1 (14½-oz/410-g) can fire-roasted whole tomatoes	1 cup (140 g) shredded cheddar cheese (dairy-free or regular) (optional)
1½ cups (355 ml) chicken bone broth	2 medium Hass avocados, peeled, pitted, and sliced (about 8 oz/220 g of flesh)
1 cup (240 ml) full-fat coconut milk	Handful of fresh cilantro leaves
1 tablespoon apple cider	

1. Heat the oil in a large saucepan over medium heat. Add the onion, garlic, and bell pepper and sauté until fragrant, about 5 minutes. 2. Add the chicken, tomatoes, broth, coconut milk, vinegar, cumin, oregano, paprika, and salt. Stir to combine, cover, and bring to a light simmer over medium-high heat. Once simmering, reduce the heat and continue to simmer for 15 minutes, until the chicken is cooked through and the bell peppers are soft. 3. When the soup is done, divide evenly among 4 bowls. Top each bowl with ¼ cup (35 g) of the cheese (if using), one-quarter of the avocado slices, and a sprinkle of cilantro.

Per Serving:
calories: 602 | fat: 45g | protein: 31g | carbs: 21g | net carbs: 8g | fiber: 13g

Beef Reuben Soup

Prep time: 10 minutes | Cook time: 20 minutes | Serves 6

1 onion, diced	1 cup sauerkraut, shredded
6 cups beef stock	1 pound corned beef, chopped
1tsp caraway seeds	3 tbsp butter
2celery stalks, diced	1 ½ cup swiss cheese, shredded
2 garlic cloves, minced	Salt and black pepper, to taste
2 cups heavy cream	

1. Melt the butter in a large pot. Add onion and celery, and fry for 3 minutes until tender. Add garlic and cook for another minute. 2. Pour the beef stock over and stir in sauerkraut, salt, caraway seeds, and add a pinch of black pepper. Bring to a boil. Reduce the heat to low, and add the corned beef. Cook for about 15 minutes, adjust the seasoning. Stir in heavy cream and cheese and cook for 1 minute.

Per Serving:
calories: 595| fat: 37g | protein: 36g | carbs: 32g | net carbs: 29g | fiber: 3g

Butternut Squash Soup with Turmeric & Ginger

Prep time: 5 minutes | Cook time: 35 minutes | serves 8

1 small butternut squash	½ cup dry Marsala wine (optional)
3 tablespoons coconut oil	8 cups miso broth
3 shallots, coarsely chopped	1 cup coconut cream
1-inch knob fresh ginger, peeled and coarsely chopped	Cold-pressed olive oil, for drizzling
1-inch knob fresh turmeric root, peeled and coarsely chopped	Handful toasted pumpkin seeds, for garnish (optional)
1 fresh lemongrass stalk, coarsely chopped	

1. Preheat the oven to 365°F. 2. Puncture the squash skin with a fork several times to create air vents. Put the entire squash into a baking dish and bake for 30 minutes or until it is extremely tender. 3. While the squash is baking, heat the oil in a large stockpot over medium heat. Add the shallots, ginger, turmeric, and lemongrass to the pan and sauté until the spices become fragrant and the shallots are tender. 4. Deglaze the pot by pouring in the Marsala wine (if using), and stirring, scraping the bottom of the pot to loosen any stuck bits. Once the alcohol starts to reduce, add the miso broth and turn the heat to low. 5. Remove the squash from oven and poke it with a fork to check for tenderness. Carefully cut the squash in half lengthwise, allowing any liquid to drain out. 6. Once the squash is cool enough to handle, scoop out the seeds. With a paring knife, remove the skin. Roughly chop the squash and add it to the stockpot. 7. Pour the coconut cream into the pot, bring to a simmer, and remove from the heat. 8. Using an immersion blender, blend the soup thoroughly until smooth and velvety. Drizzle with olive oil, and top with toasted pumpkin seeds, if desired. Serve warm.

Per Serving:
calories: 149 | fat: 13g | protein: 2g | carbs: 10g | net carbs: 9g | fiber: 1g

Easy Chili

Prep time: 10 minutes | Cook time: 35 minutes | Serves 6 to 8

2 pounds ground beef

2 tablespoons dried minced onions

2 teaspoons minced garlic

1 (15-ounce) can tomato sauce

1 (14½-ounce) can petite diced tomatoes

1 cup water

2 tablespoons chili powder

1 tablespoon ground cumin

½ teaspoon salt

½ teaspoon ground black pepper

SUGGESTED TOPPINGS:

Sour cream

Sliced green onions or chopped white onions

Shredded cheddar cheese

1. Cook the ground beef, onions, and garlic in a stockpot over medium heat, crumbling the meat with a large spoon as it cooks, until the meat is browned, about 10 minutes. Drain the fat, if necessary. 2. Add the tomato sauce, tomatoes, water, chili powder, cumin, salt, and pepper to the pot. Bring to a boil, then reduce the heat to low and simmer for 20 minutes to allow the flavors to develop and the chili to thicken slightly. 3. Garnish with the chili topping(s) of your choice and serve. Leftovers can be stored in an airtight container in the refrigerator for up to 5 days.

Per Serving:
calories: 429 | fat: 31g | protein: 27g | carbs: 9g | net carbs: 6g | fiber: 3g

Tomato Bisque

Prep time: 10 minutes | Cook time: 40 minutes | serves 8

Nonstick coconut oil cooking spray

1 pound heirloom cherry tomatoes, coarsely chopped

1 yellow onion, coarsely chopped

2 garlic cloves, coarsely chopped

¼ cup cold-pressed olive oil,

plus more for drizzling

2 thyme sprigs

Sea salt

Freshly ground black pepper

1 lemon, halved

1 cup coconut cream

⅓ cup chopped fresh basil, for garnish

1. Preheat the oven to 400°F. Grease a baking dish with cooking spray and set aside. 2. Combine the tomatoes, onion, and garlic in the baking dish. Drizzle with the olive oil and toss in the thyme. Season with salt and pepper. Top with the lemon halves and roast for 20 minutes or until the tomatoes start to blister. 3. Remove from the oven and transfer the mixture to a large saucepan over low heat. 4. Stir in the coconut cream and bring the soup to a simmer. Cook for 20 minutes to allow the flavors to meld together. 5. Remove and discard the lemon halves. 6. Turn off the heat and blend the soup with an immersion blender until it is silky smooth (adding warm water if necessary to reach desired texture). 7. Finish with cracked black pepper, olive oil drizzle, the basil, and additional salt, if desired.

Per Serving:
calories: 142 | fat: 14g | protein: 1g | carbs: 7g | net carbs: 5g | fiber: 2g

Cabbage and Pork Soup

Prep time: 10 minutes | Cook time: 12 minutes | Serves 3

1 teaspoon butter

½ cup shredded white cabbage

½ teaspoon ground coriander

½ teaspoon salt

½ teaspoon chili flakes

2 cups chicken broth

½ cup ground pork

1. Melt the butter in the Instant Pot on Sauté mode. 2. Add cabbage and sprinkle with ground coriander, salt, and chili flakes. 3. Fold in the chicken broth and ground pork. 4. Close the lid and select Manual mode. Set cooking time for 12 minutes on High Pressure. 5. When timer beeps, use a quick pressure release. Open the lid. 6. Ladle the soup and serve warm.

Per Serving:
calories: 350 | fat: 23.9g | protein: 30.2g | carbs: 1.3g | net carbs: 1.0g | fiber: 0.3g

Bacon Broccoli Soup

Prep time: 12 minutes | Cook time: 12 minutes | Serves 6

2 large heads broccoli

2 strips bacon, chopped

2 tablespoons unsalted butter

¼ cup diced onions

Cloves squeezed from 1 head roasted garlic, or 2 cloves garlic, minced

3 cups chicken broth or beef broth

6 ounces (170 g) extra-sharp Cheddar cheese, shredded (about 1½ cups)

2 ounces (57 g) cream cheese, softened

½ teaspoon fine sea salt

¼ teaspoon ground black pepper

Pinch of ground nutmeg

1. Cut the broccoli florets off the stems, leaving as much of the stems intact as possible. Reserve the florets for another recipe. Trim the bottom end of each stem so that it is flat. Using a spiral slicer, cut the stems into "noodles." 2. Place the bacon in the Instant Pot and press Sauté. Cook, stirring occasionally, for 4 minutes, or until crisp. Remove the bacon with a slotted spoon and set aside on a paper towel-lined plate to drain, leaving the drippings in the pot. 3. Add the butter and onions to the Instant Pot and cook for 4 minutes, or until the onions are soft. Add the garlic (and, if using raw garlic, sauté for another minute). Add the broth, Cheddar cheese, cream cheese, salt, pepper, and nutmeg and sauté until the cheeses are melted, about 3 minutes. Press Cancel to stop the Sauté. 4. Use a stick blender to purée the soup until smooth. Alternatively, you can pour the soup into a regular blender or food processor and purée until smooth, then return it to the Instant Pot. If using a regular blender, you may need to blend the soup in two batches; if you overfill the blender jar, the soup will not purée properly. 5. Add the broccoli noodles to the puréed soup in the Instant Pot. Seal the lid, press Manual, and set the timer for 1 minute. Once finished, let the pressure release naturally. 6. Remove the lid and stir well. Ladle the soup into bowls and sprinkle some of the bacon on top of each serving.

Per Serving:
calories: 258 | fat: 19g | protein: 13g | carbs: 9g | net carbs: 8g | fiber: 1g

Chicken Poblano Pepper Soup

Prep time: 10 minutes | Cook time: 20 minutes | Serves 8

1 cup diced onion

3 poblano peppers, chopped

5 garlic cloves

2 cups diced cauliflower

1½ pounds (680 g) chicken breast, cut into large chunks

¼ cup chopped fresh cilantro

1 teaspoon ground coriander

1 teaspoon ground cumin

1 to 2 teaspoons salt

2 cups water

2 ounces (57 g) cream cheese, cut into small chunks

1 cup sour cream

1. To the inner cooking pot of the Instant Pot, add the onion, poblanos, garlic, cauliflower, chicken, cilantro, coriander, cumin, salt, and water. 2. Lock the lid into place. Select Manual and adjust the pressure to High. Cook for 15 minutes. When the cooking is complete, let the pressure release naturally for 10 minutes, then quick-release any remaining pressure. Unlock the lid. 3. Remove the chicken with tongs and place in a bowl. 4. Tilting the pot, use an immersion blender to roughly purée the vegetable mixture. It should still be slightly chunky. 5. Turn the Instant Pot to Sauté and adjust to high heat. When the broth is hot and bubbling, add the cream cheese and stir until it melts. Use a whisk to blend in the cream cheese if needed. 6. Shred the chicken and stir it back into the pot. Once it is heated through, serve, topped with sour cream, and enjoy.

Per Serving:

calories: 202 | fat: 10g | protein: 20g | carbs: 8g | net carbs: 5g | fiber: 3g

Keto Pho with Shirataki Noodles

Prep time: 20 minutes | Cook time: 10 minutes | Makes 4 bowls

8 ounces (227 g) sirloin, very thinly sliced

3 tablespoons coconut oil (or butter or ghee)

2 garlic cloves, minced

2 tablespoons liquid or coconut aminos

2 tablespoons fish sauce

1 teaspoon freshly grated or

ground ginger

8 cups bone broth

4 (7-ounce / 198-g) packages shirataki noodles, drained and rinsed

1 cup bean sprouts

1 scallion, chopped

1 tablespoon toasted sesame seeds (optional)

1. Put the sirloin in the freezer while you prepare the broth and other ingredients (about 15 to 20 minutes). This makes it easier to slice. 2. In a large pot over medium heat, melt the coconut oil. Add the garlic and cook for 3 minutes. Then add the aminos, fish sauce, ginger, and bone broth. Bring to a boil. 3. Remove the beef from the freezer and slice it very thin. 4. Divide the noodles, beef, and bean sprouts evenly among four serving bowls. Carefully ladle 2 cups of broth into each bowl. Cover the bowls with plates and let sit for 3 to 5 minutes to cook the meat. 5. Serve garnished with the chopped scallion and sesame seeds (if using).

Per Serving:

1 bowl: calories: 385 | fat: 29g | protein: 23g | carbs: 8g | net carbs: 4g | fiber: 4g

Greek Chicken and "Rice" Soup with Artichokes

Prep time: 10 minutes | Cook time: 15 minutes | Serves 4

4 cups chicken stock

2 cups riced cauliflower, divided

2 large egg yolks

¼ cup freshly squeezed lemon juice (about 2 lemons)

¾ cup extra-virgin olive oil,

divided

8 ounces (227 g) cooked chicken, coarsely chopped

1 (13¾-ounce / 390-g) can artichoke hearts, drained and quartered

¼ cup chopped fresh dill

1. In a large saucepan, bring the stock to a low boil. Reduce the heat to low and simmer, covered. 2. Transfer 1 cup of the hot stock to a blender or food processor. Add ½ cup raw riced cauliflower, the egg yolks, and lemon juice and purée. While the processor or blender is running, stream in ½ cup olive oil and blend until smooth. 3. Whisking constantly, pour the purée into the simmering stock until well blended together and smooth. Add the chicken and artichokes and simmer until thickened slightly, 8 to 10 minutes. Stir in the dill and remaining 1½ cups riced cauliflower. Serve warm, drizzled with the remaining ¼ cup olive oil.

Per Serving:

calories: 583 | fat: 47g | protein: 26g | carbs: 19g | fiber: 10g | sodium: 189mg

Bacon, Leek, and Cauliflower Soup

Prep time: 15 minutes | Cook time: 15 minutes | Serves 6

6 slices bacon

1 leek, remove the dark green end and roots, sliced in half lengthwise, rinsed, cut into ½-inch-thick slices crosswise

½ medium yellow onion, sliced

4 cloves garlic, minced

3 cups chicken broth

1 large head cauliflower, roughly chopped into florets

1 cup water

1 teaspoon kosher salt

1 teaspoon ground black pepper

⅔ cup shredded sharp Cheddar cheese, divided

½ cup heavy whipping cream

1. Set the Instant Pot to Sauté mode. When heated, place the bacon on the bottom of the pot and cook for 5 minutes or until crispy. 2. Transfer the bacon slices to a plate. Let stand until cool enough to handle, crumble it with forks. 3. Add the leek and onion to the bacon fat remaining in the pot. Sauté for 5 minutes or until fragrant and the onion begins to caramelize. Add the garlic and sauté for 30 seconds more or until fragrant. 4. Stir in the chicken broth, cauliflower florets, water, salt, pepper, and three-quarters of the crumbled bacon. 5. Secure the lid. Press the Manual button and set cooking time for 3 minutes on High Pressure. 6. When timer beeps, perform a quick pressure release. Open the lid. 7. Stir in ½ cup of the Cheddar and the cream. Use an immersion blender to purée the soup until smooth. 8. Ladle into bowls and garnish with the remaining Cheddar and crumbled bacon. Serve immediately.

Per Serving:

calories: 251 | fat: 18.9g | protein: 10.5g | carbs: 12.0g | net carbs: 8.6g | fiber: 3.4g

Beef and Eggplant Tagine

Prep time: 15 minutes | Cook time: 25 minutes | Serves 6

1 pound (454 g) beef fillet, chopped	4 cups beef broth
1 eggplant, chopped	1 teaspoon ground allspices
6 ounces (170 g) scallions, chopped	1 teaspoon erythritol
	1 teaspoon coconut oil

1. Put all ingredients in the Instant Pot. Stir to mix well. 2. Close the lid. Select Manual mode and set cooking time for 25 minutes on High Pressure. 3. When timer beeps, use a natural pressure release for 15 minutes, then release any remaining pressure. Open the lid. 4. Serve warm.
Per Serving:
calories: 158 | fat: 5.3g | protein: 21.1g | carbs: 8.2g | net carbs: 4.7g | fiber: 3.5g

Broccoli Ginger Soup

Prep time: 5 minutes | Cook time: 25 minutes | Serves 4

3 tablespoons coconut oil or avocado oil	1 (2-in/5-cm) piece fresh ginger root, peeled and minced
1 small white onion, sliced	1½ teaspoons turmeric powder
2 cloves garlic, minced	¾ teaspoon finely ground sea salt
5 cups (420 g) broccoli florets	
1 (13½-oz/400-ml) can full-fat coconut milk	⅓ cup (55 g) collagen peptides (optional)
1½ cups (355 ml) chicken bone broth	¼ cup (40 g) sesame seeds

1. Melt the oil in a large frying pan over medium heat. Add the onion and garlic and cook until translucent, about 10 minutes. 2. Add the broccoli, coconut milk, broth, ginger, turmeric, and salt. Cover and cook for 15 minutes, or until the broccoli is tender. 3. Transfer the broccoli mixture to a blender or food processor. Add the collagen, if using, and blend until smooth. 4. Divide among 4 bowls, top each bowl with 1 tablespoon of sesame seeds, and enjoy!
Per Serving:
calories: 344 | fat: 26g | protein: 13g | carbs: 12g | net carbs: 7g | fiber: 5g

Slow Cooker Beer Soup with Cheddar & Sausage

Prep time: 15 minutes | Cook time: 8 hours | Serves 8

1 cup heavy cream	6 ounces beer
10 ounces sausages, sliced	16 ounces beef stock
1 cup celery, chopped	1 onion, diced
1 cup carrots, chopped	1 cup cheddar cheese, grated
4 garlic cloves, minced	Salt and black pepper, to taste
8 ounces cream cheese	Fresh cilantro, chopped, to garnish
1 tsp red pepper flakes	

1. Turn on the slow cooker. Add beef stock, beer, sausages, carrots, onion, garlic, celery, salt, red pepper flakes, and black pepper, and stir to combine. Pour in enough water to cover all the ingredients by roughly 2 inches. Close the lid and cook for 6 hours on Low. 2. Open the lid and stir in the heavy cream, cheddar, and cream cheese, and cook for 2 more hours. Ladle the soup into bowls and garnish with cilantro before serving. Yummy!
Per Serving:
calories: 387| fat: 28g | protein: 24g | carbs: 12g | net carbs: 9g | fiber: 2g

Cabbage Roll Soup

Prep time: 10 minutes | Cook time: 8 minutes | Serves 4

½ pound (227 g) 84% lean ground pork	paste
	½ cup diced tomatoes
½ pound (227 g) 85% lean ground beef	2 cups chicken broth
	1 teaspoon salt
½ medium onion, diced	½ teaspoon thyme
½ medium head cabbage, thinly sliced	½ teaspoon garlic powder
	¼ teaspoon pepper
2 tablespoons sugar-free tomato	

1. Press the Sauté button and add beef and pork to Instant Pot. Brown meat until no pink remains. Add onion and continue cooking until onions are fragrant and soft. Press the Cancel button. 2. Add remaining ingredients to Instant Pot. Press the Manual button and adjust time for 8 minutes. 3. When timer beeps, allow a 15-minute natural release and then quick-release the remaining pressure. Serve warm.
Per Serving:
calories: 304 | fat: 16g | protein: 24g | carbs: 12g | net carbs: 8g | fiber: 4g

Chili-Infused Lamb Soup

Prep time: 5 minutes | Cook time: 25 minutes | Serves 6

1 tablespoon coconut oil	2 cups coconut milk
¾ pound ground lamb	1½ tablespoons red chili paste
2 cups shredded cabbage	or as much as you want
½ onion, chopped	Zest and juice of 1 lime
2 teaspoons minced garlic	1 cup shredded kale
4 cups chicken broth	

1. Cook the lamb. In a medium stockpot over medium-high heat, warm the coconut oil. Add the lamb and cook it, stirring it often, until it has browned, about 6 minutes. 2. Cook the vegetables. Add the cabbage, onion, and garlic and sauté until they've softened, about 5 minutes. 3. Simmer the soup. Stir in the chicken broth, coconut milk, red chili paste, lime zest, and lime juice. Bring it to a boil, then reduce the heat to low and simmer until the cabbage is tender, about 10 minutes. 4. Add the kale. Stir in the kale and simmer the soup for 3 more minutes. 5. Serve. Spoon the soup into six bowls and serve.
Per Serving:
calories: 380 | fat: 32g | protein: 17g | carbs: 7g | net carbs: 6g | fiber: 1g

Vegan Pho

Prep time: 10 minutes | Cook time: 20 minutes | serves 8

8 cups vegetable broth

1-inch knob fresh ginger, peeled and chopped

2 tablespoons tamari

3 cups shredded fresh spinach

2 cups chopped broccoli

1 cup sliced mushrooms

½ cup chopped carrots

⅓ cup chopped scallions

1 (8-ounce) package shirataki noodles

2 cups shredded cabbage

2 cups mung bean sprouts

Fresh Thai basil leaves, for garnish

Fresh cilantro leaves, for garnish

Fresh mint leaves, for garnish

1 lime, cut into 8 wedges, for garnish

1. In a large stockpot over medium-high heat, bring the vegetable broth to a simmer with the ginger and tamari. 2. Once the broth is hot, add the spinach, broccoli, mushrooms, carrots, and scallions, and simmer for a few minutes, just until the vegetables start to become tender. 3. Stir in the shirataki noodles, then remove the pot from the heat and divide the soup among serving bowls. 4. Top each bowl with cabbage, sprouts, basil, cilantro, mint, and a lime wedge.

Per Serving:
calories: 47 | fat: 0g | protein: 3g | carbs: 10g | net carbs: 7g | fiber: 3g

OG Zuppa Toscana Soup

Prep time: 20 minutes | Cook time: 51 minutes | Serves 8

1 pound loose Italian sausage

1 tablespoon unsalted butter

1½ cups chopped onion

3 cloves garlic, peeled and minced

8 cups water

2 (1 teaspoon) chicken bouillon cubes

½ pound no-sugar-added bacon, cooked and crumbled

4 cups chopped cauliflower, chopped into bite-sized chunks

4 cups chopped kale

1½ cups heavy whipping cream

1. In a medium-sized skillet over medium heat, cook sausage 10–15 minutes while stirring until brown. Drain fat. 2. In a large soup pot over medium heat, melt butter and then add onion. Sauté 3–5 minutes until soft and clear. Add garlic and cook 1 more minute. Add water and bouillon cubes. 3. Add crumbled bacon, cauliflower, and cooked sausage to pot. 4. When water reaches boil, reduce heat to low, cover pot, and simmer 15–20 minutes, stirring regularly until cauliflower reaches desired softness. 5. Add kale and cream. Cook, stirring regularly, for 10 minutes. 6. Let cool 10 minutes and then serve.

Per Serving:
calories: 488| fat: 39g | protein: 21g | carbs: 10g | net carbs: 8g | fiber: 2g

Chicken Zucchini Soup

Prep time: 8 minutes | Cook time: 14 minutes | Serves 6

¼ cup coconut oil or unsalted butter

1 cup chopped celery

¼ cup chopped onions

2 cloves garlic, minced

1 pound (454 g) boneless, skinless chicken breasts, cut into 1-inch cubes

6 cups chicken broth

1 tablespoon dried parsley

1 teaspoon fine sea salt

½ teaspoon dried marjoram

½ teaspoon ground black pepper

1 bay leaf

2 cups zucchini noodles

1. Place the coconut oil in the Instant Pot and press Sauté. Once melted, add the celery, onions, and garlic and cook, stirring occasionally, for 4 minutes, or until the onions are soft. Press Cancel to stop the Sauté. 2. Add the cubed chicken, broth, parsley, salt, marjoram, pepper, and bay leaf. Seal the lid, press Manual, and set the timer for 10 minutes. Once finished, let the pressure release naturally. 3. Remove the lid and stir well. Place the noodles in bowls, using ⅓ cup per bowl. Ladle the soup over the noodles and serve immediately; if it sits too long, the noodles will get too soft.

Per Serving:
calories: 253 | fat: 15g | protein: 21g | carbs: 11g | net carbs: 10g | fiber: 1g

Chapter 9 Snacks and Appetizers

Parmesan Artichoke

Prep time: 1 minute | Cook time: 30 minutes | Serves 2

1 large artichoke

1 cup water

¼ cup grated Parmesan cheese

¼ teaspoon salt

¼ teaspoon red pepper flakes

1. Trim artichoke. Remove stem, outer leaves and top. Gently spread leaves. 2. Add water to Instant Pot and place steam rack on bottom. Place artichoke on steam rack and sprinkle with Parmesan, salt, and red pepper flakes. Click lid closed. Press the Steam button and adjust time for 30 minutes. 3. When timer beeps, allow a 15-minute natural release and then quick-release the remaining pressure. Enjoy warm topped with additional Parmesan.
Per Serving:
calories: 90 | fat: 3g | protein: 6g | carbs: 10g | net carbs: 6g | fiber: 4g

Chicken Tinga Wings

Prep time: 10 minutes | Cook time: 30 minutes | Serves 6

1 to 2 cups coconut oil, for frying

1 pound (454 g) chicken wings (about 12 wings)

Fine sea salt and freshly ground black pepper, to taste

Tinga Sauce:

1 pound (454 g) Mexican-style fresh (raw) chorizo

½ large white onion, chopped

1 clove garlic, minced

3 cups chopped tomatoes

1 cup chopped husked tomatillos

2 tablespoons puréed chipotles in adobo sauce

1½ teaspoons fine sea salt

1 teaspoon freshly ground black pepper

½ teaspoon dried oregano leaves

1 sprig fresh thyme

½ cup chicken bone broth, homemade or store-bought

1. Preheat the oil to 350ºF (180ºC) in a deep-fryer or a 4-inch-deep (or deeper) cast-iron skillet over medium heat. The oil should be at least 3 inches deep; add more oil if needed. 2. While the oil heats, make the sauce: Cook the chorizo, onion, and garlic in a large cast-iron skillet over medium heat until the meat is crumbled and cooked through, about 5 minutes. Add the tomatoes, tomatillos, chipotles, salt, pepper, and herbs and stir to combine. Continue cooking for 5 minutes. Add the chicken broth and cook for 5 more minutes. Remove the thyme sprig and set the sauce aside. 3. Fry about six wings at a time until golden brown on all sides and cooked through, about 8 minutes. Remove from the oil and sprinkle with salt and pepper. Repeat with the remaining wings. 4. Place the wings on a serving platter and serve with the sauce, or toss the wings in the sauce before serving. They are best served fresh. Store extra wings

and sauce separately in airtight containers in the fridge for up to 3 days. To reheat, place the chicken wings on a rimmed baking sheet and heat in a preheated 400ºF (205ºC) oven for 4 minutes, or until warmed. Heat the sauce in a saucepan over medium-low heat until warmed.
Per Serving:
calories: 247 | fat: 17g | protein: 19g | carbs: 5g | net carbs: 3g | fiber: 2g

Bone Broth Fat Bombs

Prep time: 5 minutes | Cook time: 0 minutes | Makes 12 fat bombs

1 tablespoon grass-fed powdered gelatin

2 cups homemade bone broth, any type, warmed

Special Equipment:

Silicone mold with 12 (1⅛-ounce / 53-g) cavities

1. Sprinkle the gelatin over the broth and whisk to combine. 2. Place the silicone mold on a rimmed sheet pan (for easy transport). Pour the broth into the mold. Place in the fridge or freezer until the gelatin is fully set, about 2 hours. To release the fat bombs from the mold, gently push on the mold to pop them out. 3. Store in an airtight container in the fridge for up to 5 days or in the freezer for several months.
Per Serving:
calories: 27 | fat: 5g | protein: 2g | carbs: 2g | net carbs: 2g | fiber: 0g

Bacon-Wrapped Avocados

Prep time: 10 minutes | Cook time: 15 minutes | Serves 4

8 bacon slices

1 ripe avocado, peeled and cut into 8 wedges

Salt and freshly ground black

pepper, to taste

1 or 2 lime wedges

Ground cayenne pepper

1. Wrap 1 bacon slice around each avocado wedge. If needed, use a toothpick to secure them. 2. Heat a nonstick skillet over medium-high heat. Evenly space the bacon-wrapped wedges around the skillet. If you aren't using a toothpick, place the loose end of the bacon facing down to create a seal as it cooks. Cook for 6 to 8 minutes, turning every couple of minutes until the bacon is cooked. 3. Remove from the heat and finish with a sprinkle of salt, pepper, lime juice, and cayenne. Serve warm.
Per Serving:
calories: 314 | fat: 26g | protein: 15g | carbs: 5g | net carbs: 2g | fiber: 3g

Cheese and Charcuterie Board

Prep time: 15 minutes | Cook time: 0 minutes | Serves 7

4 ounces prosciutto, sliced

4 ounces Calabrese salami, sliced

4 ounces capicola, sliced

7 ounces Parrano Gouda cheese

7 ounces aged Manchego

cheese

7 ounces Brie cheese

½ cup roasted almonds

½ cup mixed olives

12 cornichons (small, tart pickles)

1 sprig fresh rosemary or other herbs of choice, for garnish Arrange the meats, cheeses, and almonds on a large wooden cutting board. Place the olives and pickles in separate bowls and set them on or alongside the cutting board. Garnish with a spring of rosemary or other fresh herbs of your choice.

Per Serving:
calories: 445 | fat: 35g | protein: 31g | carbs: 3g | net carbs: 2g | fiber: 1g

Pickled Herring

Prep time: 4 minutes | Cook time: 5 minutes | Serves 12

4 pounds (1.8 kg) herring or skinned Northern Pike fillets, cut into 2-inch pieces

Saltwater Brine:

10 cups water

½ cup fine sea salt

Pickling Brine:

½ cup thinly sliced red onions

Handful of fresh dill

2 cups water

2½ cups coconut vinegar

½ cup Swerve confectioners'-style sweetener or equivalent amount of liquid or powdered sweetener

2 teaspoons ground allspice

1 teaspoon dry mustard or mustard seeds

½ teaspoon grated fresh ginger

½ teaspoon prepared horseradish

½ teaspoon peppercorns

For Serving:

Hard-boiled eggs, halved or quartered

Pickled ginger

Capers

Fermented pickles

Sliced red onions

Fresh dill sprigs

1. Place the fish in a large bowl with the 10 cups of water. Add the salt and stir. Cover and refrigerate for 24 hours, then drain the fish and rinse it well. 2. Place the drained and rinsed fish in a clean 2-liter glass jar, layering it with the sliced onions and dill. 3. In a large pot over medium heat, heat the 2 cups of water, coconut vinegar, sweetener, allspice, mustard, ginger, horseradish, and peppercorns. Once the sweetener has dissolved, about 5 minutes, allow the brine to cool a little, then pour over the fish packed in the jar. Cover and refrigerate overnight to allow the flavors to meld; the longer the better for stronger flavors. If you let it sit for 5 days, the bones will dissolve. The pickled fish will keep in an airtight container in the fridge for up to 1 month. 4. To serve, arrange the pickled fish on a platter with hard-boiled eggs, pickled ginger, capers, fermented pickles, sliced red onions, and fresh dill.

Per Serving:
calories: 240 | fat: 14g | protein: 27g | carbs: 2g | net carbs: 2g | fiber: 0g

Grandma's Meringues

Prep time: 10 minutes | Cook time: 1 hour | Makes 12 meringues

2 large egg whites, room temperature

¼ teaspoon cream of tartar

Pinch of finely ground sea salt

½ cup (80 g) confectioners'-style erythritol

½ teaspoon vanilla extract

FOR SERVING:

24 fresh strawberries, sliced

¾ cup (190 g) coconut cream

12 fresh mint leaves

1. Preheat the oven to 225°F (108°C). Line a rimmed baking sheet with parchment paper or a silicone baking mat. 2. Place the egg whites, cream of tartar, and salt in a very clean large bowl. Make sure that the bowl does not have any oil residue in it. Using a handheld electric mixer or stand mixer, mix on low speed until the mixture becomes foamy. 3. Once foamy, increase the speed to high. Slowly add the erythritol, 1 tablespoon at a time, mixing all the while. Add a tablespoon about every 20 seconds. 4. Keep beating until the mixture is shiny and thick and peaks have formed; it should be nearly doubled in volume. (The peaks won't be as stiff as in a traditional meringue.) Fold in the vanilla. 5. Using a large spoon, dollop the meringue mixture onto the lined baking sheet, making a total of 12 meringues. 6. Bake for 1 hour without opening the oven door. After 1 hour, turn off the oven and keep the meringues in the cooling oven for another hour, then remove. 7. To serve, place 2 meringues on each plate. Top each serving with 4 sliced strawberries, 2 tablespoons of coconut cream, and 2 mint leaves.

Per Serving:
calories: 100 | fat: 8g | protein: 2g | carbs: 6g | net carbs: 4g | fiber: 2g

Goat Cheese–Mackerel Pâté

Prep time: 10 minutes | Cook time: 0 minutes | Serves 4

4 ounces (113 g) olive oil-packed wild-caught mackerel

2 ounces (57 g) goat cheese

Zest and juice of 1 lemon

2 tablespoons chopped fresh parsley

2 tablespoons chopped fresh arugula

1 tablespoon extra-virgin olive oil

2 teaspoons chopped capers

1 to 2 teaspoons fresh horseradish (optional)

Crackers, cucumber rounds, endive spears, or celery, for serving (optional)

1. In a food processor, blender, or large bowl with immersion blender, combine the mackerel, goat cheese, lemon zest and juice, parsley, arugula, olive oil, capers, and horseradish (if using). Process or blend until smooth and creamy. 2. Serve with crackers, cucumber rounds, endive spears, or celery. 3. Store covered in the refrigerator for up to 1 week.

Per Serving:
calories: 142 | fat: 10g | protein: 11g | carbs: 1g | fiber: 0g | sodium: 203mg

Tuna Cucumber Boats

Prep time: 5 minutes | Cook time: 0 minutes | Serves 1

1 English cucumber (about 12 in/30.5 cm long)	onions
1 (5-oz/142-g) can flaked tuna packed in water, drained	2 teaspoons finely chopped fresh parsley
1 dill pickle, finely diced	1 teaspoon lemon juice
3 tablespoons mayonnaise	1 clove garlic, minced
2 tablespoons finely diced red	½ teaspoon Dijon mustard

1. Cut the cucumber in half lengthwise, scoop out the seeds, and then cut each piece in half crosswise. Set aside. 2. Place the remaining ingredients in a medium-sized bowl and mix until incorporated. 3. Spoon the tuna mixture into the hollowed-out cucumber pieces, piling it high. Set on a plate and enjoy!
Per Serving:
calories: 527 | fat: 34g | protein: 40g | carbs: 13g | net carbs: 9g | fiber: 4g

Cheese Stuffed Mushrooms

Prep time: 15 minutes | Cook time: 8 minutes | Serves 4

1 cup cremini mushroom caps	1 ounce (28 g) Monterey Jack cheese, shredded
1 tablespoon chopped scallions	
1 tablespoon chopped chives	1 teaspoon butter, softened
1 teaspoon cream cheese	½ teaspoon smoked paprika
1 teaspoon sour cream	1 cup water, for cooking

1. Trim the mushroom caps if needed and wash them well. 2. After this, in the mixing bowl, mix up scallions, chives, cream cheese, sour cream, butter, and smoked paprika. 3. Then fill the mushroom caps with the cream cheese mixture and top with shredded Monterey Jack cheese. 4. Pour water and insert the trivet in the instant pot. 5. Arrange the stuffed mushrooms caps on the trivet and close the lid. 6. Cook the meal on Manual (High Pressure) for 8 minutes. 7. Then make a quick pressure release.
Per Serving:
calories: 45 | fat: 4g | protein: 3g | carbs: 1g | net carbs: 1g | fiber: 0g

Curried Broccoli Skewers

Prep time: 15 minutes | Cook time: 1 minute | Serves 2

1 cup broccoli florets	2 tablespoons coconut cream
½ teaspoon curry paste	1 cup water, for cooking

1. In the shallow bowl mix up curry paste and coconut cream. 2. Then sprinkle the broccoli florets with curry paste mixture and string on the skewers. 3. Pour water and insert the steamer rack in the instant pot. 4. Place the broccoli skewers on the rack. Close and seal the lid. 5. Cook the meal on Manual mode (High Pressure) for 1 minute. 6. Make a quick pressure release.
Per Serving:
calories: 58 | fat: 4g | protein: 2g | carbs: 4g | net carbs: 2g | fiber: 2g

Cabbage and Broccoli Slaw

Prep time: 5 minutes | Cook time: 10 minutes | Serves 6

2 cups broccoli slaw	4 tablespoons butter
½ head cabbage, thinly sliced	1 teaspoon salt
¼ cup chopped kale	¼ teaspoon pepper

1. Press the Sauté button and add all ingredients to Instant Pot. Stir-fry for 7 to 10 minutes until cabbage softens. Serve warm.
Per Serving:
calories: 97 | fat: 7g | protein: 2g | carbs: 6g | net carbs: 3g | fiber: 3g

90-Second Bread

Prep time: 5 minutes | Cook time: 90 seconds | Serves 1

1 heaping tablespoon coconut flour	1 large egg
	1½ tablespoons butter, melted
½ teaspoon baking powder	Pinch salt

1. In a small, 3- to 4-inch diameter, microwave-safe bowl, combine the coconut flour, baking powder, egg, butter, and salt, and mix until well combined. 2. Place the bowl in the microwave and cook on high for 90 seconds. 3. Dump the bread from the bowl and allow to cool for a couple of minutes. 4. With a serrated knife, cut the bread in half horizontally to make two halves, if desired.
Per Serving:
calories: 204 | fat: 17g | protein: 8g | carbs: 5g | net carbs: 2g | fiber: 3g

Cauliflower Cheese Balls

Prep time: 5 minutes | Cook time: 21 minutes | Serves 8

1 cup water	2 tablespoons minced fresh chives
1 head cauliflower, broken into florets	
	1 garlic clove, minced
1 cup shredded Asiago cheese	½ teaspoon cayenne pepper
½ cup grated Parmesan cheese	Coarse sea salt and white pepper, to taste
2 eggs, beaten	
2 tablespoons butter	

1. Pour the water into the Instant Pot and insert a steamer basket. Place the cauliflower in the basket. 2. Lock the lid. Select the Manual mode and set the cooking time for 3 minutes at High Pressure. 3. When the timer beeps, perform a quick pressure release. Carefully remove the lid. 4. Transfer the cauliflower to a food processor, along with the remaining ingredients. Pulse until everything is well combined. 5. Form the mixture into bite-sized balls and place them on a baking sheet. 6. Bake in the preheated oven at 400°F (205°C) for 18 minutes until golden brown. Flip the balls halfway through the cooking time. Cool for 5 minutes before serving.
Per Serving:
calories: 161 | fat: 12.6g | protein: 9.3g | carbs: 3.8g | net carbs: 3g | fiber: 0.8g

Sesame Mushrooms

Prep time: 2 minutes | Cook time: 10 minutes | Serves 6

3 tablespoons sesame oil	½ teaspoon smoked paprika
¾ pound (340 g) small button mushrooms	½ teaspoon cayenne pepper
1 teaspoon minced garlic	Salt and ground black pepper, to taste

1. Set your Instant Pot to Sauté and heat the sesame oil. 2. Add the mushrooms and sauté for 4 minutes until just tender, stirring occasionally. 3. Add the remaining ingredients to the Instant Pot and stir to mix well. 4. Lock the lid. Select the Manual mode and set the cooking time for 5 minutes at High Pressure. 5. When the timer beeps, perform a quick pressure release. Carefully remove the lid. 6. Serve warm.

Per Serving:
calories: 77 | fat: 7.6g | protein: 1.9g | carbs: 1.8g | net carbs: 1.0g | fiber: 0.8g

Bacon Avocado Mousse Cups

Prep time: 10 minutes | Cook time: 20 minutes | Serves 6

12 bacon slices	Juice of ½ lime
2 or 3 ripe avocados, halved and pitted	Salt and freshly ground black pepper, to taste
½ cup plain Greek yogurt	

1. Preheat the oven to 425°F (220°C). 2. Wrap each piece of bacon around the sides and bottom of the wells of a mini muffin tin to create little bacon cups. Bake for 15 to 20 minutes or until the bacon is cooked through and crisp. 3. While the bacon cooks, in a medium bowl, combine the avocado flesh, yogurt, and lime juice. Mix well until combined and smooth. Season with salt and pepper and transfer to a piping bag (or a plastic bag with the tip cut off). 4. Remove the bacon from the oven and cool slightly. Pipe each bacon cup full of avocado mousse. Serve immediately.

Per Serving:
2 filled cups: calories: 530 | fat: 38g | protein: 31g | carbs: 16g | net carbs: 9g | fiber: 7g

Garlic Herb Butter

Prep time: 10 minutes | Cook time: 8 minutes | Serves 4

⅓ cup butter	½ teaspoon minced garlic
1 teaspoon dried parsley	¼ teaspoon dried thyme
1 tablespoon dried dill	

1. Preheat the instant pot on Sauté mode. 2. Then add butter and melt it. 3. Add dried parsley, dill, minced garlic, and thyme. Stir the butter mixture well. 4. Transfer it in the butter mold and refrigerate until it is solid.

Per Serving:
calories: 138 | fat: 15g | protein: 0g | carbs: 1g | net carbs: 1g | fiber: 0g

Mac Fatties

Prep time: 10 minutes | Cook time: 0 minutes | Makes 20 fat cups

1¾ cups (280 g) roasted and salted macadamia nuts	¼ teaspoon cayenne pepper
⅓ cup (70 g) coconut oil	TURMERIC FLAVOR:
ROSEMARY LEMON FLAVOR:	½ teaspoon turmeric powder
1 teaspoon finely chopped fresh rosemary	¼ teaspoon ginger powder
	GARLIC HERB FLAVOR:
¼ teaspoon lemon juice	1¼ teaspoons dried oregano leaves
SPICY CUMIN FLAVOR:	½ teaspoon paprika
½ teaspoon ground cumin	½ teaspoon garlic powder

1. Place the macadamia nuts and oil in a blender or food processor. Blend until smooth, or as close to smooth as you can get it with the equipment you're using. 2. Divide the mixture among 4 small bowls, placing ¼ cup (87 g) in each bowl. 3. To the first bowl, add the rosemary and lemon juice and stir to combine. 4. To the second bowl, add the cumin and cayenne and stir to combine. 5. To the third bowl, add the turmeric and ginger and stir to combine. 6. To the fourth bowl, add the oregano, paprika, and garlic powder and stir to combine. 7. Set a 24-well silicone or metal mini muffin pan on the counter. If using a metal pan, line 20 of the wells with mini foil liners. (Do not use paper; it would soak up all the fat.) Spoon the mixtures into the wells, using about 1 tablespoon per well. 8. Place in the freezer for 1 hour, or until firm. Enjoy directly from the freezer.

Per Serving:
calories: 139 | fat: 14g | protein: 1g | carbs: 2g | net carbs: 1g | fiber: 1g

Colby Cheese and Pepper Dip

Prep time: 5 minutes | Cook time: 5 minutes | Serves 8

1 tablespoon butter	2 garlic cloves, minced
2 red bell peppers, sliced	1 teaspoon red Aleppo pepper flakes
2 cups shredded Colby cheese	
1 cup cream cheese, room temperature	1 teaspoon sumac
1 cup chicken broth	Salt and ground black pepper, to taste

1. Set your Instant Pot to Sauté and melt the butter. 2. Add the bell peppers and sauté for about 2 minutes until just tender. 3. Add the remaining ingredients to the Instant Pot and gently stir to incorporate. 4. Lock the lid. Select the Manual mode and set the cooking time for 3 minutes at High Pressure. 5. When the timer beeps, perform a quick pressure release. Carefully remove the lid. 6. Allow to cool for 5 minutes and serve warm.

Per Serving:
calories: 241 | fat: 20.8g | protein: 10.6g | carbs: 3.0g | net carbs: 2.6g | fiber: 0.4g

Bok Choy Salad Boats with Shrimp

Prep time: 8 minutes | Cook time: 2 minutes | Serves 8

26 shrimp, cleaned and deveined	⅓ cup olives, pitted and sliced
2 tablespoons fresh lemon juice	4 tablespoons olive oil
1 cup water	2 tablespoons apple cider vinegar
Sea salt and ground black pepper, to taste	8 Bok choy leaves
4 ounces (113 g) feta cheese, crumbled	2 tablespoons fresh basil leaves, snipped
2 tomatoes, diced	2 tablespoons chopped fresh mint leaves

1. Toss the shrimp and lemon juice in the Instant Pot until well coated. Pour in the water. 2. Lock the lid. Select the Manual mode and set the cooking time for 2 minutes at Low Pressure. 3. When the timer beeps, perform a quick pressure release. Carefully remove the lid. 4. Season the shrimp with salt and pepper to taste, then let them cool completely. 5. Toss the shrimp with the feta cheese, tomatoes, olives, olive oil, and vinegar until well incorporated. 6. Divide the salad evenly onto each Bok choy leaf and place them on a serving plate. Scatter the basil and mint leaves on top and serve immediately.

Per Serving:
calories: 129 | fat: 10.7g | protein: 4.9g | carbs: 3.0g | net carbs: 2.4g | fiber: 0.6g

Keto Crackers-Two Ways

Prep time: 15 minutes | Cook time: 6 minutes | Serves 2

Simple Keto Crackers	Keto Cheddar Cheese Crackers
½ cup shredded mozzarella cheese	½ cup shredded cheddar cheese
⅓ cup blanched almond flour	⅓ cup blanched almond flour
⅛ teaspoon garlic powder	⅛ teaspoon garlic powder
Dash of salt	Dash of salt
1 large egg yolk	1 large egg yolk

1 Preheat the oven to 425°F. 2 In a microwave-safe bowl, combine the cheese, almond flour, garlic powder, and salt. Microwave for 30 seconds. 3 Use your hands to knead the dough until fully mixed. Add the egg yolk and knead until it's blended into the dough. 4 Lay a piece of parchment paper on a flat surface, place the dough on top, and place another piece of parchment on top of the dough. Press down and spread the dough (with your hands or a rolling pin) into a very thin, even rectangle. 5 Using a fork, gently poke holes in the dough to prevent it from bubbling while baking. (Don't skip this step!) 6 Use a knife to cut the dough into 1-inch squares. 7 Line a baking sheet with parchment paper and lay the squares on the parchment with a bit of space between them. Bake for 5 to 6 minutes, until golden brown. 8 For extra-crunchy crackers, flip them over and bake for an additional 2 to 4 minutes, watching closely to ensure that they don't burn!

Per Serving:
calories: 234 | fat: 20g | protein: 12g | carbs: 5g | net carbs: 3g | fiber: 2g

Gourmet "Cheese" Balls

Prep time: 1 hour 20 minutes | Cook time: 0 minutes | serves 6

1 cup raw hazelnuts, soaked overnight	1 teaspoon miso paste
¼ cup water	1 teaspoon mustard
2 tablespoons nutritional yeast	½ cup almond flour
1 teaspoon apple cider vinegar	1 cup slivered almonds
	1 teaspoon dried oregano

1. In a high-powered blender, combine the hazelnuts, water, nutritional yeast, vinegar, miso paste, and mustard, and blend until well combined, thick, and creamy. 2. Transfer the mixture to a medium bowl. 3. Slowly stir in the almond flour until the mixture forms a dough-like consistency. Set aside. 4. In a separate, small bowl, toss the almonds and oregano together and set aside. 5. Using a soup spoon or tablespoon, scoop some mixture into your hand and shape it into a bite-size ball. Place the ball on a baking sheet. Repeat until you have used all the mixture (about 2 dozen balls). 6. One by one, roll the hazelnut balls in the almond and oregano mixture until thoroughly coated, placing each coated ball back on the baking sheet. 7. Place the sheet in the refrigerator for 1 hour to allow the balls to set.

Per Serving:
calories: 308 | fat: 27g | protein: 10g | carbs: 11g | net carbs: 5g | fiber: 6g

Salami Chips with Pesto

Prep time: 10 minutes | Cook time: 12 minutes | Serves 6

CHIPS:	¼ cup raw walnuts
6 ounces sliced Genoa salami	¼ teaspoon pink Himalayan salt
PESTO:	¼ teaspoon ground black pepper
1 cup fresh basil leaves	½ cup extra-virgin olive oil
3 cloves garlic	
¼ cup grated Parmesan cheese	

1. Make the chips: Preheat the oven to 375°F and line 2 rimmed baking sheets with parchment paper. 2. Arrange the salami in a single layer on the lined baking sheets. Bake for 10 to 12 minutes, until crisp. Transfer to a paper towel–lined plate to absorb the excess oil. Allow to cool and crisp up further. 3. Make the pesto: Put all the pesto ingredients, except for the olive oil, in a food processor and pulse until everything is roughly chopped and a coarse paste has formed. 4. With the food processor running, slowly pour in the olive oil. Process until all of the oil has been added and the ingredients are fully incorporated. Taste and season with additional salt and pepper, if desired. 5. Pour the pesto into a small serving bowl and serve the salami chips alongside. Store leftover pesto in a sealed container in the refrigerator for up to 2 weeks; store the chips in a zip-top plastic bag in the refrigerator for up to 5 days.

Per Serving:
calories: 202 | fat: 9g | protein: 8g | carbs: 1g | net carbs: 1g | fiber: 0g

Bacon-Wrapped Avocado Fries

Prep time: 10 minutes | Cook time: 18 minutes | Serves 4

2 medium Hass avocados, peeled and pitted (about 8 oz/220 g of flesh)

16 strips bacon (about 1 lb/455 g), cut in half lengthwise

1. Cut each avocado into 8 fry-shaped pieces, making a total of 16 fries. 2. Wrap each avocado fry in 2 half-strips of bacon. Once complete, place in a large frying pan. 3. Set the pan over medium heat and cover with a splash guard. Fry for 6 minutes on each side and on the bottom, or until crispy, for a total of 18 minutes. 4. Remove from the heat and enjoy immediately!

Per Serving:
calories: 723 | fat: 58g | protein: 43g | carbs: 6g | net carbs: 3g | fiber: 4g

Keto Taco Shells

Prep time: 5 minutes | Cook time: 20 minutes | Serves 4

6 ounces (170 g) shredded cheese

1. Preheat the oven to 350°F (180°C). 2. Line a baking sheet with a silicone baking mat or parchment paper. 3. Separate the cheese into 4 (1½-ounce / 43-g) portions and make small circular piles a few inches apart (they will spread a bit in the oven). Pat the cheese down so all the piles are equally thick. Bake for 10 to 12 minutes or until the edges begin to brown. Cool for just a couple of minutes. 4. Lay a wooden spoon or spatula across two overturned glasses. Repeat to make a second setup, and carefully transfer a baked cheese circle to drape over the length of each spoon or spatula. Let them cool into the shape of a taco shell. 5. Fill with your choice of protein and top with chopped lettuce, avocado, salsa, sour cream, or whatever else you like on your tacos. These taco shells will keep refrigerated in an airtight container for a few days, but they are best freshly made and still a little warm.

Per Serving:
1 taco shell: calories: 168 | fat: 14g | protein: 11g | carbs: 1g | net carbs: 1g | fiber: 0g

Lemon-Butter Mushrooms

Prep time: 10 minutes | Cook time: 4 minutes | Serves 2

1 cup cremini mushrooms, sliced

½ cup water

1 tablespoon lemon juice

1 teaspoon almond butter

1 teaspoon grated lemon zest

½ teaspoon salt

½ teaspoon dried thyme

1. Combine all the ingredients in the Instant Pot. 2. Secure the lid. Select the Manual mode and set the cooking time for 4 minutes at High Pressure. 3. Once cooking is complete, do a natural pressure release for 5 minutes, then release any remaining pressure. Carefully open the lid. 4. Serve warm.

Per Serving:
calories: 63 | fat: 4.8g | protein: 2.9g | carbs: 3.3g | net carbs: 2.1g | fiber: 1.2g

Bacon-Cheddar Dip Stuffed Mushrooms

Prep time: 10 minutes | Cook time: 35 minutes | Serves 12

24 ounces (680 g) baby portobello mushrooms

2 tablespoons avocado oil

3 ounces (85 g) cream cheese

¼ cup sour cream

2 cloves garlic, minced

1 tablespoon chopped fresh dill

1 tablespoon chopped fresh parsley

¾ cup (3 ounces / 85 g) shredded Cheddar cheese

⅓ cup cooked bacon bits

3 tablespoons sliced green onions

1. Preheat the oven to 400°F (205°C). Line a sheet pan with foil or parchment paper and grease lightly. 2. Remove the stems from the mushrooms and place cavity side up on the baking sheet. Drizzle with the avocado oil. 3. Roast the mushrooms for 15 to 20 minutes, until soft. 4. Meanwhile, in a microwave-safe bowl or a saucepan, melt the cream cheese in the microwave or over low heat on the stove until it's soft and easy to stir. Remove from the heat. 5. Stir the sour cream, garlic, dill, and parsley into the cream cheese. Stir in the Cheddar, bacon, and green onions. 6. When the mushrooms are soft, remove from the oven but leave the oven on. Drain any liquid from the pan and from inside the mushrooms. Pat the cavities dry with paper towels. Use a small cookie scoop or spoon to fill them with the dip mixture. 7. Bake the stuffed mushrooms for 10 to 15 minutes, until hot.

Per Serving:
calories: 107 | fat: 8g | protein: 4g | carbs: 3g | net carbs: 3g | fiber: 0g

Antipasto Skewers

Prep time: 10 minutes | Cook time: 0 minutes | Makes 8 skewers

8 ounces (227 g) fresh whole Mozzarella

16 fresh basil leaves

16 slices salami (4 ounces / 113 g)

16 slices coppa or other cured meat like prosciutto (4 ounces / 113 g)

8 artichoke hearts, packed in water (8 ounces / 227 g)

¼ cup vinaigrette made with olive oil or avocado oil and apple cider vinegar

Flaky salt and freshly ground black pepper, to taste

1. Cut the Mozzarella into 16 small chunks. 2. Skewer 2 pieces each of the Mozzarella, basil leaves, salami slices, and coppa slices, along with one artichoke heart, on each skewer. You'll probably want to fold the basil leaves in half and the salami and coppa in fourths (or more depending on size) before skewering. 3. Place the skewers in a small shallow dish and drizzle with the dressing, turning to coat. If possible, let them marinate for 30 minutes or more. Sprinkle lightly with flaky salt and the pepper before serving.

Per Serving:
calories: 200 | fat: 15g | protein: 11g | carbs: 4g | net carbs: 4g | fiber: 0g

Citrus-Marinated Olives

Prep time: 10 minutes | Cook time: 0 minutes | Makes 2 cups

2 cups mixed green olives with pits	or 1 large orange
¼ cup red wine vinegar	1 teaspoon red pepper flakes
¼ cup extra-virgin olive oil	2 bay leaves
4 garlic cloves, finely minced	½ teaspoon ground cumin
Zest and juice of 2 clementines	½ teaspoon ground allspice

1. In a large glass bowl or jar, combine the olives, vinegar, oil, garlic, orange zest and juice, red pepper flakes, bay leaves, cumin, and allspice and mix well. Cover and refrigerate for at least 4 hours or up to a week to allow the olives to marinate, tossing again before serving.

Per Serving:
¼ cup: calories: 112 | fat: 10g | protein: 1g | carbs: 5g | fiber: 2g | sodium: 248mg

Egg Custard Tarts

Prep time: 10 minutes | Cook time: 20 minutes | Serves 2

¼ cup almond flour	1 tablespoon erythritol
1 tablespoon coconut oil	1 teaspoon vanilla extract
2 egg yolks	1 cup water, for cooking
¼ cup coconut milk	

1. Make the dough: Mix up almond flour and coconut oil. 2. Then place the dough into 2 mini tart molds and flatten well in the shape of cups. 3. Pour water in the instant pot. Insert the steamer rack. 4. Place the tart mold in the instant pot. Close and seal the lid. 5. Cook them for 3 minutes on Manual mode (High Pressure). Make a quick pressure release. 6. Then whisk together vanilla extract, erythritol, coconut milk, and egg yolks. 7. Pour the liquid in the tart molds and close the lid. 8. Cook the dessert for 7 minutes on Manual mode (High Pressure). 9. Then allow the natural pressure release for 10 minutes more.

Per Serving:
calories: 208 | fat: 20g | protein: 4g | carbs: 3g | net carbs: 2g | fiber: 1g

Chocolate-Covered Coffee Bites

Prep time: 10 minutes | Cook time: 0 minutes | Serves 8

BITES:	regular or decaf)
¼ cup plus 2 tablespoons (90 g) cacao butter	2 tablespoons collagen peptides
	CHOCOLATE TOPPING:
½ cup (75 g) macadamia nuts, roasted	¼ cup (56 g) stevia-sweetened chocolate chips, melted
1 tablespoon confectioners'-style erythritol or 1 or 2 drops liquid stevia ½ teaspoon instant coffee (medium or light roast,	GARNISH:
	About ¼ teaspoon large flake sea salt
	SPECIAL EQUIPMENT:

Silicone mold with eight 1-ounce (30-ml) semispherical cavities

1. Place the cacao butter, macadamia nuts, erythritol, and instant coffee in a high-powered blender or food processor. Blend on high speed until the nuts have broken down quite a bit but are still chunky, about 20 seconds. 2. Add the collagen and pulse to combine. 3. Using a spoon, scoop and press the mixture into 8 cavities of a silicone mold. Place the mold in the fridge for 2 hours or in the freezer for 1 hour, until the bites are set. 4. Meanwhile, line a baking sheet with parchment paper or a silicone baking mat and set aside. 5. Remove the mold from the fridge or freezer and pop out the bites onto the prepared baking sheet. Drizzle the melted chocolate over the top, then sprinkle each bite with a pinch of salt. Return the bites to the fridge until the chocolate is set, about 10 minutes. Enjoy!

Per Serving:
calories: 213 | fat: 20g | protein: 4g | carbs: 4g | net carbs: 2g | fiber: 2g

Broccoli Cheese Dip

Prep time: 5 minutes | Cook time: 10 minutes | Serves 6

4 tablespoons butter	½ cup mayonnaise
½ medium onion, diced	½ cup chicken broth
1½ cups chopped broccoli	1 cup shredded Cheddar cheese
8 ounces (227 g) cream cheese	

1. Press the Sauté button and then press the Adjust button to set heat to Less. Add butter to Instant Pot. Add onion and sauté until softened, about 5 minutes. Press the Cancel button. 2. Add broccoli, cream cheese, mayo, and broth to pot. Press the Manual button and adjust time for 4 minutes. 3. When timer beeps, quick-release the pressure and stir in Cheddar. Serve warm.

Per Serving:
calories: 411 | fat: 37g | protein: 8g | carbs: 4g | net carbs: 3g | fiber: 1g

3-Ingredient Almond Flour Crackers

Prep time: 5 minutes | Cook time: 12 minutes | Serves 6

2 cups (8 ounces / 227 g) blanched almond flour	½ teaspoon sea salt
	1 large egg, beaten

1. Preheat the oven to 350°F (180°C). Line a large baking sheet with parchment paper. 2. In a large bowl, mix together the almond flour and sea salt. Add the egg and mix well, until a dense, crumbly dough forms. (You can also mix in a food processor if you prefer.) 3. Place the dough between two large pieces of parchment paper. Use a rolling pin to roll out to a very thin rectangle, about 1/16 inch thick. (It will tend to roll into an oval shape, so just rip off pieces of dough and re-attach to form a more rectangular shape.) 4. Cut the cracker dough into rectangles. Place on the lined baking sheet. Prick with a fork a few times. Bake for 8 to 12 minutes, until golden.

Per Serving:
calories: 226 | fat: 19g | protein: 9g | carbs: 8g | net carbs: 4g | fiber: 4g

Keto Trail Mix

Prep time: 5 minutes | Cook time: 0 minutes | Serves 4

¼ cup pumpkin seeds	1 cup crunchy cheese snack
¼ cup salted almonds	¼ cup sugar-free chocolate
¼ cup salted macadamia nuts	chips
¼ cup salted walnuts	

1. In a resealable 1-quart plastic bag, combine the pumpkin seeds, almonds, macadamia nuts, walnuts, cheese snack, and chocolate chips. Seal the bag and shake to mix.

Per Serving:
calories: 253 | fat: 23g | protein: 7g | carbs: 5g | net carbs: 2g | fiber: 3g

Crispy Bacon Wrapped Onion Rings

Prep time: 15 minutes | Cook time: 40 minutes | Serves 6

1 extra-large (1 pound / 454 g) onion, sliced into ½-inch-thick rings	lengthwise
	Avocado oil cooking spray
12 slices bacon, halved	½ cup (2 ounces / 57 g) grated Parmesan cheese

1. Preheat the oven to 400ºF (205ºC). Line a sheet pan with foil. If you have an ovenproof nonstick cooling rack, place it over the pan. (This is optional, but recommended for the crispiest bacon.) Grease the sheet pan or rack. 2. Wrap each onion ring tightly in a thin strip of bacon, trying to cover the whole ring without overlapping. As you finish each ring, place it on a large cutting board in a single layer. (You can also just use the baking sheet without the rack for this step and the next, then use the rack starting at step 5.) 3. Spray the onion rings with avocado oil spray, then sprinkle lightly with half of the grated Parmesan. Flip and repeat on the other side. 4. Place the onion rings on the prepared baking sheet. Bake for 30 to 35 minutes, flipping halfway through, until the bacon is cooked through and starting to get a little crispy on the edges. Drain the bacon grease from the pan occasionally if not using a rack. 5. Switch the oven to broil. Broil the onion rings for 3 to 5 minutes, until crispy. To crisp up more, let the onion rings cool from hot to warm.

Per Serving:
calories: 141 | fat: 8g | protein: 9g | carbs: 7g | net carbs: 6g | fiber: 1g

Brownie Cake

Prep time: 10 minutes | Cook time: 25 minutes | Serves 8

¾ cup (120 g) confectioners'-style erythritol, divided	2 teaspoons vanilla extract
½ cup plus 3 tablespoons (143 g) coconut oil, ghee, or cacao butter, melted, divided	¾ cup (85 g) blanched almond flour
	¼ cup plus 2 tablespoons (30 g) cocoa powder, divided
2 large eggs	1 teaspoon baking powder

1. Preheat the oven to 350°F (177°C). Line an 8-inch (20-cm) round cake pan or square baking pan with parchment paper. 2. Combine ½ cup (95 g) of the erythritol, ½ cup (120 ml) of the melted oil, the eggs, and vanilla in a large mixing bowl. 3. In a separate bowl, place the almond flour, ¼ cup (20 g) of the cocoa powder, and the baking powder and whisk with a fork. 4. Add the dry mixture to the wet mixture and mix until smooth. 5. Transfer the batter to the lined pan and smooth with the back of a spoon. Bake for 23 to 25 minutes, until a toothpick inserted in the middle comes out clean. Allow to cool for 30 minutes. 6. Meanwhile, prepare the frosting: Place the remaining ¼ cup (25 g) of erythritol, 3 tablespoons of melted oil, and 2 tablespoons of cocoa powder in a small bowl. Whisk to combine. 7. If you're serving the cake right away, as soon as it's cool, cut into 8 equal pieces, place on plates, and drizzle with the frosting. If you're serving it later, cover the entire cake with the frosting while it's still in the pan and set in the fridge for at least 20 minutes before serving.

Per Serving:
calories: 207 | fat: 22g | protein: 3g | carbs: 3g | net carbs: 2g | fiber: 2g

Easy Peasy Peanut Butter Cookies

Prep time: 15 minutes | Cook time: 7 to 12 minutes | Makes 15 cookies

½ cup coconut flour	2 tablespoons butter, at room temperature
¼ cup sugar-free sweetener	
½ teaspoon baking soda	2 large eggs
4 tablespoons (low-carb or handmade) peanut butter	1 teaspoon vanilla extract

1. Preheat the oven to 350°F (180°C). Line a baking sheet with parchment paper and set aside. 2. In a bowl, combine the flour, sweetener, and baking soda, mixing to blend. 3. Add the peanut butter, butter, eggs, and vanilla, and mix well to incorporate. 4. Drop by even spoonfuls onto the prepared baking sheet to make 15 cookies. 5. Using the back of a fork, press the cookies down a little and make decorative criss-cross marks. 6. Cook for 7 to 8 minutes for soft cookies or 10 to 12 minutes for crispy cookies.

Per Serving:
1 cookie: calories: 70 | fat: 5g | protein: 3g | carbs: 3g | net carbs: 2g | fiber: 1g

Parmesan Crisps

Prep time: 5 minutes | Cook time: 5 minutes | Makes about 25 crisps

2 cups grated Parmesan cheese

1. Heat the oven to 400°F (205°C). Line a baking sheet with a silicone mat or parchment paper. Scoop a generous tablespoon of the cheese onto the sheet and flatten it slightly. Repeat with the rest of the cheese, leaving about 1 inch (2.5 cm) space in between them. 2. Bake for 3 to 5 minutes, until crisp.

Per Serving:
calories: 169 | fat: 11g | protein: 11g | carbs: 6g | net carbs: 6g | fiber: 0g

Salmon-Stuffed Cucumbers

Prep time: 10 minutes | Cook time: 0 minutes | Serves 4

2 large cucumbers, peeled	Zest and juice of 1 lime
1 (4-ounce / 113-g) can red salmon	3 tablespoons chopped fresh cilantro
1 medium very ripe avocado, peeled, pitted, and mashed	½ teaspoon salt
1 tablespoon extra-virgin olive oil	¼ teaspoon freshly ground black pepper

1. Slice the cucumber into 1-inch-thick segments and using a spoon, scrape seeds out of center of each segment and stand up on a plate. 2. In a medium bowl, combine the salmon, avocado, olive oil, lime zest and juice, cilantro, salt, and pepper and mix until creamy. 3. Spoon the salmon mixture into the center of each cucumber segment and serve chilled.

Per Serving:
calories: 173 | fat: 13g | protein: 8g | carbs: 8g | fiber: 4g | sodium: 420mg

Low-Carb Granola Bars

Prep time: 10 minutes | Cook time: 15 to 20 minutes | Makes about 12 bars

1 cup almonds	¼ cup unsweetened peanut butter
1 cup hazelnuts	
1 cup unsweetened coconut flakes	½ cup dark chocolate chips
	1 tablespoon vanilla extract
1 egg	1 tablespoon ground cinnamon
¼ cup coconut oil, melted	Pinch salt

1. Preheat the oven to 350ºF (180ºC). 2. In a food processor, pulse together the almonds and macadamia nuts for 1 to 2 minutes until roughly chopped. (You want them pretty fine but not turning into nut butter.) Transfer them to a large bowl. 3. Stir in the coconut, egg, coconut oil, peanut butter, chocolate chips, vanilla, cinnamon, and salt. Transfer the mixture to an 8- or 9-inch square baking dish and gently press into an even layer. Bake for 15 to 20 minutes or until golden brown. Cool and cut into 12 bars. Refrigerate in an airtight container for up to 2 weeks.

Per Serving:
1 bar: calories: 588 | fat: 58g | protein: 11g | carbs: 6g | net carbs: 5g | fiber: 1g

Granola Clusters

Prep time: 5 minutes | Cook time: 15 minutes | Serves 2

¼ cup almonds	melted
¼ cup pecans	1 tablespoon pumpkin seeds
¼ cup macadamia nuts	1 tablespoon chia seeds
1 large egg white	1 tablespoon unsweetened
2 tablespoons ground flaxseed	coconut flakes
1 tablespoon coconut oil,	1 tablespoon granulated

erythritol
¼ teaspoon vanilla extract

⅛ teaspoon pink Himalayan sea salt

1. Preheat the oven to 325ºF (163ºC). Line a baking sheet with parchment paper. 2. In a food processor, combine the almonds, pecans, macadamia nuts, egg white, flaxseed, coconut oil, pumpkin seeds, chia seeds, coconut flakes, erythritol, vanilla, and salt. Pulse until the largest chunks of nuts are about the size of a pea. 3. Spread the mixture evenly on the baking sheet. Bake for 15 to 18 minutes, until the granola is lightly browned. 4. Let cool for about 20 minutes, then break into clusters.

Per Serving:
calories: 482 | fat: 45g | protein: 12g | carbs: 15g | net carbs: 5g | fiber: 10g

Greens Chips with Curried Yogurt Sauce

Prep time: 10 minutes | Cook time: 5 to 6 minutes | Serves 4

1 cup low-fat Greek yogurt	leaves cut into 2- to 3-inch pieces
1 tablespoon freshly squeezed lemon juice	
	½ bunch chard, stemmed, ribs removed and discarded, leaves cut into 2- to 3-inch pieces
1 tablespoon curry powder	
½ bunch curly kale, stemmed, ribs removed and discarded,	1½ teaspoons olive oil

1. In a small bowl, stir together the yogurt, lemon juice, and curry powder. Set aside. 2. In a large bowl, toss the kale and chard with the olive oil, working the oil into the leaves with your hands. This helps break up the fibers in the leaves so the chips are tender. 3. Air fry the greens in batches at 390ºF (199ºC) for 5 to 6 minutes, until crisp, shaking the basket once during cooking. Serve with the yogurt sauce.

Per Serving:
calories: 98 | fat: 4g | protein: 7g | carbs: 13g | fiber: 4g | sodium: 186mg

Crunchy Jicama Fries

Prep time: 5 minutes | Cook time: 40 minutes | Serves 4

1 medium jicama (about 1 lb/455 g), peeled and cut into fry-like pieces	1 teaspoon finely chopped fresh parsley
	½ cup (105 g) mayonnaise or sugar-free ketchup, for serving (optional)
2 tablespoons avocado oil	
½ teaspoon paprika	
Pinch of finely ground sea salt	

1. Preheat the oven to 400°F (205°C). Line a rimmed baking sheet with parchment paper or a silicone baking mat. 2. Place the jicama pieces on the baking sheet and toss with the oil and paprika. Bake for 40 minutes, flipping the fries over halfway through baking. 3. Remove from the oven, sprinkle the fries with the salt and parsley, and enjoy immediately. Serve with the mayonnaise on the side for dipping, if desired.

Per Serving:
calories: 96 | fat: 4g | protein: 1g | carbs: 15g | net carbs: 7g | fiber: 8g

Stuffed Party Shrooms

Prep time: 15 minutes | Cook time: 23 minutes | Serves 4

12 large whole mushrooms, approximately 2" wide	softened
2 tablespoons unsalted butter	½ cup full-fat mayonnaise
8 ounces cooked no-sugar-added bacon, crumbled (approximately 8 strips)	1 medium green onion, finely chopped
7 ounces full-fat cream cheese,	1 teaspoon paprika
	⅛ teaspoon salt
	⅛ teaspoon black pepper

1. Preheat oven to 400°F. Line a baking sheet with parchment paper. 2. Remove mushroom stems from caps, being very careful not to break edges of cap, and scrape out the black gills if the mushroom is mature enough for the gills to be visible. Chop the trimmed stem pieces finely. 3. In a small frying pan over medium heat, fry mushroom trimmings with butter for 3 minutes until soft. 4. Place caps on baking sheet, rounded-side down. 5. In a medium bowl, combine fried mushroom trimmings with remaining ingredients. Scoop the mixture evenly into the caps. 6. Bake 20 minutes until filling bubbles and turns golden brown.

Per Serving:
calories: 690| fat: 59g | protein: 25g | carbs: 6g | net carbs: 5g | fiber: 1g

Savory Broccoli Cheddar Waffles

Prep time: 15 minutes | Cook time: 20 minutes | Serves 4

1 head broccoli, florets separated, stalk reserved for another use	1 teaspoon salt
	Freshly ground black pepper, to taste
1 shallot, minced	1 cup shredded Cheddar cheese
3 eggs	Nonstick olive oil cooking spray, or olive oil, for the waffle iron
1 teaspoon chopped fresh chives	
3 garlic cloves, minced	Sliced scallion, for garnish

1. In a food processor, pulse the broccoli florets until roughly chopped (don't overprocess—you want it to be rough). Transfer to a microwave-safe container and microwave, uncovered, on high power for 2 minutes. Cool slightly. Place the broccoli in a thin cloth or piece of cheesecloth and twist to remove any water (not a lot will come out but the little that's there needs to be removed). Transfer to a medium bowl and add the shallot. Stir to combine. 2. In a small bowl, whisk together the eggs, chives, garlic, and salt, and season with pepper. Pour the egg mixture over the broccoli and mix together until well incorporated. 3. Add the Cheddar and continue to mix gently. 4. Turn on your waffle iron. Grease it well with cooking spray (if you don't have cooking spray, use a little olive oil on a paper towel). 5. Separate the broccoli mixture into 4 portions. Spoon the mixture onto the prepared waffle iron. Cook for 4 to 5 minutes (or follow the manufacturer's instructions if you're unsure) or until the waffle "batter" is firm and golden brown. Top with sliced scallion and serve.

Per Serving:
calories: 224 | fat: 14g | protein: 16g | carbs: 12g | net carbs: 8g | fiber: 4g

Extreme Fudge Brownies

Prep time: 10 minutes | Cook time: 52 minutes | Makes 9 brownies

¼ cup cocoa powder	¾ cup (1½ sticks) unsalted butter
2 tablespoons coconut flour	
¼ teaspoon pink Himalayan salt	2 ounces unsweetened baking chocolate (100% cacao)
3 large eggs	
½ cup granular erythritol	Powdered erythritol, for topping (optional)
½ teaspoon vanilla extract	

1. Preheat the oven to 325°F and grease an 8-inch square brownie pan with coconut oil spray. 2. Put the cocoa powder, coconut flour, and salt in a small bowl and whisk using a fork. Set aside. 3. In a large bowl, whisk together the eggs, erythritol, and vanilla extract. Set aside. 4. In a small microwave-safe bowl, combine the butter and chocolate. Microwave until fully melted, about 1 minute, stirring every 30 seconds. Add the melted chocolate mixture to the egg mixture and whisk to combine. 5. Add the dry mixture to the wet mixture in 2 batches, whisking after each addition until fully combined. 6. Pour the batter into the greased pan and bake for 50 minutes, or until a toothpick inserted in the center comes out clean. Allow to cool in the pan for 20 minutes, then cut into 9 pieces. If desired, dust with powdered erythritol before serving. 7. Store leftovers in a sealed container in the refrigerator for up to a week or freeze for up to a month.

Per Serving:
calories: 210 | fat: 20g | protein: 4g | carbs: 4g | net carbs: 1g | fiber: 3g

Rhubarb Microwave Cakes

Prep time: 5 minutes | Cook time: 0 minutes | Serves 2

1 large egg	1 teaspoon ground cinnamon
3 tablespoons refined avocado oil or macadamia nut oil	¼ teaspoon ground nutmeg
	¼ teaspoon baking powder
1 tablespoon plus 1 teaspoon confectioners'-style erythritol	1 (2½-in/6.5-cm) piece rhubarb, diced
¼ teaspoon vanilla extract or powder	1 to 2 fresh strawberries, hulled and sliced, for garnish (optional)
¼ cup (32 g) roughly ground flax seeds	

1. Place the egg, oil, erythritol, and vanilla in a small bowl. Whisk to combine. 2. In a separate small bowl, place the flax seeds, cinnamon, nutmeg, and baking powder. Stir to combine, then add to the bowl with the wet ingredients. 3. Add the diced rhubarb to the bowl and stir until coated. 4. Divide the mixture between two 8-ounce (240-ml) ramekins, coffee cups, or other small microwave-safe containers. Microwave for 2 to 2½ minutes, until a toothpick inserted in the middle comes out clean. Garnish with strawberry slices, if desired.

Per Serving:
calories: 303 | fat: 28g | protein: 6g | carbs: 7g | net carbs: 2g | fiber: 6g

Peanut Butter Fat Bomb

Prep time: 10 minutes | Cook time: 0 minutes | Serves 2

1 tablespoon butter, at room temperature	butter or almond butter
1 tablespoon coconut oil	2 teaspoons Swerve natural sweetener or 2 drops liquid
2 tablespoons all-natural peanut	stevia

1. In a microwave-safe medium bowl, melt the butter, coconut oil, and peanut butter in the microwave on 50 percent power. Mix in the sweetener. 2. Pour the mixture into fat bomb molds. (I use small silicone cupcake molds.) 3. Freeze for 30 minutes, unmold them, and eat! Keep some extras in your freezer so you can eat them anytime you are craving a sweet treat.

Per Serving:
calories: 196 | fat: 20g | protein: 3g | carbs: 8g | net carbs: 3g | fiber: 1g

Classic Cheesecake

Prep time: 5 minutes | Cook time: 50 minutes | Serves 16

Almond Flour Crust:	32 ounces (907 g) cream
2 cups (8 ounces / 227 g) blanched almond flour	cheese, softened at room temperature
5 tablespoons plus 1 teaspoon (⅔ stick) butter, melted	1¼ cups powdered erythritol
3 tablespoons erythritol	3 large eggs, at room
1 teaspoon vanilla extract	temperature
Cheesecake Filling:	1 tablespoon lemon juice
	1 teaspoon vanilla extract

1. Position a rack in the center of the oven and preheat the oven to 350°F (180°C). Grease the sides of a 9-inch springform pan and line the bottom with a circle of parchment paper. 2. Make the almond flour crust: In a medium bowl, stir the almond flour, melted butter, erythritol, and vanilla until well combined. The dough will be slightly crumbly. Press the dough into the bottom of the prepared pan. Bake for 10 to 12 minutes, until barely golden. Let cool at least 10 minutes. Leave the oven on. 3. Meanwhile, make the cheesecake filling: In a bowl, with an electric hand mixer, beat the cream cheese and powdered erythritol together at low to medium speed for about 2 minutes, until fluffy. Keeping the mixer at low to medium the whole time (too high a speed will introduce too many air bubbles, which we don't want), beat in the eggs, one at a time. Finally, beat in the lemon juice and vanilla, scraping down the sides of the bowl periodically. 4. Pour the filling into the pan over the crust. Smooth the top with a spatula (use an icing spatula for a smoother top if you have one). Tap the pan on the counter to release any air bubbles. 5. Bake for 40 to 55 minutes, until the center is almost set, but still jiggly. 6. Remove the cheesecake from the oven. If the edges are stuck to the pan, run a knife around the edge (don't remove the springform edge yet). Cool in the pan on the counter to room temperature, then refrigerate for at least 4 hours, preferably overnight, until completely set. (Do not try to remove the cake from the pan before chilling.)

Per Serving:
calories: 328 | fat: 31g | protein: 7g | carbs: 18g | net carbs: 5g | fiber: 13g

Strawberry Cheesecake

Prep time: 20 minutes | Cook time: 10 minutes | Serves 2

1 tablespoon gelatin	1 strawberry, chopped
4 tablespoon water (for gelatin)	¼ cup coconut milk
4 tablespoon cream cheese	1 tablespoon Swerve

1. Mix up gelatin and water and leave the mixture for 10 minutes. 2. Meanwhile, pour coconut milk in the instant pot. 3. Bring it to boil on Sauté mode, about 10 minutes. 4. Meanwhile, mash the strawberry and mix it up with cream cheese. 5. Add the mixture in the hot coconut milk and stir until smooth. 6. Cool the liquid for 10 minutes and add gelatin. Whisk it until gelatin is melted. 7. Then pour the cheesecake in the mold and freeze in the freezer for 3 hours.

Per Serving:
calories: 155 | fat: 14g | protein: 5g | carbs: 4g | net carbs: 3g | fiber: 1g

Fresh Cream-Filled Strawberries

Prep time: 10 minutes | Cook time: 0 minutes | Serves 6

1 cup heavy (whipping) cream	12 large strawberries, hulled
Sweetener of choice (optional)	and hollowed out

1. In a large bowl, whisk the cream and sweetener (if using) until thickened into whipped cream, about 5 minutes. 2. Spoon the whipped cream into the hollowed strawberries or use a pastry tube to pipe it inside. Serve immediately. 3. Optional garnishes could include lime zest, finely chopped mint, or shaved dark chocolate.

Per Serving:
calories: 153 | fat: 15g | protein: 1g | carbs: 3g | net carbs: 3g | fiber: 0g

After-Dinner Parfait

Prep time: 10 minutes | Cook time: 0 minutes | Serves 4

1 small (9-gram) package sugar-free Jell-O, any flavor	softened
1 cup boiling water	2 tablespoons canned whipped cream
1 cup cold water	1 tablespoon crushed salty
4 ounces full-fat cream cheese,	peanuts

1 In a medium bowl, add Jell-O to boiling water. Stir in cold water until mixture starts to thicken, 2–3 minutes. Refrigerate until firm, about 30 minutes. 2 Using a mixer in a medium mixing bowl, beat softened cream cheese until smooth. Going slowly at first, combine firm Jell-O with cream cheese. Gradually increase speed until desired consistency is reached. 3 Scoop into serving bowls and top with whipped cream and dusting of crushed peanuts.

Per Serving:
calories: 122 | fat: 10g | protein: 3g | carbs: 2g | net carbs: 2g | fiber: 0g

Baked Crab Dip

Prep time: 15 minutes | Cook time: 25 minutes |

Serves 4 to 6

4 ounces cream cheese, softened

½ cup shredded Parmesan cheese, plus ½ cup extra for topping (optional) ⅓ cup mayonnaise

¼ cup sour cream

1 tablespoon chopped fresh parsley

2 teaspoons fresh lemon juice

1½ teaspoons Sriracha sauce

½ teaspoon garlic powder

8 ounces fresh lump crabmeat

Salt and pepper

1 Preheat the oven to 375°F. 2 Combine all the ingredients except for the crabmeat in a mixing bowl and use a hand mixer to blend until smooth. 3 Put the crabmeat in a separate bowl, check for shells, and rinse with cold water, if needed. Pat dry or allow to rest in a strainer until most of the water has drained. 4 Add the crabmeat to the bowl with the cream cheese mixture and gently fold to combine. Taste for seasoning and add salt and pepper to taste, if needed. Pour into an 8-inch round or square baking dish and bake for 25 minutes, until the cheese has melted and the dip is warm throughout. 5 If desired, top the dip with another ½ cup of Parmesan cheese and broil for 2 to 3 minutes, until the cheese has melted and browned slightly.

Per Serving:
calories: 275 | fat: 23g | protein: 16g | carbs: 1g | net carbs: 1g | fiber: 0g

Almond Sesame Crackers

Prep time: 15 minutes | Cook time: 15 minutes |

Makes about 36 (1-inch-square) crackers

1½ cups almond flour

1 egg

3 tablespoons sesame seeds,

divided

Salt and freshly ground black pepper, to taste

1. Preheat the oven to 350°F (180°C). 2. Line a baking sheet with parchment paper. 3. In a large bowl, mix together the almond flour, egg, and 1½ tablespoons of sesame seeds. Transfer the dough to a sheet of parchment and pat it out flat with your clean hands. Cover with another piece of parchment paper and roll it into a large square, at least 10 inches wide. 4. Remove the top piece of parchment and use a pizza cutter or sharp knife to cut the dough into small squares, about 1 inch wide. Season with salt and pepper and sprinkle with the remaining 1½ tablespoons of sesame seeds. 5. Remove the crackers from the parchment and place them on the prepared baking sheet. Bake for about 15 minutes or until the crackers begin to brown. Cool before serving, and store any leftovers in an airtight bag or container on your counter for up to 2 weeks.

Per Serving:
10 crackers: calories: 108 | fat: 9g | protein: 5g | carbs: 3g | net carbs: 1g | fiber: 2g

Cucumber Finger Sandwiches

Prep time: 10 minutes | Cook time: 0 minutes | serves 4

1 medium English cucumber

2 ounces cream cheese (¼ cup), softened

2 to 3 slices sharp cheddar

cheese, cut into 1-inch pieces

4 slices bacon, cooked and cut crosswise into 1-inch pieces

1. Slice the cucumber crosswise into rounds about ¼ inch thick. Spread the cream cheese on half of the cucumber slices, then top each with a piece of cheese and a piece of bacon. Place the remainder of the cucumber slices on top to make sandwiches. Serve immediately or cover and refrigerate before serving. These sandwiches should be eaten the day they are made or they will become soggy.

Per Serving:
calories: 187 | fat: 14g | protein: 10g | carbs: 3g | net carbs: 3g | fiber: 0g

Caponata Dip

Prep time: 15 minutes | Cook time: 35 minutes |

Makes about 2 cups

1 large eggplant (about 1¼ pounds / 567 g), cut into ½-inch pieces

1 large yellow onion, cut into ½-inch pieces

4 large cloves garlic, peeled and smashed with the side of a knife

4 tablespoons extra-virgin olive oil, divided, plus extra for garnish

½ teaspoon sea salt

¼ teaspoon ground black pepper

¼ teaspoon ground cumin

1 medium tomato, chopped into 1-inch chunks

Juice of 1 lemon

2 tablespoons chopped fresh cilantro leaves

For Garnish:

Extra-virgin olive oil

Fresh cilantro leaves

Pinch of paprika (optional)

Pine nuts (optional)

For Serving (Optional):

Low-carb flax crackers

Sliced vegetables

1. Preheat the oven to 375°F (190°C). 2. Place the eggplant, onion, garlic, 2 tablespoons of the olive oil, salt, pepper, and cumin in a large bowl and toss to combine. 3. Spread the mixture out on a rimmed baking sheet and bake for 30 to 35 minutes, until the eggplant is softened and browned, tossing halfway through. 4. Remove the eggplant mixture from the oven and transfer it to a food processor. Add the tomato, lemon juice, cilantro, and remaining 2 tablespoons of olive oil. Pulse until the mixture is just slightly chunky. Add salt and pepper to taste. 5. Scoop the dip into a serving dish and garnish with additional olive oil, cilantro, paprika (if desired), and pine nuts (optional). Serve with low-carb crackers and sliced vegetables, if desired.

Per Serving:
calories: 90 | fat: 7g | protein: 1g | carbs: 7g | net carbs: 4g | fiber: 3g

Pecan Butter Cookies

Prep time: 5 minutes | Cook time: 24 minutes |
Makes 12 cookies

1 cup chopped pecans

½ cup salted butter, melted

½ cup coconut flour

¾ cup erythritol, divided

1 teaspoon vanilla extract

1. In a food processor, blend together pecans, butter, flour, ½ cup erythritol, and vanilla 1 minute until a dough forms. 2. Form dough into twelve individual cookie balls, about 1 tablespoon each. 3. Cut three pieces of parchment to fit air fryer basket. Place four cookies on each ungreased parchment and place one piece parchment with cookies into air fryer basket. Adjust air fryer temperature to 325ºF (163ºC) and set the timer for 8 minutes. Repeat cooking with remaining batches. 4. When the timer goes off, allow cookies to cool 5 minutes on a large serving plate until cool enough to handle. While still warm, dust cookies with remaining erythritol. Allow to cool completely, about 15 minutes, before serving.

Per Serving:
calories: 121 | fat: 13g | protein: 1g | carbs: 2g | net carbs: 1g | fiber: 1g

Key Lime Pie Cupcakes

Prep time: 5 minutes | Cook time: 50 minutes |
Makes 12 cupcakes

Crust:

¾ cup (3 ounces / 85 g) coconut flour

2 tablespoons erythritol

4 tablespoons (½ stick) butter, melted

2 large eggs

Filling:

6 tablespoons (¾ stick) butter

3 cups heavy cream

¾ cup powdered erythritol

½ cup sour cream

1 tablespoon lime zest, plus more for garnish (optional)

½ cup lime juice

1 teaspoon vanilla extract

Sugar-free whipped cream, for garnish (optional)

1. Preheat the oven to 350ºF (180ºC). Line 12 cups of a muffin tin with paper liners. 2. Make the crust: In a large bowl, stir together the coconut flour and erythritol. Stir in the melted butter and egg, until evenly combined. The dough will be crumbly, but you should be able to pinch it together. 3. Press a thin layer of the dough into the bottoms of the lined muffin cups. Bake for 10 to 12 minutes, until firm and slightly golden on the edges. Set aside to cool. 4. Meanwhile, make the filling: In a large sauté pan (not a saucepan), melt the butter over medium heat. Whisk in the heavy cream and powdered erythritol to combine. Bring to a boil, then reduce to a simmer and simmer for 30 to 45 minutes, stirring occasionally, until the mixture is thick, coats the back of a spoon, and the volume is reduced by half. It will also pull away from the pan as you tilt it. (This process will go faster if you use a larger pan.) Remove from the heat and set aside to cool for about 10 minutes, until warm but no longer hot. Meanwhile, preheat the oven to 350ºF (180ºC) again. 5. Stir the sour cream, lime zest, lime juice, and vanilla into the condensed milk. 6. Pour the filling into the muffin cups over the crust, which should have cooled enough and no longer be hot. 7. Return the pan to the oven for 5 to 10 minutes, until bubbles

form on top and the cupcakes start to set on the edges but not in the center. Do not let the filling fully set or brown. 8. Remove the pan from the oven and cool completely on the counter, then chill for at least 1 to 2 hours, until set. (If possible, chilling overnight is even better.) 9. If desired, top with sugar-free whipped cream and/or additional lime zest.

Per Serving:
calories: 337 | fat: 33g | protein: 3g | carbs: 6g | net carbs: 4g | fiber: 2g

Lemon and Ricotta Torte

Prep time: 15 minutes | Cook time: 35 minutes |
Serves 12

Cooking spray

Torte:

1⅓ cups Swerve

½ cup (1 stick) unsalted butter, softened

2 teaspoons lemon or vanilla extract

5 large eggs, separated

2½ cups blanched almond flour

1¼ (10-ounce / 284-g) cups whole-milk ricotta cheese

¼ cup lemon juice

1 cup cold water

Lemon Glaze:

½ cup (1 stick) unsalted butter

¼ cup Swerve

2 tablespoons lemon juice

2 ounces (57 g) cream cheese (¼ cup)

Grated lemon zest and lemon slices, for garnish

1. Line a baking pan with parchment paper and spray with cooking spray. Set aside. 2. Make the torte: In the bowl of a stand mixer, place the Swerve, butter, and extract and blend for 8 to 10 minutes until well combined. Scrape down the sides of the bowl as needed. 3. Add the egg yolks and continue to blend until fully combined. Add the almond flour and mix until smooth, then stir in the ricotta and lemon juice. 4. Whisk the egg whites in a separate medium bowl until stiff peaks form. Add the whites to the batter and stir well. Pour the batter into the prepared pan and smooth the top. 5. Place a trivet in the bottom of your Instant Pot and pour in the water. Use a foil sling to lower the baking pan onto the trivet. Tuck in the sides of the sling. 6. Seal the lid, press Pressure Cook or Manual, and set the timer for 30 minutes. Once finished, let the pressure release naturally. 7. Lock the lid. Select the Manual mode and set the cooking time for 30 minutes at High Pressure. 8. When the timer beeps, perform a natural pressure release for 10 minutes. Carefully remove the lid. 9. Use the foil sling to lift the pan out of the Instant Pot. Place the torte in the fridge for 40 minutes to chill before glazing. 10. Meanwhile, make the glaze: Place the butter in a large pan over high heat and cook for about 5 minutes until brown, stirring occasionally. Remove from the heat. While stirring the browned butter, add the Swerve. 11. Carefully add the lemon juice and cream cheese to the butter mixture. Allow the glaze to cool for a few minutes, or until it starts to thicken. 12. Transfer the chilled torte to a serving plate. Pour the glaze over the torte and return it to the fridge to chill for an additional 30 minutes. 13. Scatter the lemon zest on top of the torte and arrange the lemon slices on the plate around the torte. 14. Serve.

Per Serving:
calories: 367 | fat: 32.8g | protein: 11.5g | carbs: 10.0g | net carbs: 7.0g | fiber: 3.0g

Garlic Meatballs

Prep time: 20 minutes | Cook time: 15 minutes | Serves 6

7 ounces (198 g) ground beef	1 teaspoon chili flakes
7 ounces (198 g) ground pork	1 teaspoon dried parsley
1 teaspoon minced garlic	1 tablespoon coconut oil
3 tablespoons water	¼ cup beef broth

1. In the mixing bowl, mix up ground beef, ground pork, minced garlic, water, chili flakes, and dried parsley. 2. Make the medium size meatballs from the mixture. 3. After this, heat up coconut oil in the instant pot on Sauté mode. 4. Put the meatballs in the hot coconut oil in one layer and cook them for 2 minutes from each side. 5. Then add beef broth and close the lid. 6. Cook the meatballs for 10 minutes on Manual mode (High Pressure). 7. Then make a quick pressure release and transfer the meatballs on the plate.

Per Serving:
calories: 131 | fat: 6g | protein: 19g | carbs: 0g | net carbs: 0g | fiber: 0g

Zucchini Bread

Prep time: 10 minutes | Cook time: 40 minutes |

Serves 12

2 cups coconut flour	1 teaspoon vanilla extract
2 teaspoons baking powder	3 eggs, beaten
¾ cup erythritol	1 zucchini, grated
½ cup coconut oil, melted	1 teaspoon ground cinnamon
1 teaspoon apple cider vinegar	

1. In the mixing bowl, mix coconut flour with baking powder, erythritol, coconut oil, apple cider vinegar, vanilla extract, eggs, zucchini, and ground cinnamon. 2. Transfer the mixture into the air fryer basket and flatten it in the shape of the bread. 3. Cook the bread at 350ºF (177ºC) for 40 minutes.

Per Serving:
calories: 135 | fat: 14g | protein: 2g | carbs: 4g | net carbs: 3g | fiber: 1g

Southern Almond Pie

Prep time: 10 minutes | Cook time: 35 minutes |

Serves 12

2 cups almond flour	1 egg
1½ cups powdered erythritol	1 teaspoon vanilla extract
1 teaspoon baking powder	Cooking spray
Pinch of salt	1½ teaspoons ground cinnamon
½ cup sour cream	1½ teaspoons Swerve
4 tablespoons butter, melted	1 cup water

1. In a large bowl, whisk together the almond flour, powdered erythritol, baking powder, and salt. 2. Add the sour cream, butter, egg, and vanilla and whisk until well combined. The batter will be very thick, almost like cookie dough. 3. Grease the baking dish with cooking spray. Line with parchment paper, if desired. 4.

Transfer the batter to the dish and level with an offset spatula. 5. In a small bowl, combine the cinnamon and Swerve. Sprinkle over the top of the batter. 6. Cover the dish tightly with aluminum foil. Add the water to the pot. Set the dish on the trivet and carefully lower it into the pot. 7. Set the lid in place. Select the Manual mode and set the cooking time for 35 minutes on High Pressure. When the timer goes off, do a quick pressure release. Carefully open the lid. 8. Remove the trivet and pie from the pot. Remove the foil from the pan. The pie should be set but soft, and the top should be slightly cracked. 9. Cool completely before cutting.

Per Serving:
calories: 221 | fat: 19.0g | protein: 5.6g | carbs: 4.8g | net carbs: 2.4g | fiber: 2.4g

Fried Cabbage Wedges

Prep time: 5 minutes | Cook time: 15 minutes | Serves 6

1 large head green or red cabbage (about 2½ lbs/1.2 kg)	salt
2 tablespoons coconut oil or avocado oil	¾ cup (180 ml) green goddess dressing
2 teaspoons garlic powder	SPECIAL EQUIPMENT:
½ teaspoon finely ground sea	12 (4-in/10-cm) bamboo skewers

1. Cut the cabbage in half through the core, from top to bottom. Working with each half separately, remove the core by cutting a triangle around it and pulling it out. Then lay the half cut side down and cut into 6 wedges. Press a bamboo skewer into each wedge to secure the leaves. Repeat with the other half. 2. Heat the oil in a large frying pan over medium-low heat. 3. Place the cabbage wedges in the frying pan and sprinkle with the garlic powder and salt. Cook for 10 minutes on one side, or until lightly browned, then cook for 5 minutes on the other side. Serve with the dressing on the side.

Per Serving:
calories: 252 | fat: 20g | protein: 3g | carbs: 12g | net carbs: 7g | fiber: 5g

Blueberry Fat Bombs

Prep time: 10 minutes | Cook time: 0 minutes |

Makes 12 fat bombs

½ cup coconut oil, at room temperature	½ cup blueberries, mashed with a fork
½ cup cream cheese, at room temperature	6 drops liquid stevia
	Pinch ground nutmeg

1. Line a mini muffin tin with paper liners and set aside. 2. In a medium bowl, stir together the coconut oil and cream cheese until well blended. 3. Stir in the blueberries, stevia, and nutmeg until combined. 4. Divide the blueberry mixture into the muffin cups and place the tray in the freezer until set, about 3 hours. 5. Place the fat bombs in an airtight container and store in the freezer until you wish to eat them.

Per Serving:
calories: 115 | fat: 12g | protein: 1g | carbs: 1g | net carbs: 1g | fiber: 0g

Lemon-Ricotta Cheesecake

Prep time: 10 minutes | Cook time: 30 minutes | Serves 6

Unsalted butter or vegetable oil, for greasing the pan	ricotta cheese, at room temperature
8 ounces (227 g) cream cheese, at room temperature	Zest of 1 lemon
¼ cup plus 1 teaspoon Swerve, plus more as needed	Juice of 1 lemon
⅓ cup full-fat or part-skim	½ teaspoon lemon extract
	2 eggs, at room temperature
	2 tablespoons sour cream

1. Grease a 6-inch springform pan extremely well. I find this easiest to do with a silicone basting brush so I can get into all the nooks and crannies. Alternatively, line the sides of the pan with parchment paper. 2. In the bowl of a stand mixer, beat the cream cheese, ¼ cup of Swerve, the ricotta, lemon zest, lemon juice, and lemon extract on high speed until you get a smooth mixture with no lumps. 3. Taste to ensure the sweetness is to your liking and adjust if needed. 4. Add the eggs, reduce the speed to low and gently blend until the eggs are just incorporated. Overbeating at this stage will result in a cracked crust. 5. Pour the mixture into the prepared pan and cover with aluminum foil or a silicone lid. 6. Pour 2 cups of water into the inner cooking pot of the Instant Pot, then place a trivet in the pot. Place the covered pan on the trivet. 7. Lock the lid into place. Select Manual and adjust the pressure to High. Cook for 30 minutes. When the cooking is complete, let the pressure release naturally. Unlock the lid. 8. Carefully remove the pan from the pot, and remove the foil. 9. In a small bowl, mix together the sour cream and remaining 1 teaspoon of Swerve and spread this over the top of the warm cake. 10. Refrigerate the cheesecake for 6 to 8 hours. Do not be in a hurry! The cheesecake needs every bit of this time to be its best.

Per Serving:
calories: 217 | fat: 17g | protein: 6g | carbs: 10g | net carbs: 10g | fiber: 0g

Candied Mixed Nuts

Prep time: 5 minutes | Cook time: 15 minutes | Serves 8

1 cup pecan halves	⅓ cup grass-fed butter
1 cup chopped walnuts	1 teaspoon ground cinnamon
⅓ cup Swerve, or more to taste	

1. Preheat your oven to 350ºF (180ºC), and line a baking sheet with aluminum foil. 2. While your oven is warming, pour ½ cup of filtered water into the inner pot of the Instant Pot, followed by the pecans, walnuts, Swerve, butter, and cinnamon. Stir nut mixture, close the lid, and then set the pressure valve to Sealing. Use the Manual mode to cook at High Pressure, for 5 minutes. 3. Once cooked, perform a quick release by carefully switching the pressure valve to Venting, and strain the nuts. Pour the nuts onto the baking sheet, spreading them out in an even layer. Place in the oven for 5 to 10 minutes (or until crisp, being careful not to overcook). Cool before serving. Store leftovers in the refrigerator or freezer.

Per Serving:
calories: 122 | fat: 12g | protein: 4g | carbs: 3g | net carbs: 1g | fiber: 2g

Breaded Mushroom Nuggets

Prep time: 15 minutes | Cook time: 50 minutes | Serves 4

24 cremini mushrooms (about 1 lb/455 g)	salt
2 large eggs	2 tablespoons avocado oil
½ cup (55 g) blanched almond flour	½ cup (120 ml) honey mustard dressing, for serving (optional)
1 teaspoon garlic powder	SPECIAL EQUIPMENT (optional):
1 teaspoon paprika	Toothpicks
½ teaspoon finely ground sea	

1. Preheat the oven to 350°F (177°C). Line a rimmed baking sheet with parchment paper or a silicone baking mat. 2. Break the stems off the mushrooms or cut them short so that the stems are level with the caps. 3. Crack the eggs into a small bowl and whisk. 4. Place the almond flour, garlic powder, paprika, and salt in a medium-sized bowl and whisk to combine. 5. Dip one mushroom at a time into the eggs, then use the same hand to drop it into the flour mixture, being careful not to get the flour mixture on that hand. Rotate the mushroom in the flour mixture with a fork to coat on all sides, then transfer it to the lined baking sheet. Repeat with the remaining mushrooms. 6. Drizzle the coated mushrooms with the oil. Bake for 50 minutes, or until the tops begin to turn golden. 7. Remove from the oven and serve with the dressing, if using. If serving to friends and family, provide toothpicks.

Per Serving:
calories: 332 | fat: 29g | protein: 8g | carbs: 9g | net carbs: 7g | fiber: 2g

Vanilla Poppy Seed Cake

Prep time: 10 minutes | Cook time: 25 minutes | Serves 6

1 cup almond flour	¼ cup heavy cream
2 eggs	⅛ cup sour cream
½ cup erythritol	½ teaspoon baking powder
2 teaspoons vanilla extract	1 cup water
1 teaspoon lemon extract	¼ cup powdered erythritol, for garnish
1 tablespoon poppy seeds	
4 tablespoons melted butter	

1. In large bowl, mix almond flour, eggs, erythritol, vanilla, lemon, and poppy seeds. 2. Add butter, heavy cream, sour cream, and baking powder. 3. Pour into 7-inch round cake pan. Cover with foil. 4. Pour water into Instant Pot and place steam rack in bottom. Place baking pan on steam rack and click lid closed. Press the Cake button and press the Adjust button to set heat to Less. Set time for 25 minutes. 5. When timer beeps, allow a 15-minute natural release, then quick-release the remaining pressure. Let cool completely. Sprinkle with powdered erythritol for serving.

Per Serving:
calories: 221 | fat: 21g | protein: 3g | carbs: 5g | net carbs: 3g | fiber: 2g

Double Chocolate Brownies

Prep time: 5 minutes | Cook time: 15 to 20 minutes | Serves 8

1 cup almond flour
½ cup unsweetened cocoa powder
½ teaspoon baking powder
⅓ cup Swerve
¼ teaspoon salt

½ cup unsalted butter, melted and cooled
3 eggs
1 teaspoon vanilla extract
2 tablespoons mini semisweet chocolate chips

1. Preheat the air fryer to 350ºF (177ºC). Line a cake pan with parchment paper and brush with oil. 2. In a large bowl, combine the almond flour, cocoa powder, baking powder, Swerve, and salt. Add the butter, eggs, and vanilla. Stir until thoroughly combined. (The batter will be thick.) Spread the batter into the prepared pan and scatter the chocolate chips on top. 3. Air fry for 15 to 20 minutes until the edges are set. (The center should still appear slightly undercooked.) Let cool completely before slicing. To store, cover and refrigerate the brownies for up to 3 days.

Per Serving:
calories: 191 | fat: 17g | protein: 6g | carbs: 7g | net carbs: 3g | fiber: 4g

Chocolate Pecan Clusters

Prep time: 5 minutes | Cook time: 5 minutes | Makes 8 clusters

3 tablespoons butter
¼ cup heavy cream
1 teaspoon vanilla extract

1 cup chopped pecans
¼ cup low-carb chocolate chips

1. Press the Sauté button and add butter to Instant Pot. Allow butter to melt and begin to turn golden brown. Once it begins to brown, immediately add heavy cream. Press the Cancel button. 2. Add vanilla and chopped pecans to Instant Pot. Allow to cool for 10 minutes, stirring occasionally. Spoon mixture onto parchment-lined baking sheet to form eight clusters, and scatter chocolate chips over clusters. Place in fridge to cool.

Per Serving:
calories: 194 | fat: 18g | protein: 2g | carbs: 7g | net carbs: 6g | fiber: 1g

Lemon Berry Cream Pops

Prep time: 10 minutes | Cook time: 5 minutes | Makes 8 ice pops

Cream Pops:
2 cups coconut cream
1 tablespoon unsweetened vanilla extract
Optional: low-carb sweetener, to taste
2 cups raspberries, fresh or

frozen and defrosted
Coating:
1⅓ cups coconut butter
¼ cup virgin coconut oil
Zest from 2 lemons, about 2 tablespoons
1 teaspoon unsweetened vanilla

extract

1. To make the cream pops: In a bowl, whisk the coconut cream with the vanilla and optional sweetener until smooth and creamy. In another bowl, crush the raspberries using a fork, then add them to the bowl with the coconut cream and mix to combine. 2. Divide the mixture among eight ⅓-cup ice pop molds. Freeze until solid for 3 hours, or until set. 3. To easily remove the ice pops from the molds, fill a pot as tall as the ice pops with warm (not hot) water and dip the ice pop molds in for 15 to 20 seconds. Remove the ice pops from the molds and then freeze again. 4. Meanwhile, prepare the coating: Place the coconut butter and coconut oil in a small saucepan over low heat. Stir until smooth, remove from the heat, and add the lemon zest and vanilla. Let cool to room temperature. 5. Remove the ice pops from the freezer, two at a time, and, holding the ice pops over the saucepan, use a spoon to drizzle the coating all over. Return to the freezer until fully set, about 10 minutes. Store in the freezer in a resealable bag for up to 3 months.

Per Serving:
calories: 549 | fat: 8g | protein: 3g | carbs: 58g | fiber: 3g | sodium: 7mg

Fudge Pops

Prep time: 5 minutes | Cook time: 0 minutes | serves 4

1 (14-ounce) can full-fat coconut cream
3 avocados, peeled, pitted, and chopped
⅓ cup cacao powder

5 or 6 drops liquid stevia
⅓ cup freshly grated orange zest
Sea salt

1. In a high-powered blender, combine the coconut cream with the avocados, cacao powder, and stevia. 2. Whip the mixture in the blender for 5 minutes until it becomes airy. 3. Stir in the orange zest and salt and pour the mixture into popsicle molds. 4. Place the molds in the freezer overnight to set. 5. To serve, run warm water over the popsicle molds to loosen the fudge pops.

Per Serving:
calories: 434 | fat: 40g | protein: 4g | carbs: 21g | net carbs: 9g | fiber: 12g

Chocolate Lava Cakes

Prep time: 5 minutes | Cook time: 15 minutes | Serves 2

2 large eggs, whisked
¼ cup blanched finely ground almond flour

½ teaspoon vanilla extract
2 ounces (57 g) low-carb chocolate chips, melted

1. In a medium bowl, mix eggs with flour and vanilla. Fold in chocolate until fully combined. 2. Pour batter into two ramekins greased with cooking spray. Place ramekins into air fryer basket. Adjust the temperature to 320ºF (160ºC) and bake for 15 minutes. Cakes will be set at the edges and firm in the center when done. Let cool 5 minutes before serving.

Per Serving:
calories: 313 | fat: 23g | protein: 11g | carbs: 16g | fiber: 5g | sodium: 77mg

Strawberry Shortcakes

Prep time: 10 minutes | Cook time: 15 minutes | serves 6

1½ cups fresh strawberries
¾ cup finely ground blanched almond flour
1 teaspoon baking powder
⅛ teaspoon salt
1 large egg
⅓ cup granular erythritol
2 tablespoons heavy whipping cream
2 tablespoons salted butter, melted but not hot
½ teaspoon vanilla extract
1½ cups whipped cream, for serving

1. Preheat the oven to 375°F. Line a baking sheet with parchment paper. 2. Hull and slice the strawberries and set aside. 3. In a small bowl, whisk together the almond flour, baking powder, and salt. 4. In a medium-sized mixing bowl, whisk the egg, then stir in the erythritol, cream, melted butter, and vanilla extract. While stirring, slowly add the dry ingredients; continue stirring until well blended. 5. Drop spoonfuls of the batter onto the prepared baking sheet, spacing the shortcakes 2 inches apart, to make a total of 6 shortcakes. Bake for 13 to 15 minutes, until the shortcakes are golden brown on the tops and a toothpick or tester inserted in the middle of a shortcake comes out clean. Allow to completely cool on the pan. 6. To serve, top the shortcakes with whipped cream and the sliced strawberries. Leftover shortcakes can be stored in an airtight container in the refrigerator for up to 5 days.

Per Serving:

calories: 154 | fat: 13g | protein: 4g | carbs: 5g | net carbs: 3g | fiber: 2g

Lemon Coconut Cake

Prep time: 5 minutes | Cook time: 40 minutes | Serves 9

Base:
6 large eggs, separated
⅓ cup melted ghee or virgin coconut oil
1 tablespoon fresh lemon juice
Zest of 2 lemons
2 cups almond flour
½ cup coconut flour
¼ cup collagen powder
1 teaspoon baking soda
1 teaspoon vanilla powder or 1 tablespoon unsweetened vanilla extract
Optional: low-carb sweetener, to taste
Topping:
½ cup unsweetened large coconut flakes
1 cup heavy whipping cream or coconut cream
¼ cup mascarpone, more heavy whipping cream, or coconut cream
½ teaspoon vanilla powder or 1½ teaspoons unsweetened vanilla extract

1. Preheat the oven to 285°F (140°C) fan assisted or 320°F (160°C) conventional. Line a baking tray with parchment paper (or use a silicone tray). A square 8 × 8–inch (20 × 20 cm) or a rectangular tray of similar size will work best. 2. To make the base: Whisk the egg whites in a bowl until stiff peaks form. In a separate bowl, whisk the egg yolks, melted ghee, lemon juice, and lemon zest. In a third bowl, mix the almond flour, coconut flour, collagen, baking soda, vanilla and optional sweetener. 3. Add the whisked egg yolk–ghee mixture into the dry mixture and combine well. Gently fold in the egg whites, trying not to deflate them. 4. Pour into the baking tray. Bake for 35 to 40 minutes, until lightly golden on top and set inside. Remove from the oven and let cool completely before adding the topping. 5. To make the topping: Preheat the oven to 350°F (175°C) fan assisted or 380°F (195°C) conventional. Place the coconut flakes on a baking tray and bake for 2 to 3 minutes. Remove from the oven and set aside to cool. 6. Once the cake is cool, place the cream, mascarpone, and vanilla in a bowl. Whip until soft peaks form. Spread on top of the cooled cake and top with the toasted coconut flakes. 7. To store, refrigerate for up to 5 days or freeze for up to 3 months. Coconut flakes will soften in the fridge. If you want to keep them crunchy, sprinkle on top of each slice before serving.

Per Serving:

calories: 342 | fat: 31g | protein: 9g | carbs: 10g | fiber: 4g | sodium: 208mg

"Frosty" Chocolate Shake

Prep time: 10 minutes | Cook time: 0 minutes | Serves 2

¾ cup heavy (whipping) cream
4 ounces coconut milk
1 tablespoon Swerve natural sweetener
¼ teaspoon vanilla extract
2 tablespoons unsweetened cocoa powder

1. Pour the cream into a medium cold metal bowl, and with your hand mixer and cold beaters, beat the cream just until it forms peaks. 2. Slowly pour in the coconut milk, and gently stir it into the cream. Add the sweetener, vanilla, and cocoa powder, and beat until fully combined. 3. Pour into two tall glasses, and chill in the freezer for 1 hour before serving. I usually stir the shakes twice during this time.

Per Serving:

calories: 444 | fat: 47g | protein: 4g | carbs: 15g | net carbs: 7g | fiber: 2g

Hazelnut Butter Cookies

Prep time: 30 minutes | Cook time: 20 minutes | Serves 10

4 tablespoons liquid monk fruit
½ cup hazelnuts, ground
1 stick butter, room temperature
2 cups almond flour
1 cup coconut flour
2 ounces (57 g) granulated Swerve
2 teaspoons ground cinnamon

1. Firstly, cream liquid monk fruit with butter until the mixture becomes fluffy. Sift in both types of flour. 2. Now, stir in the hazelnuts. Now, knead the mixture to form a dough; place in the refrigerator for about 35 minutes. 3. To finish, shape the prepared dough into the bite-sized balls; arrange them on a baking dish; flatten the balls using the back of a spoon. 4. Mix granulated Swerve with ground cinnamon. Press your cookies in the cinnamon mixture until they are completely covered. 5. Bake the cookies for 20 minutes at 310ºF (154ºC). 6. Leave them to cool for about 10 minutes before transferring them to a wire rack. Bon appétit!

Per Serving:

calories: 244 | fat: 24g | protein: 5g | carbs: 6g | net carbs: 2g | fiber: 4g

Mint–Chocolate Chip Ice Cream

Prep time: 10 minutes | Cook time: 30 minutes | Serves 2

½ tablespoon butter	(whipping) cream, divided
1 tablespoon Swerve natural sweetener	¼ teaspoon peppermint extract
10 tablespoons heavy	2 tablespoons sugar-free chocolate chips (I use Lily's)

1. Put a medium metal bowl and your hand-mixer beaters in the freezer to chill. 2. In a small, heavy saucepan over medium heat, melt the butter. Whisk in the sweetener and 5 tablespoons of cream. 3. Turn the heat up to medium-high and bring the mixture to a boil, stirring constantly. Turn the heat down to low and simmer, stirring occasionally, for about 30 minutes. You want the mixture to be thick, so it sticks to the back of a spoon. 4. Stir in the peppermint extract. 5. Pour the thickened mixture into a medium bowl and refrigerate to cool. 6. Remove the metal bowl and the mixer beaters from the freezer. Pour the remaining 5 tablespoons of cream into the bowl. With the electric beater, whip the cream until it is thick and fluffy and forms peaks. Don't overbeat, or the cream will turn to butter. Take the cream mixture out of the refrigerator. 7. Using a rubber scraper, gently fold the whipped cream into the cooled mixture. 8. Transfer the mixture to a small metal container that can go in the freezer (I use a mini loaf pan since I only make enough for two). 9. Mix in the chocolate chips, and cover the container with foil or plastic wrap. 10. Freeze the ice cream for 4 to 5 hours before serving, stirring it twice during that time.

Per Serving:
calories: 325 | fat: 33g | protein: 3g | carbs: 17g | net carbs: 4g | fiber: 4g

Nutty Shortbread Cookies

Prep time: 10 minutes | Cook time: 10 minutes | Makes 10 cookies

½ cup butter, at room temperature, plus additional for greasing the baking sheet	vanilla extract
	1½ cups almond flour
½ cup granulated sweetener	½ cup ground hazelnuts
1 teaspoon alcohol-free pure	Pinch sea salt

1. In a medium bowl, cream together the butter, sweetener, and vanilla until well blended. 2. Stir in the almond four, ground hazelnuts, and salt until a firm dough is formed. 3. Roll the dough into a 2-inch cylinder and wrap it in plastic wrap. Place the dough in the refrigerator for at least 30 minutes until firm. 4. Preheat the oven to 350°F. Line a baking sheet with parchment paper and lightly grease the paper with butter; set aside. 5. Unwrap the chilled cylinder, slice the dough into 18 cookies, and place the cookies on the baking sheet. 6. Bake the cookies until firm and lightly browned, about 10 minutes. 7. Allow the cookies to cool on the baking sheet for 5 minutes and then transfer them to a wire rack to cool completely.

Per Serving:
1 cookie: calories: 105 | fat: 10g | protein: 3g | carbs: 2g | net carbs: 1g | fiber: 1g

Pecan Pumpkin Pie

Prep time: 5 minutes | Cook time: 40 minutes | Serves 5 to 6

Base:	½ teaspoon ground cinnamon
2 tablespoons grass-fed butter, softened	½ teaspoon ginger, finely grated
	½ teaspoon ground nutmeg
1 cup blanched almond flour	½ teaspoon ground cloves
½ cup chopped pecans	1 (14-ounce / 397-g) can
Topping:	organic pumpkin purée
½ cup Swerve, or more to taste	1 egg
⅓ cup heavy whipping cream	

1. Pour 1 cup of filtered water into the inner pot of the Instant Pot, then insert the trivet. Using an electric mixer, combine the butter, almond flour, and pecans. Mix thoroughly. Transfer this mixture into a well-greased, Instant Pot-friendly pan, and form a crust at the bottom of the pan, with a slight coating of the mixture also on the sides. Freeze for 15 minutes. In a large bowl, thoroughly combine the topping ingredients. 2. Take the pan from the freezer, add the topping evenly, and then place the pan onto the trivet. Cover loosely with aluminum foil. Close the lid, set the pressure release to Sealing, and select Manual. Set the Instant Pot to 40 minutes on High Pressure, and let cook. 3. Once cooked, let the pressure naturally disperse from the Instant Pot for about 10 minutes, then carefully switch the pressure release to Venting. 4. Open the Instant Pot and remove the pan. Cool in the refrigerator for 4 to 5 hours, serve, and enjoy!

Per Serving:
calories: 152 | fat: 14g | protein: 3g | carbs: 6g | net carbs: 4g | fiber: 2g

Lemonade Fat Bomb

Prep time: 10 minutes | Cook time: 0 minutes | Serves 2

½ lemon	2 teaspoons Swerve natural sweetener or 2 drops liquid stevia
4 ounces cream cheese, at room temperature	
2 ounces butter, at room temperature	Pinch pink Himalayan salt

1. Zest the lemon half with a very fine grater into a small bowl. Squeeze the juice from the lemon half into the bowl with the zest. 2. In a medium bowl, combine the cream cheese and butter. Add the sweetener, lemon zest and juice, and pink Himalayan salt. Using a hand mixer, beat until fully combined. 3. Spoon the mixture into the fat bomb molds. (I use small silicone cupcake molds. If you don't have molds, you can use cupcake paper liners that fit into the cups of a muffin tin.) 4. Freeze for at least 2 hours, unmold, and eat! Keep extras in your freezer in a zip-top bag so you and your loved ones can have them anytime you are craving a sweet treat. They will keep in the freezer for up to 3 months.

Per Serving:
calories: 404 | fat: 43g | protein: 4g | carbs: 8g | net carbs: 4g | fiber: 1g

Creamy Banana Fat Bombs

Prep time: 10 minutes | Cook time: 0 minutes | Makes 12 fat bombs

1¼ cups cream cheese, at room temperature

¾ cup heavy (whipping) cream

1 tablespoon pure banana extract

6 drops liquid stevia

1. Line a baking sheet with parchment paper and set aside. 2. In a medium bowl, beat together the cream cheese, heavy cream, banana extract, and stevia until smooth and very thick, about 5 minutes. 3. Gently spoon the mixture onto the baking sheet in mounds, leaving some space between each mound, and place the baking sheet in the refrigerator until firm, about 1 hour. 4. Store the fat bombs in an airtight container in the refrigerator for up to 1 week.

Per Serving:
calories: 134 | fat: 12g | protein: 3g | carbs: 1g | net carbs: 1g | fiber: 0g

Blackberry Crisp

Prep time: 5 minutes | Cook time: 5 minutes | Serves 1

10 blackberries

½ teaspoon vanilla extract

2 tablespoons powdered erythritol

⅛ teaspoon xanthan gum

1 tablespoon butter

¼ cup chopped pecans

3 teaspoons almond flour

½ teaspoon cinnamon

2 teaspoons powdered erythritol

1 cup water

1. Place blackberries, vanilla, erythritol, and xanthan gum in 4-inch ramekin. Stir gently to coat blackberries. 2. In small bowl, mix remaining ingredients. Sprinkle over blackberries and cover with foil. Press the Manual button and set time for 4 minutes. When timer beeps, quick-release the pressure. Serve warm. Feel free to add scoop of whipped cream on top.

Per Serving:
calories: 346 | fat: 31g | protein: 3g | carbs: 13g | net carbs: 5g | fiber: 8g

Halle Berries-and-Cream Cobbler

Prep time: 10 minutes | Cook time: 25 minutes | Serves 4

12 ounces (340 g) cream cheese (1½ cups), softened

1 large egg

¾ cup Swerve confectioners'-style sweetener or equivalent amount of powdered sweetener

½ teaspoon vanilla extract

¼ teaspoon fine sea salt

1 cup sliced fresh raspberries or strawberries

Biscuits:

3 large egg whites

¾ cup blanched almond flour

1 teaspoon baking powder

2½ tablespoons very cold unsalted butter, cut into pieces

¼ teaspoon fine sea salt

Frosting:

2 ounces (57 g) cream cheese (¼ cup), softened

1 tablespoon Swerve confectioners'-style sweetener or equivalent amount of powdered or liquid sweetener

1 tablespoon unsweetened, unflavored almond milk or heavy cream

Fresh raspberries or strawberries, for garnish

1. Preheat the air fryer to 400ºF (204ºC). Grease a pie pan. 2. In a large mixing bowl, use a hand mixer to combine the cream cheese, egg, and sweetener until smooth. Stir in the vanilla and salt. Gently fold in the raspberries with a rubber spatula. Pour the mixture into the prepared pan and set aside. 3. Make the biscuits: Place the egg whites in a medium-sized mixing bowl or the bowl of a stand mixer. Using a hand mixer or stand mixer, whip the egg whites until very fluffy and stiff. 4. In a separate medium-sized bowl, combine the almond flour and baking powder. Cut in the butter and add the salt, stirring gently to keep the butter pieces intact. 5. Gently fold the almond flour mixture into the egg whites. Use a large spoon or ice cream scooper to scoop out the dough and form it into a 2-inch-wide biscuit, making sure the butter stays in separate clumps. Place the biscuit on top of the raspberry mixture in the pan. Repeat with remaining dough to make 4 biscuits. 6. Place the pan in the air fryer and bake for 5 minutes, then lower the temperature to 325ºF (163ºC) and bake for another 17 to 20 minutes, until the biscuits are golden brown. 7. While the cobbler cooks, make the frosting: Place the cream cheese in a small bowl and stir to break it up. Add the sweetener and stir. Add the almond milk and stir until well combined. If you prefer a thinner frosting, add more almond milk. 8. Remove the cobbler from the air fryer and allow to cool slightly, then drizzle with the frosting. Garnish with fresh raspberries. 9. Store leftovers in an airtight container in the refrigerator for up to 3 days. Reheat the cobbler in a preheated 350ºF (177ºC) air fryer for 3 minutes, or until warmed through.

Per Serving:
calories: 535 | fat: 14g | protein: 13g | carbs: 14g | net carbs: 10g | fiber: 4g

Quick Blackberry Cobbler for Two

Prep time: 5 minutes | Cook time: 2 minutes | serves 2

1½ cups fresh blackberries

¼ teaspoon liquid stevia

¼ teaspoon vanilla extract

¼ cup finely ground blanched almond flour

¼ cup (½ stick) cold salted butter, cubed

½ teaspoon baking powder

Whipped cream, for serving (optional)

1. Grease a 2-cup microwave-safe baking dish. 2. In a small bowl, gently combine the blackberries, stevia, and vanilla extract, then pour the mixture into the prepared baking dish. 3. In a small bowl, use a fork to stir together the almond flour and baking powder, then add the butter and continue stirring with the fork until a crumbly mixture forms. Sprinkle the mixture evenly over the blackberries. 4. Microwave for 1½ to 2 minutes, checking every 30 seconds, until the blackberries are bubbly and the topping is lightly browned; microwave cook times vary according to wattage. Allow the cobbler to cool for 10 minutes. Serve with whipped cream, if desired.

Per Serving:
calories: 328 | fat: 30g | protein: 4g | carbs: 13g | net carbs: 6g | fiber: 7g

Cookies-and-Cream Fat Bomb

Prep time: 10 minutes | Cook time: 1 to 3 minutes | Serves 2

1¾ ounces (50 g) cacao butter

4 teaspoons powdered erythritol

4 teaspoons heavy cream powder

Pinch of pink Himalayan sea salt

2 teaspoons cacao nibs

1. In a small microwave-safe bowl, heat the cacao butter on high power in 30-second increments until it is liquid. Make sure to stir between intervals of microwaving. 2. Add the powdered erythritol, heavy cream powder, and salt to the cacao butter. Whisk until the mixture is well combined. 3. Line 2 cups of a muffin pan with paper cupcake liners. Split the liquid between the cups. 4. Pour 1 teaspoon of cacao nibs into each cup, then place the muffin pan in the refrigerator to cool for about 1 hour. (The cups can be stored in the refrigerator until ready to enjoy.)

Per Serving:

calories: 242 | fat: 24g | protein: 1g | carbs: 5g | net carbs: 4g | fiber: 1g

Almond Butter Keto Fat Bombs

Prep time: 3 minutes | Cook time: 3 minutes | Serves 6

¼ cup coconut oil

¼ cup no-sugar-added almond butter

2 tablespoons cacao powder

¼ cup powdered erythritol

1. Press the Sauté button and add coconut oil to Instant Pot. Let coconut oil melt completely and press the Cancel button. Stir in remaining ingredients. Mixture will be liquid. 2. Pour into 6 silicone molds and place into freezer for 30 minutes until set. Store in fridge.

Per Serving:

calories: 142 | fat: 14g | protein: 3g | carbs: 9g | net carbs: 7g | fiber: 2g

Olive Oil Cake

Prep time: 10 minutes | Cook time: 30 minutes | Serves 8

2 cups blanched finely ground almond flour

5 large eggs, whisked

¾ cup extra-virgin olive oil

⅓ cup granular erythritol

1 teaspoon vanilla extract

1 teaspoon baking powder

1. In a large bowl, mix all ingredients. Pour batter into an ungreased round nonstick baking dish. 2. Place dish into air fryer basket. Adjust the temperature to 300°F (149°C) and bake for 30 minutes. The cake will be golden on top and firm in the center when done. 3. Let cake cool in dish 30 minutes before slicing and serving.

Per Serving:

calories: 363 | fat: 35g | protein: 9g | carbs: 6g | net carbs: 3g | fiber: 3g

Chewy Chocolate Chip Cookies

Prep time: 10 minutes | Cook time: 20 minutes | Makes 16 cookies

1½ cups blanched almond flour

½ cup granular erythritol

1 tablespoon unflavored beef gelatin powder

1 teaspoon baking powder

½ cup (1 stick) unsalted butter,

melted but not hot

1 large egg

1 teaspoon vanilla extract

½ cup sugar-free chocolate chips

1. Preheat the oven to 350°F and line 2 baking sheets with parchment paper. 2. Put the almond flour, erythritol, gelatin, and baking powder in a medium-sized bowl and whisk using a fork. Set aside. 3. Put the melted butter, egg, and vanilla extract in a large bowl and combine using a hand mixer or whisk. Add the dry mixture to wet mixture in 2 batches and combine until you have a soft dough that can easily be rolled between your hands without sticking. 4. Fold the chocolate chips into the dough with a rubber spatula. Using a cookie scoop or spoon, scoop 16 even-sized balls of the dough onto the baking sheets, leaving 2 inches of space between them. Using your hand or the spatula, flatten the cookies a little. They will spread slightly in the oven. 5. Bake for 20 minutes, or until golden brown. Allow to cool on the baking sheets for 15 minutes prior to handling. 6. Store leftovers in a sealed container in the refrigerator for up to a week or freeze for up to a month.

Per Serving:

calories: 125 | fat: 12g | protein: 3g | carbs: 3g | net carbs: 1g | fiber: 2g

Pecan Clusters

Prep time: 10 minutes | Cook time: 8 minutes | Serves 8

3 ounces (85 g) whole shelled pecans

1 tablespoon salted butter, melted

2 teaspoons confectioners' erythritol

½ teaspoon ground cinnamon

½ cup low-carb chocolate chips

1. In a medium bowl, toss pecans with butter, then sprinkle with erythritol and cinnamon. 2. Place pecans into ungreased air fryer basket. Adjust the temperature to 350°F (177°C) and air fry for 8 minutes, shaking the basket two times during cooking. They will feel soft initially but get crunchy as they cool. 3. Line a large baking sheet with parchment paper. 4. Place chocolate in a medium microwave-safe bowl. Microwave on high, heating in 20-second increments and stirring until melted. Place 1 teaspoon chocolate in a rounded mound on ungreased parchment-lined baking sheet, then press 1 pecan into top, repeating with remaining chocolate and pecans. 5. Place baking sheet into refrigerator to cool at least 30 minutes. Once cooled, store clusters in a large sealed container in refrigerator up to 5 days.

Per Serving:

calories: 104 | fat: 10g | protein: 1g | carbs: 3g | net carbs: 2g | fiber: 1g

Lemon-Poppyseed Cookies

Prep time: 5 minutes | Cook time: 10 minutes | serves 4

Nonstick cooking spray

1 cup almond butter

¾ cup monk fruit sweetener

4 tablespoons chia seeds

3 tablespoons fresh grated lemon zest

Juice of 1 lemon

1 tablespoon poppy seeds

1. Preheat the oven to 350°F. Grease a baking sheet with cooking spray and set aside. 2. In a large mixing bowl, combine the almond butter with the monk fruit sweetener, chia seeds, lemon zest, lemon juice, and poppy seeds. Mix well, kneading the mixture with your hands. 3. Roll pieces of the dough into cookie-size balls and place them on the prepared baking sheet, spacing them evenly, as some spreading will occur during baking. 4. Bake the cookies for 8 minutes, until golden. 5. Transfer the cookies to a cooling rack. 6. Serve as is or paired with your favorite unsweetened, plant-based milk.

Per Serving:

calories: 460 | fat: 39g | protein: 13g | carbs: 21g | net carbs: 9g | fiber: 12g

Lemon Coconut Truffles

Prep time: 30 minutes | Cook time: 0 minutes | Makes 16 truffles

3 cups shredded unsweetened coconut, divided

½ cup pecans

2 tablespoons coconut oil

Zest and juice of 1 lemon

½ cup monk fruit sweetener, granulated form

Pinch sea salt

1. Make the truffle base. Put 2 cups of the coconut and the pecans in a food processor and pulse until the mixture looks like a paste, about 5 minutes. 2. Add the remaining ingredients. Add the coconut oil, lemon zest, lemon juice, sweetener, and salt to the processor and pulse until the mixture forms a big ball, about 2 minutes. 3. Form the truffles. Scoop the mixture out with a tablespoon and roll it into 16 balls. Roll the truffles in the remaining 1 cup of coconut. 4. Store. Store the truffles in a sealed container in the refrigerator for up to one week or in the freezer for up to one month.

Per Serving:

calories: 160 | fat: 16g | protein: 2g | carbs: 5g | net carbs: 2g | fiber: 3g

Appendix 1: Measurement Conversion Chart

MEASUREMENT CONVERSION CHART

VOLUME EQUIVALENTS(DRY)

US STANDARD	METRIC (APPROXIMATE)
1/8 teaspoon	0.5 mL
1/4 teaspoon	1 mL
1/2 teaspoon	2 mL
3/4 teaspoon	4 mL
1 teaspoon	5 mL
1 tablespoon	15 mL
1/4 cup	59 mL
1/2 cup	118 mL
3/4 cup	177 mL
1 cup	235 mL
2 cups	475 mL
3 cups	700 mL
4 cups	1 L

VOLUME EQUIVALENTS(LIQUID)

US STANDARD	US STANDARD (OUNCES)	METRIC (APPROXIMATE)
2 tablespoons	1 fl.oz.	30 mL
1/4 cup	2 fl.oz.	60 mL
1/2 cup	4 fl.oz.	120 mL
1 cup	8 fl.oz.	240 mL
1 1/2 cup	12 fl.oz.	355 mL
2 cups or 1 pint	16 fl.oz.	475 mL
4 cups or 1 quart	32 fl.oz.	1 L
1 gallon	128 fl.oz.	4 L

TEMPERATURES EQUIVALENTS

FAHRENHEIT(F)	CELSIUS(C) (APPROXIMATE)
225 °F	107 °C
250 °F	120 °C
275 °F	135 °C
300 °F	150 °C
325 °F	160 °C
350 °F	180 °C
375 °F	190 °C
400 °F	205 °C
425 °F	220 °C
450 °F	235 °C
475 °F	245 °C
500 °F	260 °C

WEIGHT EQUIVALENTS

US STANDARD	METRIC (APPROXIMATE)
1 ounce	28 g
2 ounces	57 g
5 ounces	142 g
10 ounces	284 g
15 ounces	425 g
16 ounces (1 pound)	455 g
1.5 pounds	680 g
2 pounds	907 g

Appendix 2: The Dirty Dozen and Clean Fifteen

The Dirty Dozen and Clean Fifteen

The Environmental Working Group (EWG) is a nonprofit, nonpartisan organization dedicated to protecting human health and the environment Its mission is to empower people to live healthier lives in a healthier environment. This organization publishes an annual list of the twelve kinds of produce, in sequence, that have the highest amount of pesticide residue-the Dirty Dozen-as well as a list of the fifteen kinds ofproduce that have the least amount of pesticide residue-the Clean Fifteen.

THE DIRTY DOZEN	THE CLEAN FIFTEEN
• The 2016 Dirty Dozen includes the following produce. These are considered among the year's most important produce to buy organic:	• The least critical to buy organically are the Clean Fifteen list. The following are on the 2016 list:

THE DIRTY DOZEN

• The 2016 Dirty Dozen includes the following produce. These are considered among the year's most important produce to buy organic:

Strawberries	Spinach
Apples	Tomatoes
Nectarines	Bell peppers
Peaches	Cherry tomatoes
Celery	Cucumbers
Grapes	Kale/collard greens
Cherries	Hot peppers

• *The Dirty Dozen list contains two additional itemskale/collard greens and hot peppers-because they tend to contain trace levels of highly hazardous pesticides.*

THE CLEAN FIFTEEN

• The least critical to buy organically are the Clean Fifteen list. The following are on the 2016 list:

Avocados	Papayas
Corn	Kiw
Pineapples	Eggplant
Cabbage	Honeydew
Sweet peas	Grapefruit
Onions	Cantaloupe
Asparagus	Cauliflower
Mangos	

• *Some of the sweet corn sold in the United States are made from genetically engineered (GE) seedstock. Buy organic varieties of these crops to avoid GE produce.*

Made in the USA
Las Vegas, NV
10 April 2023

70426898R00057